Studies in International Economics and Institutions

Studies in International Economics and Institutions

H.-J. Vosgerau (Ed.), New Institutional Arrangements for the World Economy
IX, 482 pages. 1989

Michael Rauscher

OPEC and the Price of Petroleum

Theoretical Considerations
and Empirical Evidence

With 29 Figures

Springer-Verlag Berlin Heidelberg New York
London Paris Tokyo Hong Kong

Michael Rauscher
Sonderforschungsbereich 178
Universität Konstanz
Postfach 55 60
D-7750 Konstanz, FRG

ISBN 3-540-51654-9 Springer-Verlag Berlin Heidelberg New York Tokyo
ISBN 0-387-51654-9 Springer-Verlag New York Heidelberg Berlin Tokyo

© Springer-Verlag Berlin · Heidelberg 1989
Printed in Germany

Printing: Weihert-Druck GmbH, Darmstadt
Bookbinding: J. Schäffer GmbH u. Co. KG., Grünstadt
2142/7130-543210

Acknowledgements

I would like to thank my supervisor, Prof. Dr. Horst Siebert, for his advice and critique. Moreover, I am indebted to Prof. Dr. Gerd Ronning, Prof. Dr. Murray C. Kemp and to my colleagues Jesko Hentschel, Joachim Keck, Peter König, Anke Meyer, Dr. Ernst Mohr, and Jonathan Thomas for helpful comments, discussions, and criticism. Comments by Dr. Franz Wirl on another paper of mine led me to detect a substantial mathematical error in Chapter 4 in the first version of this study. I gratefully acknowlege research grants given by the Deutsche Forschungsgemeinschaft in the framework of the SFB 178 programme. My work profitted a lot from the intellectual atmosphere at the Faculty of Economics and Statistics and the Sonderforschungsbereich 178 in Konstanz. The responsibility for what became of all the help and good advice is mine.

Contents

3. The price of petroleum in economic theory

4. An intertemporal model of OPEC's pricing policy

5. A simplified version of the model

6. An econometric model of the world petroleum market

7. Final remarks

Appendix: Optimal control theory

References

List of figures

List of tables

1. Introduction

1.1. Oil price fluctuations and their impact on economic performance

Drastic oil price fluctuations have been a major characteristic of the world petroleum market since the beginning of the seventies. The oil crises of 1973/74 and 1979/80 were followed by a dramatic drop of the oil price during the first two quarters of 1986. Starting from a level less than 2 $ per barrel in 1972, the spot market price of Arabian Light crude oil increased to some 35 $ in 1980, then slowly decreased, and finally fell to 13 $ in 1986 (annual averages). If monthly data are considered, the peaks of the oil price movement look even more dramatic. In December 1980 Arabian crude was traded for more than 40 $ a barrel, and in August 1986 the price was down at 8 $ (see Fig. 1.1).

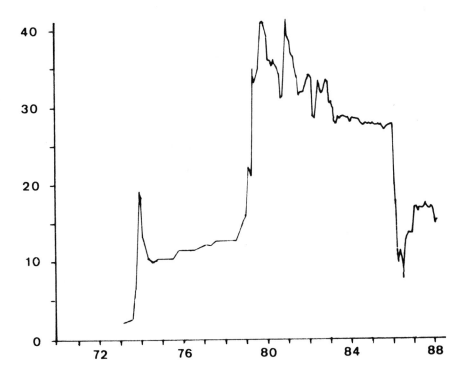

Figure 1.1: The spot market price of Saudi-Arabian Light crude oil[1]

---

[1] Data are taken from the *Petroleum Economist* and the *OPEC Bulletin*, various issues.

After the Second World War petroleum has become the most important energy resource. During the fifties and sixties its price was relatively low compared to other energy sources like coal and firewood and it tended to drive them out of the market.[2] In 1967 petroleum became the main source of energy worldwide, and at the time of the first oil crisis its share in global primary energy supply amounted to nearly 50%. When petroleum suddenly appeared to be expensive after the 1973/74 price shock, the main objective of energy policy in most countries was to reduce the dependence on imported oil. The strategy was to increase domestic oil production, to substitute other kinds of energy like coal and nuclear fuels for petroleum, and to invest in energy-saving capital (insulation etc.). All of these measures, however, are capital intensive and many of the techniques have long gestation periods, for instance coal liquefication and nuclear power utilisation. In order to accelerate the substitution process, petroleum-saving measures were heavily subsidised in many countries. The Iranian revolution in 1979 led to new price increases and thus stimulated further petroleum-saving measures.

Because of high capital intensities, an energy-conserving policy has a high degree of irreversibility. After the recent drop in the oil price, the 'departure from oil' appears to be an over-reaction: coal liquification plants that have been planned a decade ago in the expectation of a continuous growth of the oil price will probably not meet their expenses, and ambitious projects for the development of tar sands and oil shale in Canada have largely been abandoned. There are numerous examples of resources that have been mis-directed to cope with permanently increasing oil prices. The acceleration of nuclear power utilisation might turn out to be another case.

But not only the energy sector has suffered from the leap-frogging of the petroleum price. There is strong evidence that worldwide recession and unemployment during the eighties have at least in part been a result of the oil price rise. The influence of the oil price on economic performance of petroleum-importing countries is twofold. We can distinguish demand-side and supply-side effects.

First, the impact of oil price fluctuations on the demand side shall be discussed.[3] An oil price increase reduces the income available for domestic consumption. Such a loss of real purchasing power is not necessarily a problem since the oil-exporting countries gain what the importing countries lose. After the oil crises, however, it turned out that the redistribution of purchasing power was not a zero-sum game. Oil-exporting countries had massive problems in finding appropriate investment possibilities for their sudden wealth. In the literature, this topic

---

[2] For the history of the utilisation of different kinds of energy see *Ray* (1979) and *Griffin/Steele* (1980), pp. 2-19. *Maurice/Smithson* (1984) even go back to prehistoric energy crises.

[3] For a good survey and additional references see *Pindyck/Rotemberg* (1984).

has been dealt with under the heading 'petrodollar recycling'.[4] Thus, the net effect of the oil price increase was a loss of real purchasing power in the oil-importing countries. Probably, this was one of the decisive factors in creating stagflationary tendencies in the seventies and eighties. Rigidities in wages and non-energy prices accelerated inflation and unemployment. The opposite scenario can be observed for an oil price drop as it occurred in 1986: it strengthens domestic demand and, therefore, has a positive impact on output and employment.[5]

The second influence that oil price fluctuations have on the economy is due to the role of petroleum as an energy input in the production process, and it is closely related to the recent discussion about the productivity slowdown.[6] *Bruno* (1984) argues that an oil price shock leads to a downward shift in the factor price frontier if capital and labour are substituted for energy. In a neoclassical model, augmentation of a factor of production ceteris paribus lowers its marginal productivity. An approach which takes the difference between short- and long-run elasticities into account has been proposed by *Berndt/Wood* (1984). Similar models have been studied by *Saunders* (1984a) and *Struckmeyer* (1986). In these models, capital is composed of different putty-clay vintages, each vintage having a special capital-energy ratio. If an oil price shock occurs, energy-inefficient capital, which still is physically intact, becomes economically obsolete.[7] New investment is undertaken in order to replace this capital instead of expanding production capacity. Since in the process of computing the capital stock economic statistics in general use constant rates of depreciation or booking values, that have not much in common with genuine depreciation, there is a tendency towards over-estimation of existing capital. What seems to be an underutilisation of production capacity and a productivity slowdown is in reality a lack of expans-

---

[4] On the recycling problem see *Schneider* (1983), p. 271-281, *Bird* (1984), *Oweiss* (1984) and *Koopmann/Matthies/Reszat* (1984), ch. 3.

[5] In West Germany for instance, the 1986 oil price collapse is said to have set free purchasing power of approximately 2% of GDP. See *Siebert* (1986b), p. 202. Simulation results for the USA are discussed in *Hickman/Huntington/Sweeney* (1987). According to this study (pp. 44-46), a reduction in the oil price of 20% increases GNP by 1.2%.

[6] For a comparison of the different approaches see *Berndt/Wood* (1986).

[7] The revaluation can easily be measured in the case of used cars. See *Daly/Mayer* (1983). For the capital stock of an economy, it is by far harder to obtain significant evidence, but the results of *Berndt/Wood* (1984) suggest that the revaluation hypothesis is realistic.

ive investment. The effect, however, is the same: the rate of output growth declines.[8] This in turn leads to increased unemployment.[9]

Finally it should be noted that even those who should have benefitted from the oil price rise, the resource-rich countries, have got reason to complain. They suffer from de-industrialisation, also labelled Dutch disease.[10] The price increase leads to a boom in the resource sector. This boom in turn causes purchasing power to expand. The prices of non-traded goods increase while the prices of traded goods are fixed by the world market, given the country is sufficiently small. This change in relative prices makes domestic production of the tradable goods less attractive and the sector reduces its output. On the input side, the booming sector now has an advantage in the competition for factors of production. As a consequence, there is a tendency towards increasing factor remuneration, which puts the non-tradables sector under another pressure - be it by narrowing the gap between input and output prices, be it by an appreciation of the domestic currency. Both the 'spending effect' and the 'resource-movement effect' lead to a decline of the traded goods sector, traditionally the manufacturing sector of the economy. This process can be aggravated by stickiness of wages and immobility of production factors among sectors.

Non-foreseeable oil price fluctuations and uncertainty about future developments have produced frictions and high adjustment costs in the energy sector as well as in the economy as a whole. Part of these frictions could have been avoided by employing the adequate energy and stabilisation policy measures had the oil price changes been predicted in time. In the past fifteen years, however, many of the supposedly most reliable forecasts turned out to be wrong or they were surpassed by reality unexpectedly fast. As *Jacoby/Paddock* (1983), p. 31, put it:

> "*The world oil market is the forecaster's nightmare: seldom have so many knowledgeable observers been so wrong so often.*"

The reason lies with the absence of historical experience and the lack of empirical data on drastic oil price fluctuations. Before 1973, the price of petroleum had been nearly constant for two decades. There was no variance in the data. So it was almost impossible to identify interdependencies and causal relationships among variables - not to speak of reasonable estimates for important parameters, e.g. the elasticities of demand and supply and the costs of backstop technologies. Only the oil price fluctuations of the past two decades provided the variance which was

---

[8] *Struckmeyer* (1986) obtains a decrease of 0.3 percentage points in the rate of output growth after a 30% increase in the energy price.

[9] According to *Koopman/Matthies/Reszat* (1984), pp. 268-275, however, this effect can be offset partly by price-induced substitution between energy and labour. But in the short run substitution elasticities are small and so is the labour-augmenting effect of an oil price shock.

[10] See *Corden* (1984) and *Neary/van Wijnbergen* (1986) for a more detailed analysis.

needed to compute useful estimates. Having made the experience of the oil price collapse in 1986, economists should now be able to produce better forecasts of future developments in the world petroleum market.[11]

1.2. Plan of the study

This study attempts to provide a theoretical framework for such forecasts. It tries to identify variables and critical parameters that have been crucial in the process of oil price formation since the seventies. Special emphasis will be placed on the role of the Organization of Petroleum Exporting Countries, OPEC. In the late sixties and beginning of the seventies, OPEC member countries managed to establish their influence on the world petroleum markets. Since then, their production and pricing decisions have crucially affected the conduct of the market, and it has become a widely accepted view among economists that OPEC has - sometimes more, sometimes less - monopoly power and, therefore, is able to determine the price unilaterally. The theoretical framework that will be chosen for this study models OPEC as the swing producer or dominant firm in the international petroleum market. As another inegredient of such a model, one should take the sluggishness of demand reactions into account. By putting these features together and adding some other building stones, one obtains an economic model of oil price formation that explains optimal and real price paths.

While the optimal paths are smooth and nicely behaved, the real paths are characterised by significant discontinuities. A great deal of these drastic price changes is interpreted as a result of corrections of OPEC's pricing policies that became necessary because the original plans had been made on the basis of incorrect assumptions on the behaviour of demand. This is the central theoretical hypothesis of this study. It will be derived from a theoretical model, subjected to empirical analyses, and used to forecast future developments.

In order to get there, it is not sufficient to develop a merely monocausal model which gives a single answer to a complex problem. The theoretical model has to be embedded into an analysis of the history of the world petroleum market, its institutions, and the balance of political and economic power. Moreover, the approach has to be compared to other models of the world petroleum market. These are the purposes of the following two chapters.

Chapter 2 contains a descriptive portrait of the development of the world petroleum market during the last decades. Here, non-economic factors (e.g. geological and political issues) will be discussed, and special emphasis will be placed on changes in the institutional arrangements that are closely related to the development of the oil price. The alteration of property

---

[11] We are, however, probably still far away from what *Morrison* (1987), p. 399, calls *"the pot of gold at the energy economist's rainbow: an accurate forecast of the price of oil."*

rights and the creation of new contractual arrangements in the upstream sector are of particular interest. Another part of the chapter is devoted to the markets on which petroleum is traded. The interrelation of these markets and their relative importance in different phases of the history will be discussed. The creation of new arrangements, such as petroleum futures and netback contracts, as a response to changes in the economic and political environment is of special interest. Besides the analysis of institutional and political factors, this chapter serves the purpose to illustrate the cartel hypothesis historically.

Chapter 3 gives a survey of the economic literature on oil price formation. This literature is vast: so the survey cannot be complete. The aim is to summarise and compare the essential approaches to the topic. Special consideration is devoted to the economic theory of exhaustible resources, which has its origin in the seminal article by *Hotelling* (1931) and was re-discovered in the early seventies when one became conscious of the finiteness of the world's resources. This theory has produced several hypotheses that can explain the price of a depletable resource like petroleum. Besides the intertemporal approach of the theory of exhaustible resources, there are other approaches that have to be evaluated, e.g. static monopoly theory or the hypothesis of the backward-bending supply curve for crude oil. Some of the theoretical models under consideration have been examined empirically. The results of these investigations will be discussed, and it will be shown that empirical tests eliminate some of the theoretical models from the set of promising candidates for a theory of oil price formation.

Chapter 4 presents a theoretical model of oil price formation. A residual supplier or dominant firm sets the oil price. The adjustment processes of demand and competitive supply to changing prices are assumed to be sluggish. On the demand side, the underlying argument is the putty-clay nature of the capital stock that is used to transform energy into services. On the supply side, the duration of exploration and development of new oil fields defer the reaction to oil price changes. Taking these rigidities into account, the residual supplier employs a pricing policy which is in some respects different from that of a dominant firm in a static model. Additionally, the special structure of the model as a two-state-variable problem produces some new and interesting results that do not occur in simpler models.

In Chapter 5, the one-state-variable version of the model will be investigated. The simpler specification of the model allows for a more intuitive economic interpretation of the results and a deeper investigation of parameter variations. Variations of parameters that affect the demand function are of particular interest. If the price setter's expectations on the behaviour of demand are erroneous, she chooses a wrong price path. If, after a while, the decision about the pricing policy turns out to be wrong, a new price path will be chosen. This leads to discontinuous price changes or, more colloquially speaking, price shocks and oil crises. An increasing long-term price trend can be obtained if the exhaustibility of petroleum is introduced into the model. Medium-term price fluctuations, as have been experienced during the seventies and eighties, however, are independent of the scarcity effect.

In Chapter 6, the theoretical model is tested empirically by means of nonlinear regression methods. Since the underlying theoretical model is an optimisation model, special requirements on the shape of the functions have to be met. Another problem is that the price path in the theoretical model does not depend on observable variables and parameters but on OPEC's perceptions of these variables and parameters. Therefore, it is necessary to follow a rule-of-the-thumb approach in specifying the price equation. The other moduls of the econometric model are equations for global petroleum demand and non-OPEC crude oil supply. The obtained estimates are used to forecast future price paths.

Finally, in Chapter 7, the model will be evaluated and conclusions concerning economic policy implications will be drawn.

The appendix contains a short exposition of *Pontryagin's* maximum principle. Special emphasis is placed on the dynamics of opimal paths in control models with more than one state variable.

2. The world petroleum market: History and institutions

2.1. Petroleum as an exhaustible resource

After World War II, petroleum has become the predominant energy source worldwide. From 1945 to 1973, its production increased eightfold and its share in energy consumption rose from 23 to 47%.[12] This tremendous increase did not cause any problems as long as huge oil findings were made that increased the stock of known reserves even faster. It was in the early seventies when the finiteness of natural resources became an issue of public interest. The most popular publication was "Limits to Growth" by *Meadows et al.* (1972). They reported (p. 58) that, given a growth rate of 3.9% per year, which at that time seemed to be a realistic forecast, proven petroleum reserves would be exhausted within twenty years. In the meantime, this estimate of the exhaustion period has turned out to be by far too pessimistic because of new additions to reserves and the demand slowdown. However, exhaustibility remains one of the major characteristics of the natural resource petroleum.

The following sections will evaluate the importance of exhaustibility in the case of petroleum. In order to do this, it is necessary to first clarify some technical concepts that are essential for the understanding of the economics of the world petroleum market. In a second step, the data that underly the theoretical considerations of the following sections will be discussed.

2.1.1. Some basic concepts[13]

Crude oil is a mixture of different hydrocarbons, ranging from light, fluid components to heavy, paraffin-like substances. Crude oils from different oil fields usually vary in their composition. These differences (amongst other variables, e.g. the sulfur content) constitute the basis for price differentials. The heavier components, which are predominantly used in electricity generation, face intense competition by coal and natural gas. So the elasticity of demand for these products is relatively high. For lighter products such as motor gasoline there are no direct substitutes and demand is less elastic. This is reflected in higher prices for these products. Therefore, light crude oils are usually more expensive than heavier ones.

---

[12] Data from *Jenkins* (1985), pp. 72 and 76, and *BP Statistical Review of World Energy 1984*, pp. 7 and 28.

[13] For a simple introduction into technical aspects of petroleum exploration, recovery, and refining see *Welker* (1985).

In order to obtain petroleum products from crude oil, it has to be refined. By heating the crude oil, its components can be separated with respect to their boiling points.[14] The lightest components, called naphta, serve as a feedstock in the petrochemical industry. Components with higher boiling points are the base substances for jet fuel and motor gasoline. Heavy components range from fuel oil, mainly used in electricity generation, to asphalt. Since the heavier components face substantial competition, their price has been below that of crude oil during some periods in the eighties. This provided incentives for restructuring the refinery sector. Cracking facilities, that brake down the heavy products into gas and light products, have increased their share in the refinery sector substantially.[15]

Quantities of oil can be measured either in imperial or in metric units. In what follows imperial units will be used. A barrel (abbreviated b or bbl) contains 159 litres. Taking account of the fact that different types of crude oil and petroleum products are characterised by different specific gravities, barrels can be converted into tons. A rule-of-the-thumb conversion factor for crude oil is seven (more accurately: 7.3). The same can be done for production figures. So one barrel per day (b/d) corresponds to approximately 50 tons per year.

2.1.2. Measurement of reserves

Petroleum is an exhaustible resource. Since the availability of oil is considered to be essential for modern civilisation, much effort has been devoted to the determination of reserves. For the measurement of reserves different concepts are used. They are listed below with descending degree of accessibility:[16]

- Proven reserves are those that can economically be extracted with known technology and at present prices. So this concept neglects the impact of exploration, price increases, and new recovery techniques. Of all concepts of reserves this is the most conservative and the one which is most widely used. In some respects its application can lead to wrong conclusions, e.g. when reserves-to-production ratios are interpreted as depletion times.[17]

---

[14] For a short description of the refining process see *Molle/Wever* (1984), pp. 9-14.

[15] See *Fesharaki/Isaak* (1984), pp. 39, 44, and 50.

[16] For these different concepts of determining the availability of reserves see *Colitti* (1981) and *Riva* (1983), pp. 123-133. The following classification is based on *Colitti* (1981), p. 9-10.

[17] For specific fields or oil-producing areas these reserves-to-production ratios can be usefully applied, however. They can serve as an indicator of the degree of depletion: with numbers less than eight to ten, declines in production should be expected. See *Riva* (1983), p. 131.

- Reserves consist of proven reserves plus probable reserves. The latter include probable extensions in the size of known oil fields and the effects of enhanced recovery.

- Ultimately recoverable reserves additionally include undiscovered reserves that can be estimated by means of various methods.[18] Of course, these estimates are characterised by a certain degree of ambiguity.

- Petroleum in place is the amount of petroleum present. It depends on technical parameters such as pressure, viscosity and rock porosity how much of it can be recovered. Advanced techniques (secondary and tertiary recovery) can yield recovery rates of approximately 40-50%.

The most relevant of these concepts is proven reserves. It refers to known resources, i.e. the minimum available, and its advantage is the availability of detailed data. It should be noted that according to this concept reserves depend on the price. Price variations can thus cause significant revaluations of the reserves stock although nothing changes in the physical sense. While proven reserves are currently (in 1988) being reported to amount to more than 800 billion barrels,[19] the ultimately recoverable reserves are estimated to be some 1600 billion barrels.[20] Given a current rate of extraction of approximately 55 million barrels per day, these figures correspond to a reserves-to-production ratio of 40 and 80 years, respectively.

2.1.3. The development of production and reserves

As stated above, production and reserves increased at high rates during the fifties, sixties, and the early seventies. The combination of these effects is depicted in Figure 2.1. It showns annual data with five-year intervals until 1970. For the seventies and eighties, some characteristic years are chosen.[21] There were substantial increases in reserves and production until the the early seventies. The next decade was characterised by smaller changes. In 1986/87 there was a drastic increase in reserves. According to OPEC figures, proven reserves went up by

---

[18] For a survey of these methods that range from rather simple life-cycle models of oilfields to econometric and geological approaches see *Kaufman* (1983).

[19] The data on proven reserves are not always reliable: reporting the volume of reserves is not only a means of keeping the statistics up to date but also a matter of politics. This can bias the statistics considerably.

[20] See *Colitti* (1981), p. 21, and *Riva* (1983), p. 336. The World Energy Outlook, published by the *International Energy Agency* (1982), p. 210, reports a range of 1500-2240 billion barrels.

[21] Data are taken from the *OPEC Statistical Bulletin* (various issues) and *Jenkins* (1985).

almost 100 billion barrels or 12.7% in 1986. The increase is shared by two countries, the United Arab Emirates with a 200% expansion and Iran with 60%.[22]

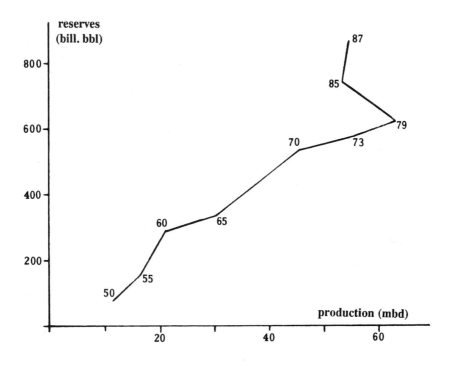

Figure 2.1.: Petroleum reserves and production

2.1.4. The regional distribution of consumption, production, and reserves

The levels of consumption, production and reserves of petroleum are unevenly distributed in the world. From a trade-theory viewpoint this simply reflects differences in endowments and tastes among countries and regions, and free trade will provide an efficient solution. Viewed in the context of the north-south conflict, the differences constitute a source of interregional injustice. Countries that consume more oil than they produce are said to exploit the natural resources wealth of the Third World.[23] The third argument is an intertemporal one: countries or

---

[22] See *OPEC Statistical Bulletin 1986*, p. 36.

[23] See for instance *Massarat* (1980), ch. 4.

regions that extract their resources at a high current rate will be dependent on imports in the future. This increases the vulnerability to supply shocks.[24]

Table 2.1.: Regional distribution of reserves, production and consumption[25]

	share of reserves	share of production	share of consumption
OPEC:			
1963	0.749	0.443	0.016
1973	0.725	0.559	0.022
1979	0.691	0.492	0.043
1987	0.759	0.309	0.055
North America			
1963	0.121	0.315	0.473
1973	0.077	0.197	0.336
1979	0.058	0.160	0.312
1987	0.034	0.177	0.287
Western Europe			
1963	0.008	0.015	0.220
1973	0.030	0.008	0.255
1979	0.027	0.036	0.226
1987	0.025	0.073	0.189
Centr. pl. economies			
1963	0.091	0.165	0.138
1973	0.112	0.173	0.169
1979	0.130	0.226	0.200
1987	0.089	0.279	0.219

The shares of reserves, production and consumption of petroleum held by different country groups are listed in Table 2.1. When interpreting these figures, the levels should be kept in mind. Reserves increased over the whole period with the greatest increases in the sixties and in 1986. Production and consumption grew rapidly until the first oil crisis and much slower during the second half of the seventies. They finally declined in the eighties. Now the following conclusions can be drawn from Table 2.1.:

- OPEC's share in production decreased dramatically after the first oil crisis and reached its lowest level of less than 30% in 1985. The fact that the reserves share significantly exceeds the

---

[24] On the relationship between import dependence and vulnerability see *Plaut* (1983).

[25] Data from *OPEC Annual Statistical Bulletin* (various issues).

production share, however, indicates that OPEC will probably have more market power in the future than it has today.

- North American reserves declined both in their level and, more significantly, in their share. The production share also declined, and the seventies and eighties brought about substantial reductions in consumption which are due to energy saving-measures and substitution processes. The comparison of the reserves and production shares, however, indicates an increasing potential of future import dependency. This hypothesis is supported by the fact that the North American reserves-to-production ratio is very low. It is only eight years.

- In Western Europe, demand has also declined substantially after the first oil shock. The 1973 increase in reserves and the subsequent increase in production are due to the discovery and development of the North Sea oil fields. Thus, the degree of dependency has declined slightly. By now, the production share, however, exceeds the reserves share by a factor of three. A substantial decline in production of North Sea oil is expected for the middle of the nineties.[26]

- The Centrally Planned Economies are characterised by increasing production and consumption. The latter indicates that international price relationships have only a minor impact on demand if any. The reserves-to-production ratio is similar to the one reported for Western Europe. Production and consumption figures indicate that there have been small exports during the observation period.

Probably, the most important observation is the fact that the major oil-consuming regions are characterised by a reserves-to-production ratio which is lower than the world average. The discrepancy between production and reserves has increased after the second oil crisis when domestic production was increased in order to reduce import dependency. In the long run, such a policy of import substitution can lead to the opposite of what has been intended: increased dependency in the future. So one can expect OPEC to gain additional market power in the future.

2.2. The Organization of Petroleum Exporting Countries

Since in this study special emphasis will be placed on the description and investigation of OPEC behaviour, it is necessary to provide a short characterisation of the Organization and its member countries. The Organization of Petroleum Exporting Countries was founded in 1960 by five of the major Third World oil-producing nations as a response to reductions in the posted prices which were announced by the major oil companies in 1959/60. OPEC's primary target at

---

[26] See *Mabro et al.* (1986), p. 6.

that time was to avoid further price reductions and to ensure an acceptable price level.[27] By now OPEC has thirteen member countries: Algeria, Ecuador, Gabon, Indonesia, Iran, Iraq, Kuwait, Libya, Nigeria, Qatar, Saudi Arabia, the United Arab Emirates (UAE), and Venezuela. These countries vary considerably with respect to size, income, and petroleum reserves.

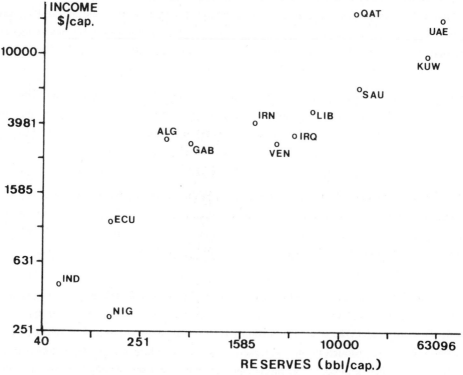

Figure 2.2.: Income and wealth in OPEC member countries

Figure 2.2. is a graphical representation of the distibution of wealth among the OPEC countries. The combinations of income (GNP) per capita and resource endowment per capita are shown in this diagram.[28] While the first variable represents current wealth from various sources, the second measures the potential of future wealth from petroleum exports. Countries close to the origin are relatively poor both in terms of current income and petroleum reserves. Since domestic absorption of their oil revenues is high, they are termed 'high absorbers'. Examples are Ecuador, Indonesia and Nigeria. On the other hand, countries with a small population have difficulties to absorb their oil revenues during times of rising prices. They are called 'low absorbers'. Notwithstanding the fact that there are many other sources for quarrels, the

---

[27]   See *Schneider* (1983), pp. 83-85, and *Terzian* (1985), pp. 40-45.

[28]   Data on population and reserves for 1986 taken from *OPEC Annual Statistical Bulletin 1986*, pp. 3 and 36.

heterogeneity of OPEC member countries constitutes a major source for a conflict of interests. One can argue that high-absorber countries are more short-term oriented whereas low absorbers rather follow long-term strategies.[29] These diverging interests have played an important part in the process of oil price formation during and following the second oil crisis.[30]

2.3. The price of petroleum

This section defines the other subject of the analysis: the price of oil. This is not a simple matter since there exists a variety of oil prices. Crude petroleum is not a homogeneous good. From the different types of crude oil, distinguished from each other by specific gravities and their sulfur contents, one has to be chosen as the marker. Due to its abundance in both production and reserves, Saudi-Arabian Light oil has widely been used for this purpose. The importance of Arabian Light, however, has declined substantially during the middle of the eighties and other crudes like the North Sea crude Brent took over this role.[31] In spite of this problem, the price of Arabian Light will be used below as the relevant reference.

The price of Arabian Light crude is not unique. There exist official prices, which are determined on OPEC conferences, and spot market prices, that are formed on free markets by the forces of supply and demand. Moreover, futures markets have to be considered. Finally, so-called netback contracts have become very important in the middle of the eighties, and they played a major role in bringing the oil price down to one third of its former level in spring and summer 1986. The following sections will discuss the different prices of petroleum and the markets on which they are determined.

2.3.1. Long-term contracts with fixed prices

Long-term contractual relationships governed the world petroleum market from the beginning of the century to the late sixties. The major oil companies owned concessions with durations of fifty or even more years. The crude oil was refined and retailed via the vertically integrated networks of the multinational oil companies. Even after the nationalisation of the reserves had taken place in the late sixties and early seventies, the long-term character of international trade in petroleum remained unchanged for some years. The producing countries sold

---

[29] See *Razavi* (1984) and *Siebert* (1985), p. 25.

[30] Chapter 5.5.3. presents a theoretical argument for endogenous oil price fluctuations caused by the heterogeneity of OPEC member countries.

[31] On the emergence of marker crudes see *Fesharaki/Razavi* (1986), pp. 59-60.

the bulk of their petroleum to the former concessionaires and, as a response to the supply disruptions, the share of government-government deals increased. Most of these transactions were made on a contractual basis that fixed the price and the term of duration of the relationship.

Long-term contracts exist since in some situations they are advantageous to the parties involved. In the contract-theory literature the insurance motive and the problem of relation-specific investments have been discussed intensively.[32] Both of these arguments are important in the case of petroleum sales contracts. Long-term contracts are useful to secure supplies, i.e. for a refiner or a import-dependent country, and they provide the seller with a predictable income. OPEC countries used fixed-price contracts to sell their petroleum since they were bound to official prices. On the other hand, many long-term sales contracts are due to relation-specific investments: the investing firm is guaranteed to obtain a certain share of petroleum as a remuneration of its exploration and development efforts.[33]

A fixed-price sales contract implies a risk allocation which insures the seller against all market risks. The buyer bears both the crude-oil-price risk and the product-price risk. The crude-oil-price risk is associated with the difference between the contract price and the spot price. The product-price risk arises from the uncertainty about the product prices prevailing at the time the crude oil has been refined. It can be shifted to a third party by selling the crude oil on the spot market.

Increased volatility of oil prices has led to more flexible contracts. The long-term orientation of sales contracts has by and large been abandoned.[34] Price indexation and escape clauses have been introduced to bring contract prices closer to spot market prices. In the extreme, long-term sales contracts have been substituted by spot market transactions.

2.3.2. The spot market

The most important spot market for petroleum and refined products is the Rotterdam market.[35] It gained public attention for the first time during the oil crises of 1973/74 and 1979/80

---

[32] For a survey see *Hart/Holmström* (1987), on the advantages and disadvantages of contracting especially pp. 118-134. For long-term contracts in the resources industry, see *Roberts* (1980), especially p. 246, and *Siebert* (1988a).

[33] This applies to the traditional concession as well as to modern production sharing contracts.

[34] *Hartshorn* (1985), p. 62, states that since the second oil shock most of the contracts have not exceeded a year's duration.

[35] The following description of the Rotterdam spot market is based on *Prast/Lax* (1983), pp. 61-70, *Niering* (1984), *Nasmyth/Brinks* (1986) and *Fesharaki/Razavi* (1986), pp. 19-27. *Gjoberg*

when it became the barometer of oil scarcity and when oil prices reached new peaks from day to day. The Rotterdam market is an unofficial telephone market for crude oil and refined products. It covers northwest Europe (the British Isles, Scandinavia, France, West Germany, Belgium, Luxemburg, and the Netherlands). Due to its geographical extension and the unofficial character of transactions, the market is difficult to monitor.[36] Another problem is the occurrence of so-called daisy chains, i.e. series of sales that involve the same physical quantity of oil.[37] Therefore, accurate data on quantities traded on the Rotterdam market are not available. The information on prices, however, is good. There are several information services that report prices on a daily basis.

Before the second oil crisis, spot markets for crude oil were rather unimportant in terms of their share in global petroleum trade.[38] The spot market primarily served the purpose of balancing surpluses and deficits of traders who had bound themselves to long-term contracts. Less than five percent of internationally traded petroleum were traded via spot markets. In the eighties this situation changed dramatically. In the middle of the eighties 30-35% of petroleum were traded on the spot market. This can be attributed to the severe pressure the refining industry was facing at that time. Due to the decline in demand, capacity utilisation decreased on average and refiners tended to use more flexible ways of buying their crude and selling their re-fined products.[39] Besides spot-market transactions, spot-related deals gained major significance. These deals do not use the spot market itself but only the price information provided by the spot market. Among others, the following types of transactions belong to this category:[40]

- barter deals, e.g. oil for investment goods or military arms,

- petroleum as payment for debt,

- package deals, e.g. a package of crude oil, refined products and basic petrochemicals,

- discount offers, either by reducing the price itself or indirectly by offering favourable financial terms, and

---

(1985) and *Bird* (1987) provide empirical evidence concerning the efficiency of the Rotterdam market.

[36] *Roeber* (1979), p. 49, has expressed this fact the following way: *"If there is such a thing as 'the Rotterdam market', it is not a market and it is not at Rotterdam."*

[37] *Fesharaki/Isaak* (1986), pp. 20-21, and *Mabro et al.* (1986), pp. 178-181, report the case of a cargo which was sold and bought by 24 parties in 36 deals over a period of three months.

[38] For a more detailed description of the history of the spot market see *Fesharaki/Razavi* (1986), pp. 10-12.

[39] See *Fesharaki/Razavi* (1986), p. 11.

[40] See *Fesharaki/Razavi* (1986), pp. 28-34.

- term contracts at spot prices.

These types of transactions were used by oil-exporting countries to increase their competitiveness in a situation of excess supply. Especially Iran and Iraq were engaged in spot-related transactions because of their special financial needs that arose from the involvement in the Gulf War.

In the middle of the eighties, about half of the international trade in petroleum took part in spot-related transactions. Adding the transactions that used the spot market directly, this implies that 80% of internationally traded petroleum was sold on a spot basis. Thus, the early eighties were characterised by a tendency from long-term relationships towards more flexible forms of trading.

This development may in part be attributed to the oil glut that provided some essential incentives to increase flexibility. But it also reflects the structural change in the oil market. The importance of the major oil companies and their integrated networks has decreased.[41] This implies that a bigger share of the petroleum appears on the market. Another important element is the vertical integration by the oil-exporting countries. Downstream integration exposes the producer to competition in downstream markets which traditionally have been more flexible than the market for crude oil. Moreover, the number of participants in the international oil market has increased substantially. These trends support the hypothesis that transactions on a spot basis will remain important even if the market turns into a seller's market again in some years.[42]

2.3.3. Netback contracts

Compared to long-term contracts with fixed prices, spot-market transactions and spot-related deals shift a part of the price risk to the producer of petroleum. A special type of spot-related transaction that shifts the whole price risk to the producer was introduced in the middle of the eighties: the so-called netback contract.

Netback contracts as a new form of trading crude oil emerged on the market in the middle of the eighties when new channels for marketing crude oil were sought by some of the major oil-producing countries. Though developed and applied first by other OPEC countries, netback contracting became important when Saudi Arabia started to use it as a tool for increasing its market share in the second half of 1985. Saudi Arabia had borne most of the burden of keeping OPEC's production low. When in August 1986 its production fell to nearly 2 million barrels per day, i.e. to half of the official quota or 20% of production capacity, Saudi

---

[41] This in particular concerns the upstream sector where substantial disintegration has taken place. See *Luciani* (1984), pp. 8-23.

[42] Similar conclusions are drawn by *Verleger* (1987).

Arabia abandoned its swing-producer role and increased production. As a means of marketing the increased volume, netback contracts were chosen.[43]

A netback contract relates the price of crude oil directly to the market prices of the products that are obtained from refining the oil.[44] The contract specifies the refinery yield, i.e. the mix of products. These products are evaluated by their spot market prices at a certain date, usually the date at which the refined products can be expected to be in the market. This implies a delay of some weeks between delivery (fob) and price determination, due to the transportation and refining lags. From this price of the product mix, expected transportation costs, marginal refinery costs and an appropriate profit margin for the buyer are deduced. This then is the price paid for the crude oil.

The parameters involved in the computation of the netback value are a matter of negotiation. For instance, it is in the seller's interest to keep production and refinery costs low whereas the buyer has the opposite intention. Even the refinery yield is negotiated. The product mix obtained from a barrel of crude oil is not constant but varies to a certain extent depending on the technological specifities of the refinery. The seller prefers a refinery yield with a higher share of high-price products, e.g. naphta and motor gasoline, than the buyer.[45]

The risk-allocation effect of a netback contract compared to a conventional spot market transaction is that not only the crude oil price risk but also the product price risk is transferred to the seller. This is shown in Table 2.2.

The large-scale utilisation of netback contracts, first by Saudi Arabia and then by many other oil-exporting countries, had two effects. On the one hand, in the case of Saudi Arabia it provided the opportunity to market the increased production effectively. This in turn caused the oil price collapse in the beginning of 1986 since Saudi Arabian production increases were not offset by drawbacks in the production of other oil exporters. On the other hand, the Rotterdam spot market lost much of its importance in this year. Many oils, among them the former marker crude Arabian Light, disappeared from the market for a couple of months. The North Sea crude

---

[43] Long before the invention of netback contracts other OPEC member countries, e.g. Algeria, Kuwait and Venezuela, already had the opportunity of netback pricing since a large proportion of their petroleum exports were refined products. See *Al Chalabi* (1988), pp. 7-9. Downstream integration brings the implicit crude oil price into close relation to spot-related product prices and, therefore, has the same effect as a netback contract.

[44] For a more detailed description of netback contracts see *Fesharaki/Razavi* (1986), especially pp. 35-49.

[45] Since there are seasonal fluctuations in the prices of petroleum products (e.g. the price of heating oil tends to be higher in winter), the refinery yields desired by the contracting parties may vary over time.

Brent and West Texas Intermediate became new markers. These sorts of petroleum are also traded on futures markets, which tend to gain increased importance.

Table 2.2.: Distribution of risks for different types of transactions

	term contract	spot market	netback
crude oil price risk	buyer	seller	seller
product price risk	buyer	buyer	seller

2.3.4. Futures markets for crude oil and petroleum products[46]

Increased price volatility in the seventies and eighties and the existence of transportation and refining lags have provided incentives to establish futures markets for petroleum and petroleum products. The first successful attempt was the creation of futures contracts for heating oil in New York. Meanwhile, contracts for other products have been introduced and even crude oil is traded.[47] The New-York Mercantile Exchange (NYMEX) offers futures contracts in West Texas Intermediate and at the International Petroleum Exchange in London Brent Blend is traded. After the introduction of these contracts the volume of trade has increased quickly, especially in New York. The 1987 volume of trade in crude oil futures exceeded global production.[48]

Futures markets are used for the purposes of hedging and speculation. Hedging is used to reduce the risk of making losses if there is price variablity in the cash market. The hedger takes a position in the futures market which is equal in quantity but opposite in obligation to the

---

[46] Here only a short discussion of some of the many aspects of petroleum futures markets can be provided. For more detailed analyses see *Prast/Lax* (1983), *Verleger* (1984), *Banks* (1985), *Razavi/Fesharaki* (1986), *Bohi/Toman* (1987), *Chen/Sears/Tzang* (1987), *Lymbery* (1988), and *Niering* (1988).

[47] For the history of petroleum futures markets see *Fesharaki/Razavi* (1986), pp. 61-67.

[48] See *Niering* (1988), p. 58. It should be noted, however, that the trade that takes place physically (wet barrels) is only a small proportion, usually less than 2%, of the volume of transactions (paper barrels). See *Prast/Lax* (1983), p. 90.

position she holds in the cash market.[49] Speculators demand risk and take positions according to their price expectations.

Real-world futures markets are far from being complete and perfect. Petroleum futures contracts go out only 15 to 18 months. This implies that oil producers, usually having a time horizon of more than a decade, cannot hedge all their production.[50] Therefore, existing petroleum futures markets do not solve the problem of intertemporal uncertainty which arises from the exhaustibility of resources.

They are, however, useful for hedging shorter-term risks. Moreover, they have acquired a major role in the process of oil price formation. Futures market prices are available instantaneously on a minute-by-minute basis whereas spot market prices are published with a lag of one day. So the futures market provides information that is not available from the spot market. One can argue that this increase in transparency has had a major impact on the increase of spot market transactions during the early eighties. The additional price information constitutes a basis for negotiations of spot transactions.[51]

2.3.5. Petroleum prices and scarcity

In the preceding sections we have identified four prices for petroleum: a contract price, a spot market price, a netback value and the futures market price. They reflect different aspects of the scarcity of petroleum:

- The contract price reflects the future scarcity of petroleum over a time interval, perceived at the time at which the contract is signed.

- The futures market price is an indicator of the scarcity expected to prevail at a certain future date.

- The spot market price measures the scarcity of petroleum at the date of delivery of crude oil.

- The netback value reflects the scarcity of petroleum at the time when refined products face the market.

---

[49] See *Prast/Lax* (1983), pp. 19-27, and *Chen/Sears/Tzang* (1987, pp. 502-505. Hedging is beneficial not only for those who trade petroleum in the cash market. As *Overdahl* (1987) has shown, oil-producing states that depend on oil-production tax revenues can insure these revenues by using petroleum futures contracts.

[50] See *Chen/Sears/Tzang* (1987), p. 507.

[51] See *Razavi/Fesharaki* (1986), pp. 67-71. For a theoretical analysis of the interaction of futures and spot market prices see *Bohi/Toman* (1987).

The spot price is the only one of these prices that indicates the current scarcity of crude oil at each date. It serves the purpose of clearing the crude oil market. This function of the spot market was perceived in particular during the times of drastic price changes, e.g. after the oil crises. OPEC's official prices followed the spot price with significant lags.[52] Therefore, the spot market price (fob Ras Tanura/Saudi Arabia) will be chosen as the appropriate price of petroleum in the subsequent analysis.

2.4. A brief history of the world petroleum market

On the world petroleum market there have not only been significant changes in the way the oil is traded but also changes in the balance of political and economic power and in the distribution of property rights. In what follows, these events will be briefly described in their historical context and evaluated with respect to their influence on economic variables.

Since the subject of this study is the development of the oil price during the seventies and eighties, special emphasis will be placed on this era. Recent events are, however, embedded into a long history of international petroleum trade dating back to the first decades of this century. So it is necessary to first describe the state of the world petroleum market prior to the oil crises.

2.4.1. The oil market before OPEC

After World War II, almost the entire world petroleum market was in the hands of seven major oil companies, the so-called Seven Sisters.[53] In the twenties and thirties they had acquired concessions in the major oil-producing areas of the world. These concessions had durations of sixty to seventy-five years. They specified an area (in most cases a whole country or region) in which an oil company or consortium was allowed to explore and to produce petroleum. There were no upper or lower bounds of production and exploration activities, and the obligations of the concessionaire were reduced to paying taxes and royalties to the host country.[54] To put it briefly: the role of the host country was that of a mere tax collector.

---

[52] On this see the empirical results presented by *Verleger* (1982), pp. 58-66, and *Fitzgerald/Pollio* (1984).

[53] See *Sampson* (1975) for the history of the rise of these multinationals. For a detailed analysis of the conduct of the world petroleum market after the Second World War see *Adelman* (1972).

[54] See *Mikesell* (1984), pp. 20-23, for a more detailed description of the old concession system.

Most of the crude petroleum was refined and retailed by the vertically integrated network of the oil companies. Since there was almost no market for crude oil, they also managed to determine the crude oil price. This is associated with the posted price system. In order to create a basis for the deduction of taxes and royalties, the value of the petroleum extracted in the host country was related to Texas Gulf prices taking into account the transportation costs that would have occured had the oil been transported there.[55]

The posted price was almost constant over the fifties and sixties. At the end of the fifties the concessionaires announced a decrease in the posted price which reduced the tax revenues of the host countries. As a response to this price reduction, five of the major oil-producing countries founded the Organization of Petroleum Exporting Countries. It was intended as an instrument to increase the bargaining power against the Seven Sisters and avoid further price reductions. During the first ten years this enterprise did not seem to be successful. Almost unnoticed, however, institutional changes took place which tended to erode the power of the major oil companies.

2.4.2. Alteration of property rights

There were three factors that contributed to the growth of the importance of oil producing countries in international oil business:

- growing national self-confidence of the oil exporting countries,

- the increasing dependency of the industrialised countries on imported oil, and

- the emergence of competition in the upstream sector by independent oil companies,

The first of these elements is sometimes referred to as the ideological factor underlying the structural changes of international oil business.[56] This principle says that the resource-rich country (rather than any foreign company) should be the sovereign owner of the natural resources located on its territory. This view was strongly supported by the Third World independency movement. An economic motivation for nationalising the oil industry was the fact that " *[t]he international oil industry had taken far more capital out of these countries (through repatriation of profits) than it had put in new investments*".[57]

The second factor was the world's dependency on imported oil, especially oil imported from OPEC countries. When OPEC was founded in 1960, its five member countries represented

---

[55]   See *Mikesell* (1984), p. 22.

[56]   See *Mikesell* (1984), p. 25.

[57]   *Schneider* (1983), p. 120.

38% of worldwide oil production. Thirteen years later OPEC's share was nearly 56%.[58] In the sixties and early seventies, OPEC's share in internationally traded crude oil amounted to some ninety percent. This and the abundancy of petroleum resources increased OPEC's market power.

A third factor was the increasing effort of smaller independent US oil companies to become concessionaires in the Middle East and North Africa after World War II. On the one hand, this meant a competitive pressure on the Majors. On the other hand, the independents had a weaker position in negotiations than the major oil companies whose concessions were spread over a number of countries. Many of the independents, in contrast, owned concessions only in single countries. Due to this dependency they were more vulnerable than the Majors.[59]

The weaker position of the independents had two effects. First, it was easier for the host countries to achieve favourable contractual arrangements. In a second step, it was possible to re-negotiate the contracts to obtain even more favourable conditions. This was exercised very successfully by Libya in 1969/70.[60] Once favourable conditions had been achieved by Libya, other countries followed. Thus, the power of the international oil companies in the upstream sector of the world petroleum market was eroded step by step. The change in property rights was no revolution but a long-lasting process of slowly increasing participation of the host countries in the oil industry. It started in the early fifties and was completed by and large at the end of the seventies, as far as OPEC countries are concerned.[61]

2.4.3. New contractual relationships

The alteration of property rights was instituted via the replacement of the classical concessions by new types of contracts in the upstream sector. The common feature of these contracts was that they restricted the freedom of the investor to explore and produce wherever and how

---

[58] Data from *OPEC Annual Bulletin 1979*, pp. XIV and XX.

[59] The power of the Majors can best be illustrated by the example of the Iranian nationalisation of 1951. As a response to the nationalisation, BP instituted a boycott of Iranian oil. Since the companies had sufficient alternative sources of oil, this boycott was successful. See *Schneider* (1983), pp. 31-35.

[60] For a detailed description of the Libyan case see *Sampson* (1975), pp. 208-229, *Schneider* (1983), pp. 139-148, and *Shwadran* (1986), pp. 20-21.

[61] A chronology of nationalisations is reported by *Kobrin* (1984), pp. 158-162. *Shwadran* (1986), pp. 72-77, provides a detailed description of the process of producer participation in Arab oil-exporting countries.

much she wanted. The following types of contracts can be distinguished (although the spectrum of intermediate and mixed types is nearly continuous):[62]

- Complete nationalisation: All activities (exploration, development, production, and marketing) are carried out by state-owned companies. Though desired by many oil exporting countries, nationalisation of the oil industry is often not possible since many of the countries lack the know-how and/or the capital required to operate the petroleum industry.

- Joint venture: A project is carried out jointly by the host country and a foreign investor. Both parties make equity contributions, and they share the returns and the risks of the project.

- Service contract: Foreign firms are contracted to provide certain services. If payments depend on success, this is called a risk-service contract. Service contracts are also used in nationalised industries to hire specialist services, e.g. seismic exploration.

- Production-sharing contract: A foreign firm operates a resource project. The production is shared among the host country and the contractor. The main difference compared to a risk-service contract is that the foreign firm is paid in kind.

- Modern concession agreement: The concessionaire has the right to explore and exploit a resource stock. There are royalties, taxes and other payments to be made to the host country. Some additional obligations have to be met, such as minimum exploration requirements, monitoring and preferential employment of the domestic labour force. In these respects the modern concession is more restrictive than the classical one.

There have been several attempts to analyse these different concepts and the corresponding tax regimes with respect to their effects on incentives and risk allocation.[63] For the following analysis, however, these questions are of minor importance. It is important, though, that oil-exporting countries are no longer merely tax collectors but actively participate in the operation of their oil industries. This is especially true for OPEC countries; the government share in their crude oil production has risen to 87%.[64]

While the process of *de-jure* nationalisation covered a period of thirty years (from the early fifties to the late seventies), *de-facto* nationalisation of the reserves of the major oil-exporting countries took place during a short period in the early seventies. When launching the oil embargo in October 1973, OPEC countries made clear that they claimed full sovereignity over their resources.

---

[62] See *Mikesell* (1984), ch. 3, and *Meyer* (1988), ch. 3.

[63] See *Virmani* (1988) and *Meyer* (1988), chs. 6-8.

[64] See *OPEC Annual Statistical Bulletin 1987*, p. 66.

2.4.4. OPEC and the oil price in the seventies and eighties: A chronology of events

Three drastic price jumps have been the major characteristics of the oil price development of the last one-and-a-half decades. The history of OPEC's successes, however, had already started two years before the first oil shock. In 1971 the OPEC conferences held at Teheran and Tripoli led to significant changes in the relationship among the host countries and the concessionaires. OPEC demanded increases in the oil price of more than 25% and succeeded. These were OPEC's first successful attempts to get an influence on oil prices.[65]

In October 1973 the Yom Kippur War broke out. As a response to Western military support for Israel, the Arab oil-producing states decided to cut production by 5% and to impose an embargo on the USA and the Netherlands.[66] Production was cut once again in November. This led to a reduction of Arab oil production by 5 million b/d or 24%.[67] In December the posted price for Arabian Light oil was raised by more than 400% to $11.65 per barrel. At the same time the spot market price reached $19.35.[68]

It is worthwhile to notice that it were the political motives that unified the major oil-exporting countries. Had there not been Israel as a common enemy, the Arab countries, different in their interests and political orientation, would probably not have been able or willing to synchronise their oil policies.[69] The first oil shock and the price increase, therefore, were results of politically motivated decisions rather than economic reasoning. The question why this price increase became permanent, however, demands an economic explanation.

OPEC did not need to reduce its oil production to keep the price up. It was sufficient to keep production constant. OPEC's production had increased by 84% during the six years that preceded the oil crisis, but in 1979 production was 0.2% below the 1973 level. Due to the increase in worldwide demand, OPEC's market share shrunk from 55.9 to 49.2% during these six years.[70] Over some periods, however, it was necassary to reduce production temporarily to main-

---

[65] See *Adelman* (1972), pp. 250-262, and *Schneider* (1983), pp. 149-166.

[66] For a more detailed description of the events during the first oil crisis see *Schneider* (1983), ch. 8, and *Shwadran* (1986), pp. 47-67.

[67] See *Schneider* (1983), p. 230.

[68] See *Verleger* (1982), p. 33.

[69] See *Schneider* (1983), p. 234. The political motives underlying Arab oil politicies are also emphasised by *Al-Sowayegh* (1984) from an Arab point of view.

[70] The underlying data were taken from *OPEC Annual Statistical Bulletin 1986*, p. 15.

tain the price level. E.g., Saudi Arabia cut its production substantially in 1977/78 to avoid a glut that would have eroded the price level.[71]

The five years following the first oil crisis were a period of almost constant real oil prices. In 1979 this situation changed because of the revolution in Iran.[72] In November and December 1978 there had already been strikes in the Iranian oil industry that had reduced production temporarily from six to one million barrels per day. During the first nine weeks of the year 1979, Iran did not export any petroleum.[73] This was a loss of 8% of world supply, and on the spot markets prices peaked although other oil exporters increased their production.[74] When Iranian exports were re-installed in March, increased inventory demand kept the market tight.[75]

Spot market prices doubled in 1979. During the second half of the year, they fluctuated above 30 $/b. OPEC's official selling price followed the spot price with considerable lags. During this adjustment process, conflicts of interests among OPEC member countries became obvious. While Saudi Arabia preferred to keep the price low, other member countries such as Algeria, Iran, Libya and Nigeria, the so-called hawks, increased their prices above OPEC's official prices unilaterally by adding surcharges.[76] With some delay the 'doves' followed these increases. When demand for OPEC oil fell substantially in 1980, voluntary cutbacks by some OPEC members helped to keep the price up. The reduction of supply was accelerated when the Gulf war broke out in September. During 1980 the official price of Saudi-Arabian Light oil was increased from 26 to 32 $/b, and in October 1981 this price reached its historical peak of 34 $/b.

The second oil shock reduced demand for OPEC oil dramatically. This was due to oil-saving measures and in particular to the increase in non-OPEC production.[77] OPEC's

---

[71] See *Schneider* (1983), pp. 304-307.

[72] Some of the political and religous background of this revolution is reviewed by *Schneider* (1983), pp. 417-419.

[73] See *Schneider* (1983), pp. 436.

[74] In February 1979, however, Saudi Arabia then producing near capacity cut its production by 1 million b/d which increased pressure on prices. See *Schneider* (1983), p. 437.

[75] Another explanation for market tightness might be viewed in the increased share of government-to-government oil deals in 1979/80. This made oil scarcer on the free markets. See *Wilson* (1987), p. 144.

[76] See *Shwadran* (1986), pp. 151-152.

[77] The 1979/80 oil price shock ultimately led to a decline in demand by 5.9 mbd and to an increase in non-OPEC oil production by 6.0 mbd. See *OPEC Annual Statistical Bulletin 1987*,

production fell from 30.9 million b/d 1979 to 22.6 in 1981 and tended to decrease further. This decline was much more than the production cutback due to the Gulf war. One had to think about a system of production quotas in order to defend the price. In March 1982 OPEC decided to reduce production to 18 million b/d, and in April this was reduced to 17.5 million b/d by Saudi Arabia cutting its production.[78] One year later the official price for OPEC oil was reduced by 5 $/b. This was the first reduction of the nominal oil price in the history of the Organization.

In the following years, demand for OPEC oil declined again and in 1985 daily production was near 15 million barrels. In January 1985 the official price was reduced a second time, to 28 $/b. Most of the OPEC countries exceeded their production quotas and offered price discounts. Saudi Arabia became the sole swing producer and in Summer 1985 its production was near 2 million b/d or less than 50% of the official quota (and less than 20% of production capacity). So Saudi Arabia decided to raise its production to the official quota. The increased production was sold via netback contracts. The additional supply and the close link of the crude oil price to the product spot market brought the price down very quickly. As other oil exporters also adopted the netback strategy, the market became nearly competitive; in August 1986 crude oil was traded for less than 8 $/b.

The Saudi-Arabian retaliation strategy was successful in that OPEC managed to agree on a common pricing and production strategy again in February 1987. The official price of the marker crude Arabian Light was fixed at 17.52 $/b. Spot markets reacted with price increases that, however, were not permanent. During the following one-and-a-half years the spot market price was substantially below the official price for most of the time. On the one hand, this is due to the fact that, in spite of the drastic price decline, demand for OPEC oil did not increase substantially. On the other hand, there have been problems of cartel discipline again.

Before the second oil crisis, OPEC did not have many problems of maintaining its dominant position in the world oil market. In the eighties, however, OPEC has acted as a "*clumsy cartel*".[79] A lack of cartel stability together with the problem of fine-tuning pricing and production policies at the same time in the presence of imperfect information made it difficult to find something like an optimal strategy.

---

pp. 15 and 23. The most significant increases in production occurred in the United Kingdom and Mexico. For changes in the regional distribution of production shares see also Table 2.1.

[78] See *Shwadran* (1986), p. 180.

[79] This expression is due to *Adelman* (1980).

2.5. Summary of some stylised facts

During the last twenty years, the world petroleum market has experienced significant structural changes and increasingly volatile prices.

The most important institutional change took place in the early seventies. It was the alteration of property rights: oil-exporting countries turned from tax collectors into sovereign producers. This was the institutional presupposition of OPEC's market power in the subsequent years.

In the first half of the eighties, a second major change occurred. The flexibility of international trade in petroleum increased considerably. Fixed-price term contracts were increasingly substituted by spot-related transactions, futures markets were established, and the number of market participants increased. This led to more competition and market transparency.

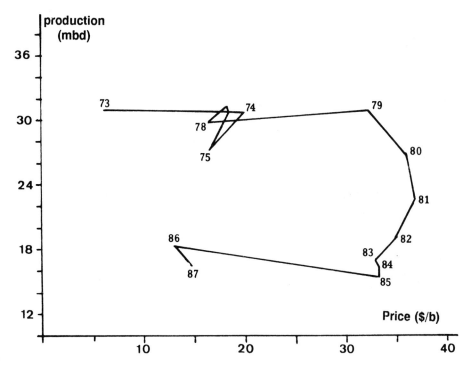

Figure 2.3.: OPEC production and the real oil price

The first two price shocks led to demand reductions and substantial increases in non-OPEC production. Demand for OPEC oil shrunk considerably, especially in the first half of the eighties. This is shown in Figure 2.3. where the real price of oil and OPEC production are plotted into one diagram.[80] Most of the following analysis is targeted at an explanation of this oil market cycle. Of course, the oil crises were due to non-economic reasons, namely the Middle East War and the Iranian revolution. Had these historical events been the only reasons for price changes, the price increases would not have been permanent. The permanency of the new prices, or what *Danielsen* (1979) calls the oil price ratchet effect, demands an economic explanation. This is the subject of the following chapters.

---

[80] The real oil price is obtained by using the exports price index for manufactured goods from industrial countries, published in the *UN Monthly Bulletin*, as a deflator. The nominal price and OPEC production are taken from *Petroleum Economist*, the *OPEC Bulletin* and the *OPEC Annual Statistical Bulletin*.

3. The price of petroleum in economic theory

3.1. Types of oil market models

There exists a vast literature on the economics of oil price formation. The spectrum ranges from insider comments on day-to-day events in specialist periodicals like the *Petroleum Economist* or the *Oil and Gas Journal* to rigorous mathematical treatments of intertemporal models in the lemma-theorem-proof mode. This chapter is an attempt to review this literature, at least the main streams of it, and to provide a synopsis of the most important and influential approaches. The analysis will focus on models that can be used to predict future oil price developments.[81] There are competing thoughts and paradigms, and the task is to evaluate them with respect to their fit to the data and their explanatory power. It will be seen that there remain some open questions that have not been answered yet, and one of these gaps will be chosen to develop a theoretical model of oil price determination in the next chapter.

Two broad categories of oil market models can be distinguished. On the one hand, there are demand models studying alternative scenarios under the assumption that the price paths are given. Examples are the oil models of *Kennedy* (1974, 1976), *Choucri* (1981) and *Choe* (1984).[82] For an explanation of the process of oil price formation, these models are of minor relevance and will not be subject to further discussion. On the other hand, there are models that introduce the oil price as an endogenous variable and allow for the identification of critical parameters. Among these models one can distinguish two sub-categories: models that involve intertemporally optimising behaviour and static or dynamic models without consideration of intertemporal aspects. The former approach is closely connected to the concepts of resource scarcity and user costs, the latter consists of a variety of models that cannot be subsumed under a common heading. The broad spectrum of both types of oil price models will be discussed on the following pages.

3.2. The economic theory of exhaustible resources

It was in the early seventies when economic theory re-discovered the exhaustibility of natural resources. Two books had been published by *Forrester* (1971) and *Meadows et al.* (1972) that predicted the doomsday to be in sight. By simulating dynamic systems, they forecasted a

---

[81] For a broader survey which also considers neo-marxist, institutionalist and other approaches that do not claim to provide quantifiable results, see *Roncaglia* (1983,1985) and *Bina* (1985), pp. 1-20.

[82] For a survey of such models see *Ulph* (1980) and *Fesharaki/Johnson* (1982).

world running out of vital resources within only decades and prophecised an era of economic decline. These results represented a fundamental challenge to the optimistic view suggested by traditional growth theory.

According to *Boulding* (1971), the concept underlying the traditional theory is that of a 'cowboy economy' (that can expand westwards to overcome limits to growth). As an alternative, he developed the paradigm of the 'spaceship earth' which is endowed with a finite stock of resources. The modern theory of exhaustible resources can be viewed as an attempt to combine the traditional growth models and the 'spaceship earth' approach. In this context, many of the earlier contributions dealt with questions like the survival of a resource-depending economy and of justice between generations.[83]

The exhaustibility of natural resources as a major concern of economic theory as well as corresponding doomsday forecasts are not new. Economists have been concerned with the scarcity of natural resources for centuries, e.g. *Malthus* (1798) and *Jevons* (1869). *Ricardo* (1817), in Chapter 3 of his 'Principles of Political Economy and Taxation', was the first to provide a satisfactory theoretical framework for an economic explanation of the increasing resource prices. The modern theory of depletable resources was established in 1931 by *Hotelling* in his seminal paper, which then was forgotten for several decades.[84] This article layed the fundaments of modern resource economics. In the following sections, the Ricardian approach, which is still influential, and *Hotelling's* model will be discussed and compared to each other.[85]

3.2.1. The Ricardian approach

Ricardo recognised that the price of a mineral resource should increase over time. He argued that there are deposits of different quality and accessibility. The current resource price is always determined by the mine with the highest cost, and the owners of mines that are cheaper to exploit enjoy a differential rent. In the first place, the low-cost deposits will be exploited. When they are exhausted, lower-quality deposits will be mined and so forth. This implies that the price of these resources, measured by the value of the labour necessary to extract them, must increase over time. Periods of decreasing prices are possible if technological progress or learning-effects

---

[83] See *Stiglitz* (1974) and *Solow* (1974a,1974b). Surveys of the economic theory of exhaustible resources are given by *Fisher/Peterson* (1977), *Withagen* (1981), and *Devarajan/Fisher* (1982).

[84] Similar ideas had already been expressed by *Gray* (1914), though in a less rigorous and more fragmentary manner.

[85] For a comparison between Ricardian and modern models of exhaustible resources see also *Roncaglia* (1983) and *Siebert* (1986a).

reduce the mining costs. In the long run, however, the scarcity effect dominates, and the price rises.

The approach will be formalised briefly before its application to oil prices is discussed. Let $q(t)$ be current and $Z(t)$ be cumulated production. Then the costs of extracting a unit of the resource, $k(Z(t))$, should be an increasing function of cumulated production, i.e. $k'(.) > 0$. The resource stock available at time t, $R(t)$, is the initial stock, R_o, minus cumulated production. Thus, the cost function can be rewritten: $k(R_o - R(t))$. The stock of the resource is reduced by the current rate of extraction. Denoting the time derivative by a dot above the variable, this can be written as:

$$(3.2.1) \qquad \dot{R}(t) \; = \; -q(t).$$

In a competitive equilibrium, supply, $q(t)$, equals demand, $D(.)$, which is inversely related to the price of the resource, $p(t)$, and the price equals the marginal extraction costs which in this case are equal to the average costs:

$$(3.2.2) \qquad q(t) \; = \; D(p(t)),$$

$$(3.2.3) \qquad p(t) \; = \; k(R_o - R(t)).$$

Some simple calculations show that

$$\dot{p}(t) \; = \; k'(R_o - R(t)) \; D(p(t))$$

and from (3.2.3)

$$(3.2.4) \qquad \dot{p}(t) \; = \; k'(k^{-1}(p(t))) \, D(p(t))$$

It is clear from (3.2.4) that the price is increasing over time. The shape of the time profile can be determined by differentiating (3.2.4) with respect to $p(t)$:

$$(3.2.5) \qquad \frac{d\dot{p}(t)}{dp(t)} \; = \; k'' D / k' \; + \; k' D'$$

where the arguments have been omitted for convenience. The sign of this expression is indeterminate since $k'D'$ is negative and the sign of the other term depends on the sign of k'', i.e. on whether the cost function is convex or concave. At least in the long run, one can reasonably assume a convex cost function since costs should go to infinity when the stock of reserves goes to zero, i.e. when cumulated production approaches R_o. If there is a choke-off price at which demand goes to zero, then $\dot{p}(t)$ goes to zero in the long run. Figure 3.1. uses the assumption that the cost function is linear in $Z(t)$. Then $\dot{p}(t)$ is proportional to demand and decreasing over time.

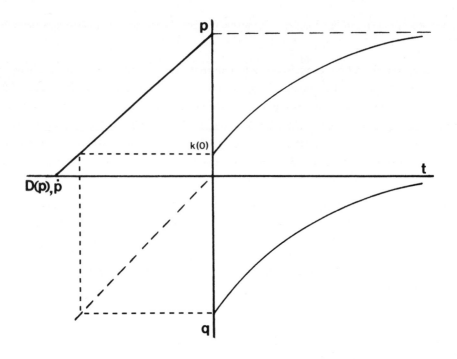

Figure 3.1.: A Ricardian price path with a linear cost function

Exploration and development of reserves can easily be introduced into this model. Under competitive conditions, the price of the resource should equal the marginal cost of mining plus the marginal cost of replacing it through exploration. If exploration costs are an increasing function of cumulated production, then the qualitative result concerning the price path remains the same: cumulated production of the resource drives its price up.

Ricardian arguments have been used in several studies to estimate future resource prices. An example for an application of the simple Ricardian model is the article by *Griffin/ Jones* (1986) who intend to determine the competitive lower bound of the oil price. They achieve this aim by considering extraction costs of Texas oil fields. Although the authors claim the method to be appropriate at least for the investigation of short-term price formation, the neglect of exploration costs is an obvious shortcoming. The costs of discovering new reserves that can replace depleted petroleum are taken into account by *Adelman* (1972), p. 6 and pp. 73-76, where he introduces the concept of 'maximum economic finding costs'. In a study on the lower bound of oil prices, *Adelman* (1986) estimates the lowest possible price to lie in a range of 2 to 5$. There are a number of other studies that, implicitly or explicitly, use Ricardian arguments and derive the price of petroleum as its marginal extraction cost plus exploration costs. Examples are

Saunders (1984b) and *Ait-Laoussine/Parra* (1985). *Devarajan/Fisher* (1982) interpret exploration costs as a measure of scarcity and show that in the US oil industry these costs have increased significantly during the decades prior to the first oil shock.[86] Their theoretical model is used by *Pakravan* (1983) to determine upper bounds for the scarcity rent for petroleum in the Middle East, and he finds values of some cents per barrel.

The conclusion one can draw from the empirical studies is that Ricardian arguments can be used to construct reference scenarios, e.g. lower bounds of oil prices. Differential rents do, however, not explain the wide gap between the price of petroleum and its costs of extraction. In the past, the price has driven costs rather than vice versa.

The major theoretical shortcoming of the Ricardian approach is that it is merely a lining-up of static models rather than a really dynamic view of the problem: the extractor does not take the intertemporal character of her decisions into account but only considers the current cost situation. The fact that current extraction affects future costs is neglected. Modern approaches try to avoid this shortcoming and model the mine as a intertemporally optimising firm.

3.2.2. A simple model of exhaustibility

The intertemporal aspect of resource extraction arises from their non-renewability. The quantity of a resource which has been extracted and used, e.g. in a production process, is not available for future use any more. Potential utilisations of the resource compete intertemporally and, therefore, constitute opportunity costs. The opportunity cost of using a unit of the resource today - or its user cost - is the utility of foregone future uses.[87]

---

[86] In their model, discovery costs only depend on current effort but not on a state variable like cumulated effort or discoveries. Due to the structure of the model, there are no limits to discoveries and complete replacement of exploited resources is always possible. If the model is extended to more than two periods, the approach turns into a renewable-resources model. *Pindyck* (1978a) shows that such a model possesses a saddle point which is attained in the long run. This saddle-point result is typical for models analysing the use of renewable resources. See for instance *Plourde* (1970) and *Fisher* (1981), ch. 3. In his critique of the *Devarajan/Fisher* model, *Lasserre* (1985) shows that the results change substantially if discovery costs depend on cumulated discoveries. He obtains a rent on future discoveries which is similar to the *Hotelling* rent that will be discussed in the next section.

[87] The concept of user cost has already be mentioned by *Keynes* (1936) in his 'General Theory', pp. 66-73. For an explanation in the context of resource economics, see textbooks like *Dasgupta/Heal* (1979), especially ch. 6, or *Fisher* (1981), pp. 12-22.

The intertemporal character of decisions concerning the use of depletable resources is usually modelled via *Pontryagin's* maximum priciple.[88] The application of this technique, however, is not necessary to derive the central result. One can also use some simpler and quite obvious economic reasoning. Let the notation be as above and let the average extraction costs, k, be not a function of cumulated production any more but a constant. The resource stock is finite and non-renewable. The firm intends to maximise its present value and future profits are discounted at a rate r. Due to the finiteness of the resource base, one unit of the resource can only be extracted at certain point of time if the firm renounces extraction of this unit at some other date. An optimal solution is reached when the firm is indifferent between extracting today and tomorrow, i.e. if the gain of extracting a marginal additional unit today equals the the loss caused by the foregone possibility of extracting it tomorrow. Let h be the time interval between today and tomorrow. Then the indifference condition is

$$(3.2.6) \qquad (p(t)\text{-}k)\, e^{-rt} = (p(t+h)\text{-}k)\, e^{-r(t+h)}$$

or, by taking logarithms and rearranging,

$$(3.2.7) \qquad r = h^{-1} \left(\log (p(t+h)\text{-}k) - \log (p(t)\text{-}k) \right).$$

Now let h go to 0 and take the limit. Applying *de l'Hospital's* rule yields the following result:

$$(3.2.8) \qquad \dot{p}(t) = r\,(p(t)\text{-}k).$$

This is the central result of the economic theory of exhaustible resources, the so-called *Hotelling* rule. There is a wedge between the price and marginal costs which increases at the firm's discount rate. This rent accrues to all producers whereas the Ricardian differential rent can only be appropriated by the owners of low-cost mines. For an interpretation of this result, two lines of arguing are possible:[89]

-   Due to its scarcity relative to needs, the resource in the ground constitutes a store of wealth. In an asset market equilibrium, holding the resource should yield the same rate of interest as holding other stores of wealth like capital or bonds. Otherwise it would be possible to realise arbitrage profits. So there must be a royalty which increases at the rate of interest or another appropriate discount rate.

-   Alternatively, the equilibrium in the resource market can be chosen as the starting point of the argument. If there is a royalty increasing at the rate of interest, then the owners of mines are

---

[88] For a survey see *Smith* (1977).

[89] Compare *Solow* (1974a), p. 2-3.

indifferent between extracing and holding the resource. Otherwise the extraction rate would
be zero or infinity. So this r-percent rule is a condition for clearance of the resource market.

Figure 3.2. shows that the price increase is small in the beginning and large towards the
end of the time horizon.[90] The shaded area is the size of the reserves stock. If, instead of an
initial price p_1, a price p_2 were chosen, then the extraction rate would be greater along the whole
path and the resource would be "overexploited". If, on the other hand, the initial price were too
high, the resource would never be exhausted. It follows that the initial price has to be chosen
such that the *Hotelling* path just depletes the initial stock of reserves. The initial gap between
marginal extraction costs and the competitive price, i.e. the level of initial user cost, measures the
scarcity of the resource.[91]

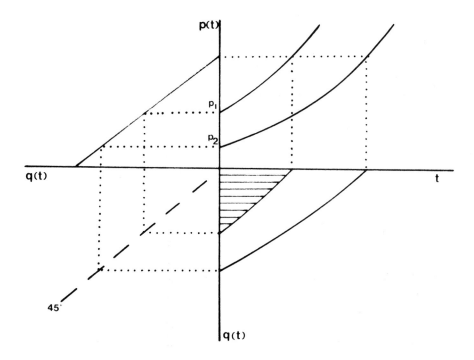

Figure 3.2.: A *Hotelling* price path

---

[90] Note that this finding is different from the Ricardian result of an ambiguous sign of the price
increase.

[91] This result has a formal analogon in control theory. There, the gap between price and
marginal costs equals the costate variable of the resource stock which can be interpreted as
its shadow price.

One of the shortcomings of this simple model is that its assumes homogeneity of the resource. In reality, however, the distribution of natural resources is characterised by a density which is decreasing with cumulative extraction. This implies increasing extraction costs. If this Ricardian element is introduced into *Hotelling's* model, the result changes significantly as *Hanson* (1980) has shown. The scarcity rent vanishes as the resource tends to be exhausted. Thus, the long-run result is a Ricardian one. If, however, stock effects do not matter so much, then *Hotelling's* model is a better approximation of the economic relationships that govern the use of exhaustible resources.[92]

3.2.3. Different market structures

It is a natural extension of this model to investigate what happens in the case of a non-competitive market structure. The simplest among these models is that of a monopolistic mining firm that has been considered by *Hotelling* (1931), pp. 146-152, himself. The result is that, as *Solow* (1974a), p. 8, has stated, *'the monopolist is the conservationist's friend'*. Monopolistic pricing leads to a higher initial price and defers the doomsday.[93] It can be derived by the same reasoning as *Hotelling's* rule for the competitive firm. At the margin, the owner of the mine must be indifferent between extracting today and tomorrow. Let $g(q(t))$ be the revenue function. Then the generalised rule is that marginal profit of the firm should be increasing at the rate of discount:

$$(3.2.9) \qquad \dot{g}'(q(t)) \;=\; r\,(g'(q(t)) - k).$$

The implications can be shown graphically as in Figure 3.3. Let g'_o be marginal revenue at time $t = 0$. It increases over time according to (3.2.9). Left of the vertical axis, the demand and the marginal-revenue schedules are depicted. Using the marginal-revenue curve, one can now construct the resource extraction path. The price path in the monopoly case can be constructed by means of the marginal revenue and the demand curve. The initial price is p_o. This price path must differ from the competitive price path. Along the competitive path, price minus marginal extraction costs increase at the discount rate. Since the discount rate and marginal costs have not changed, the path starting with p_o cannot be a competitive path. It is too flat: price minus marginal cost increase at a rate substantially lower than the discount rate. So the true competitive

---

[92] See also *Siebert* (1986a). He argues that not only stock-dependent extraction costs but also fixed costs in the extractive industry or a variable price of a substitute in the modify the *Hotelling's* result in a Ricardian direction.

[93] It should be noted that this result does not always hold. Some particular assumptions about extraction costs and the shape of the demand function have to be made. These requirements are, however, likely to be satisfied by real-world demand and cost functions.

path must be steeper. In order to exhaust the resources, the competitive path has to start at a lower initial price level. It is represented by the dashed curve in Figure 3.3. The projection into the quantity diagram shows that the competitive path exhausts the resource faster than the monopolist's path. This is just the statement made above.[94]

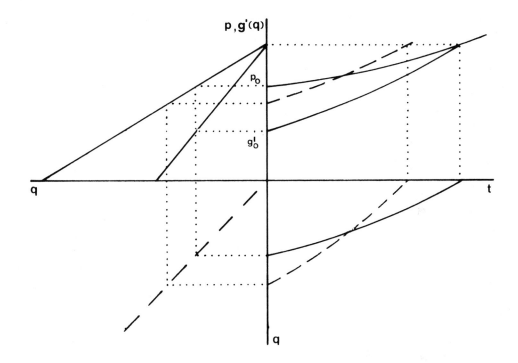

Figure 3.3.: Monopoly in the extraction of resources

For an application to the petroleum market, the model should be extended by considering a competitive fringe since OPEC's monopoly power is limited by the supply of other oil-producing countries. The higher the price, the more will these countries produce. The simplest way of modelling this is to introduce a supply function for non-OPEC oil. This has been done by *Kalymon* (1975) and *Crémer/Weitzman* (1976). They use models of this type for simulating optimal paths and obtain petroleum prices in a reasonable range. From an economic-theory viewpoint, however, these models do not go far beyond the simple monopoly model. By taking the difference between demand and non-OPEC supply, one obtains a demand-for-OPEC-oil curve, and the standard model can be applied.

---

[94] For a mathematical derivation of this result see *Dasgupta/Heal* (1979), pp. 333-334. If extraction costs are zero, then the shape of the extraction profile depends on the elasticity of demand. Only if demand becomes more elastic as the price increases, is the monopolist's path resource-saving. See also *Stiglitz* (1976).

A more satisfying approach to the competitive-fringe problem is the *Nash-Cournot* model. In this case, the optimising behaviour of the fringe is taken into account explicitly. Models of this type are considered by *Salant* (1976) and *Ulph/Folie* (1980).[95] They obtain two-phase price scenarios for the resource. In one phase, the market is competitive, in the other, a monopolistic market structure rules. When the change in the regime occurs, there is a kink in the price path. Of course, a kink is not a jump in the price and, therefore, these models cannot be used for explaining price shocks.[96] A shortcoming of the *Nash-Cournot* model is that each player takes the action of the others as given and that feedbacks are neglected. This has been noticed by *Newbery* (1981,1984) who shows that, in a *Stackelberg* setting with a leader-follower structure, the dominant-firm model can lead to dynamic inconsistency. In the beginning of the program, the dominant firm announces its extraction path. Once the game has been started, however, the monopolist might find it profitable to deviate from the announced path. So this model can be useful for the explanation of price shocks. It is, however, questionable whether in real-world actors use such a sophisticated model, and a simplified rule-of-the-thumb version is hard to be thought of.

There are an increasing number of papers that consider various types of market forms in between perfect competition and monopoly. A simple model of duopolistic behaviour of OPEC member countries has been presented by *Hnyilicza/Pindyck* (1976). They assume two different types of OPEC member countries: high absorbers, characterised by high population and a relatively small resource base, and low absorbers, with a small population and abundant reserves. They obtain an optimal program in which first the high absorbers extract all their resources and then, in a second period, the low absorbers are the sole producers. This is an unrealistic result, but it can be viewed as an extreme borderline idealisation of a smoother, less bang-bang-type reality. *Salant* (1982) considers a *Nash-Cournot* model of n independent suppliers of petroleum and presents simulation results. The price path is, of course, increasing over time and the oligopoly price path intersects the monopolistic path from below.[97] During an initial period, the extraction rate is lower than in the monopoly model. This might indicate that the oligopolistic price path is closer to a competitive price path - a result which is in accordance with intuition. *Loury* (1986) has solved the model explicitly and shows that average and marginal return of the players are inversely related to their initial endowments.

---

[95] An extension which also considers exploration has been presented by *Eswaran/Lewis* (1985).

[96] Another result of these models should be mentioned briefly. While *Salant* (1976) assumes identical cost functions, *Ulph/Folie* (1982) consider cost differences between the cartel and the fringe. *Salant's* assumption implies that the existence of a cartel increases the profits of the fringe whereas in the more general approach the effect is ambiguous.

[97] See *Salant* (1982), p. 25.

How important is non-competitive behaviour in the oil market? *Pindyck* (1987) shows that the scarcer the resource the weaker is monopoly power. Monopoly power is diminished since in the case of a finite resource stock the monopolist cannot adjust her production to the behaviour of demand in each period as she likes. There is an intertemporal restraint. The scarcer the resource, the less variable is the extraction rate in each period. Therefore, if the resource base is small, the rigidity rent dominates the monopoly rent. *Pindyck*, however, argues that in the real world the intertemporal restraint is not so important and that monopoly power explains more of the prices of most resources than intertemporal scarcity.

3.2.4. The resource-exporting country

A branch of resource economics that has attracted increased attention, especially in the late seventies and the beginning of the eighties, is the question of international trade in resources. The special interest in these questions is due to the fact that a great part of trade in natural resources is international trade. Moreover, the importance of government-owned companies in this sector has increased considerably over the the the last two decades.[98] Since one can expect the interests and objectives of governments and private firms to diverge from each other, the question arises whether there are systematic differences in the resource extraction policies. This is one of the problems the theory of trade in natural resources is dealing with. The other interesting topic is connected with development of industrialising countries. Can they transform their wealth in the ground into other assets (domestic physical capital or foreign bonds) that provide the basis for economic growth and welfare? These types of questions have been investigated by the theory of the resource-exporting country. As a second branch, there exists an increasing literature on general-equilibrium models of international trade. This line of research is devoted to an analysis of the patterns of trade and the applicability of the standard theorems of static trade theory to intertemporal models. It is the latter theory which is still in a quite fragmentary

---

[98] This is especially true for the OPEC countries where the government share in crude oil production increased from less than ten percent in the early seventies to more than eighty percent in the eighties. See *OPEC Annual Statistical Bulletin*, various issues.

and unfinished state.[99] Therefore, the following discussion will concentrate on models of the resource-exporting country.

Models of resource-exporting countries have been established by *Vousden* (1974), *Long* (1974), *Dasgupta/Eastwood/Heal* (1978), *Aarrestad* (1978,1979), *Seierstad/Sydsaeter* (1983), *Siebert* (1985), *Withagen* (1985), *Rauscher* (1987a) and *Stollery* (1987). In contrast to models of the profit-oriented resource-extracting firm, the resource-rich countries are assumed to maximise utility which in most cases is derived from consumption. Moreover, they face a balance-of-payments restriction.

Two types of models can be distinguished. On the one hand, there are models in which the resource-exporting country has access to a perfect international capital market on which it can borrow and lend at a constant interest rate.[100] If this assumption holds, then the central result concerning the shape of the price path remains unchanged. This is due to *Fisher's* separation theorem which states that, in the case of capital market perfection, production decisions are independent of consumption and savings.[101] So the growth rate of user cost is the interest rate instead of the discount rate. In this case, the main argument remains unchanged, and the model of the resource-exporting country does not provide additional insights as far as the shape of the price path is concerned. On the other hand, there are models with imperfect capital markets. In these models, *Fisher's* separation theorem does not hold, and the standard result has to be modified as will be seen below.

Siebert (1985), ch. 3, develops a model of a resource-rich country which has no access to capital markets. A country intends to maximise the sum of discounted future utility flows. Let again r be the rate of discount, $c(t)$ be consumption and $u(c(t))$ a concave utility function. A quantity $q(t)$ is extracted at a constant average cost k [102] and sold abroad at a price $p(t)$

---

[99] A survey of existing models is given by *Kemp/Long* (1984). Their models, however, do not allow for trade in the resource itself, but only in manufactured goods produced by means of the resource and other factors of production. *Djajic* (1984) uses a simple equilibrium model but does not consider any store of wealth besides the resource. Recently, more satisfying models have been promoted by *Withagen* (1985), ch. 5, *van Geldrop/Withagen* (1987), and *Djajic* (1988) who develop a general-equilibrium framework for trade in exhaustible resources which incorporates capital goods and allows for an endogenous determination of the interest rate.

[100] See *Dasgupta/Eastwood/Heal* (1978) and *Siebert* (1985), ch. 4.

[101] This theorem was established by *Fisher* (1930), ch. 11. See also *Hirshleifer* (1970), p. 63. For applications in the field of resource economics see *Long* (1977), *Kemp/Okuguchi* (1979) and *Siebert* (1985), p. 76, for instance.

[102] Think of the extraction costs as of payments for the services provided by a foreign extraction firm.

measured in units of the consumption good, which is imported. If the possibility of borrowing and lending is excluded, imports must equal exports in each period:

(3.2.10) $p(t)q(t) = c(t) + k\,q(t)$.

Like in the standard model, the optimal extraction path satisfies the condition that the owner of the mine is indifferent between extracting today and tomorrow. Shifting the exploitation of a marginal unit of the resource from a date t to a date $t+h$ leaves the target function unaffected. The loss of utility in t has to be equated to the gain of utility in $t+h$:

(3.2.11) $[\,(p(t)-k)\,u'(c(t))\,]\,e^{-rt} = [\,(p(t+h)-k)\,u'(c(t+h))\,]\,e^{-r(t+h)}$.

Rearranging and taking logarithms yields

$$r = h^{-1}\,[\,log\,(p(t+h)-k)\,u'(c(t+h)) \, - \, log\,((p(t)-k)\,u'(c(t))\,]\,.$$

If h goes to 0, then it follows from *de l'Hospital's* rule that

(3.2.12) $$r = \frac{\dot{p}\,u' + (p-k)\,u''\,\dot{c}}{(p-k)\,u'}$$

where the arguments of the functions have been omitted for convenience. A market equilibrium is reached when supply, q, equals demand, $D(p)$, where $D(.)$ is a decreasing function. The elasticities of demand and marginal utility are defined as

(3.2.13) $\varepsilon = -D'p/D$,

and

(3.2.14) $\eta = -u''c/u'$

respectively. Using these definitions and (3.2.10), equation (3.2.12) can be rewritten such that

(3.2.15) $$\widehat{p\text{-}k} = \frac{r}{\eta\,(\,\eta^{-1} + \beta\,\varepsilon\,-1\,)}$$ with $\beta = (p-k)/p$.

Although this condition looks complicated, there is an intuitive interpretation. Let extraction costs be negligible. Then $\beta=1$, and the term in brackets in the denominator of this expression can easily be interpreted. η is the elasticity of marginal utility. So its inverse, η^{-1}, can be interpreted as the elasticity of the resource-exporting country's import demand. ε is the elasticity of demand for natural resources, i.e. demand for the country's resource exports. If both demand functions are sufficiently elastic, i.e. if their sum is greater than 1, then the price increases over time. This condition is the same as the *Marshall-Lerner* condition for a normal reaction of the trade balance, which is well known from trade theory.[103] *Siebert* (1985), pp. 36-41, has derived this condition by means of control-theory methods. If the sum of the elasticities is less than 1, then the resource price should decrease over time. This implies an increasing extraction profile and, therefore, a finite time until exhaustion of the resource.[104]

The assumption that there is no store of wealth besides the resource is highly unrealistic. In reality, there are other means of storage like capital goods and financial assets. There are, however, capital market imperfections. The rate of interest is not constant and exogenous but can depend on various variables. There have been several attempts in economic theory to model this.

- *Hoel* (1981) and *Siebert* (1985), ch. 5, argue that resource exporting-countries influence the rate of interest via their extraction policies. The idea behind this hypothesis is that low extraction rates induce a substitution towards more capital-intensive production. This lowers the return on capital and, therefore, the rate of interest. To some extent, this model is similar to approaches that explicitly consider production of a final good by means of capital and the resource, for instance *Dasgupta/Heal* (1974).[105]

- The level of indebtedness has an impact on the rate of interest. Highly indebted countries face difficulties finding convenient opportunities of further borrowing. Moreover, there is a difference between the interest rate for borrowing and the interest rate for lending. The latter case has been considered by *Siebert* (1985), p. 134, who shows that there is a kink in the (continuously increasing) price path at the moment the country changes from a borrower to a lender.

- The resource-exporting country faces a problem of recycling its petrodollars. If it has high earnings, it has problems finding high-yield assets. The return on new assets decreases with the quantity of assets added to the portfolio. This has been modelled by *Rauscher* (1987a). In such a model, user costs do not increase at the rate of interest any more but at the rate of interest minus the growth rate of the interest rate. It is possible to show that U-shaped price

---

[103] Compare trade theory textbooks like *Gandolfo* (1986), ch. 12.2., and *Niehans* (1984), ch. 4.2.

[104] It should be noted that such a scenario can cause problems regarding the existence of an optimal path. If marginal utility is infinite in the origin (an assumption which is often made in economic models), then it is not optimal to terminate the program within finite time. An infinite program with an decreasing price, however, is not possible when the resource is non-renewable and finite.

[105] Simpler models with capital as the store of wealth have been constructed by *Aarrestad* (1978) and *Siebert* (1985), ch. 6. In these models, however, the resource is not a factor of production.

profiles become feasible if demand reactions are lagged. This is due to the fact that the country has to be compensated for the low returns on new assets by a very high resource price initially. As demand slowly adjusts to this price level, the resource earnings of the country decrease and the interest rate increases. This drives the price down during an initial period. In the long run, the scarcity effect dominates, and the price increases again. The initial price decrease can be interpreted as the effect of an intertemporally backward-bending resource supply schedule.

To summarise: The economic theory of the resource exporting country does not produce any new results concerning the price path as long as capital markets are perfect. Capital market imperfections can produce scenarios with temporarily decreasing prices. This result can be useful for interpreting the periods of decreasing prices that followed the oil shocks of 1973/74 and 1979/80.

3.2.5. Uncertainty

Mining and utilisation of depletable resources are connected with various risks. Usually, one distinguishes economic, technological and political risks.[106] Economic risks are related to uncertain economic variables like prices or future demand functions, technological risks occur in the engineering parts of a project, and political risks are connected with expropriation, renegotiation of contracts and changes in all kinds of institutional arrangements. All of these types of risks have been introduced into the standard model of exhaustible resources in several variations.[107]

Political risk has been considered by *Long* (1975). He shows that if a firm faces a risk of being expropriated it will extract the resource faster. The initial price is lower than in the case without risk, and the rates of extraction are higher during an initial period. This result is intuitive since the expected value of the resource stock becomes zero for the firm at the expropriation date, and there is always a positive probability of being expropriated before the exhaustion of the resource. The same reasoning can be applied if there is the possibility of a very cheap substitute to enter the market at an uncertain date.[108]

Economic risks that affect the demand for the resource can lead to different results as *Fisher* (1981), p. 46-47 has pointed out. On the one hand, one can assume that demand uncertainty is increasing over time (who knows what will happen in the distant future?). If the mining firm is risk-averse, low-risk periods have a greater weight in the objective function than periods with a

---

[106] See *Siebert* (1987b), p. 478-481.

[107] Surveys have been provided by *Fisher* (1981), pp. 44-55, 63-67, and *Long* (1984).

[108] The latter falls into the category of economic risks.

higher demand risk. Since the future is more risky than the present, the firm intends to realise a greater part of its profits in the first periods of the planning horizon. That is: risk causes a faster depletion of the resource. The opposite holds when risk is related to the extraction rate. The risk-averse entrepreneur prefers a flatter extraction path and, therefore, tends to save the resource.[109]

In economic models with exhaustible resources, technological risks are usually modelled by introducing uncertainty about the size of reserves and the success of exploration. This has been done by *Devarajan/Fisher* (1982) and *Lasserre* (1985) and others. It is shown that the price paths depend on the cost functions. Besides marginal costs and user costs there is a third component of the price which is due to risk and can be positive or negative. *Arrow/Chang* (1982) assume that exploration successes are distributed according to a *Poisson* process and they obtain the result that the resource price will be cyclical. This unconventional result is due to the assumption that extraction is costless, but there are factors required for exploration. So it is optimal to defer exploration until the latest possible date, then start to explore very intensively, use up the new reserves, explore again and so forth. This exploration-extraction cycle creates a price cycle. *Arrow/Chang* (1982), p. 10, state that the bang-bang character of the solution would be smoothed if adjustment costs or capital were introduced. Then the model might be useful for explaining a part of the ups and downs of the oil price. The stylised facts, however, appear to indicate that this part is not very important: oil price shocks have neither been correlated with major discoveries nor with failures of exploration projects.

3.2.6. Testing Hotelling's model

There have been several attempts to test the theory of exhaustible resources econo-metrically. A simple version of the model has been subjected to empirical analysis by *Slade* (1982). It is assumed that, due to technological progress, extraction costs are decreasing over time. On the other hand, the scarcity element of price formation drives the price up. The combination of these opposite effects yields a U-shaped price profile. *Slade* uses the simple approximation

$$(3.2.16) \qquad p(t) = \beta_1 + \beta_2 t + \beta_3 t^2$$

to represent this type of price path. Long time series, starting in the 19th century, are used to investigate the prices of metals and energy resources. For all of these resources she obtains positive estimates for β_3 and negative estimates for β_2, i.e. the results support the hypothesis of a U-shaped price path. While the fit of this simple model to the data is surprisingly good for some resources (e.g. silver and natural gas), the results are poor for petroleum. A conceptual

---

[109] See *Lewis* (1977).

shortcoming of this approach is that only the qualitative implication of *Hotelling's* rule is tested but not the rule itself. The same price path can be derived from a Ricardian model where stock-dependent extraction costs drive the price.

Heal/Barrow (1980) and *Barrow/Heal* (1981) were among the first to test *Hotelling's* rule empirically. They analyse markets for several metals. The first of their studies is devoted to medium-term price developments; the other uses very long time series of prices going back to the last century. The papers extend the original model by introducing the formation of expectations concerning the interest rate. Even this extension does not yield evidence in favour of *Hotelling's* model. Both investigations produce similar results: the interest rate has no significant impact on the rate of price change. Surprisingly the change of the price can rather be explained by the change in the interest rate. *Heal/Barrow* (1980), p.172, conclude *"that a constant interest rate implies more or less constant resource prices"* and according to *Barrow/Heal* (1981), p.102, *"the simple equilibrium version of Hotelling's rule (...) is rejected"*.

Similar results are reported by *Smith* (1981). He finds that *Hotelling's* rule, equation (3.2.8), does not lead to an acceptable fit to the data. The model can be improved by introducing the formation of expectations. Among various alternatives, the specification proposed by *Barrow* and *Heal* produced the best results. But they still were not convincing, and *Smith* managed to show that simple autoregressive processes were superior in forecasting future oil and gas prices.

There are a number of other studies that tend to reject the simple version of the intertemporal model of natural resources. For instance, *Frank/Babunovic* (1984), p. 88, lapidarily state that their model was *"less successful"* in the case of energy resources. It should, however, not be concealed that they claim to find evidence of depletability and *Hotelling*-type results for other resources. *Stollery* (1983) and *Farrow* (1984) examine *Hotelling's* rule using data on individual firms that are operating in the resource sector. In both cases, metallic ores are exploited. While *Stollery* finds supporting results, *Farrow* rejects the user-cost approach.

It is not surprising that the theoretical model presented in the preceding sections is not supported by empirical evidence. All intertemporal models of exhaustible resources produce variants of *Hotelling's* rule. This rule defines a price path which is smoothly increasing over time. In contrast, historical petroleum market developments have been characterised by drastic price jumps and supply disruptions. The following section will show how these discontinuities can be incorporated into *Hotelling's* model.

3.3. Parameter changes in the standard model

All the models considered up to here are characterised by perfect information of the planning institution. Be it a private firm, be it a state-owned company, the planner is assumed to know the relevant parameters accurately. According to the models, most of these parameters are constant or, if they vary, the variation is smooth (e.g. a trend) and predictable. In reality, however, we have experienced events that were unforeseeable. Examples are the three oil price shocks of the seventies and eighties. Moreover, there was variability in the interest rate, economic decline led to unanticipated draw-backs in demand, all attempts of estimating the production costs of synthetic fuels failed, and there were changes in market structure and institutional conditions.

How do these parameter changes affect the optimal paths in models with exhaustible resources? In the preceding sections, several optimality conditions have been derived. They are all defined in growth rates. The principal result is that the user cost of the resource should grow at the rate of interest or another appropriate rate of discount. The parameter changes do not only - and in many cases not even - affect these growth rates. But there are also significant and important impacts on the levels of the variables. This will be shown below for some examples. The next argument then is that if a change in a decisive parameter occurs the planner should adjust the optimal path to the new conditions instantaneously. Such adjustment processes produce discontinuities in the optimal paths and can, therefore, be useful for an explanation of oil price shocks.

3.3.1. The size of the resource stock

An obvious reason for a price shock can be an unexpected change in the resource base. Along the optimal path, the price develops according to *Hotelling's* rule. Given this price path and a certain demand schedule, the extraction path is completely determined from the beginning until the exhaustion of the resource. If there are unexpected discoveries of reserves, this path does not exhaust the resource any more. The initial price must, therefore, decrease at the point of time when the discovery is made. The opposite holds if expectations about future discoveries have been too optimistic. Then the scarcity rent must increase and, therefore, the price.

This can be seen from Figure 3.2 on p. 37. The shaded area, the integral of the extraction path, is the size of the resource stock. Corresponding to this resource endowment is a price path starting at p_1. If the resource base is extended by new discoveries, the old price path does not exhaust the resource and cannot be optimal anymore. A new price path, p_2, has to be chosen. Along this path, lower prices induce higher demand which in turn allows for a complete exhaustion of the reserves.[110]

One can argue that in the early seventies people became conscious of and concerned about the finiteness of natural resources, and that this in part was responsible for the drastic in-

---

[110] See *Roumasset/Fesharaki/Isaac* (1983) for numerical results concerning the effects of variations of the size of the resource stock.

crease in the oil price as well as the prices of other mineral resources. This may be a reasonable explanation for a part of the first price increase.

3.3.2. Changing property rights

In the beginning of the seventies, oil-exporting countries increased their influence on the production and pricing of petroleum, which by then had been dominated by the multinational oil companies. On the Teheran and Tripolis conferences in 1971 OPEC countries managed to accomplish new, higher prices. Two years later the oil embargo, the following price shock and especially OPEC's ability to keep the price up showed that the property rights for the resource had changed. They had gone from the private companies, among them the powerful Seven Sisters, into the hands of the oil-exporting nations. While the process of de-jure nationalisation extended over decades, de-facto nationalisation of two thirds of the world's petroleum reserves took place during a short period in the early seventies.

How is this change of the regime reflected in economic variables? *Long* (1975) and *Johany* (1979) argue that private firms which operate in resource-rich countries on the basis of concessions face a risk of being expropriated at some time. Thus, they do not maximise the present value of profits but the expected present value. Compared to a situation without expropriation risk, this is equivalent to an increase in the effective rate of discount. After the nationalisation of reserves, the property rights are in the hands of state-owned oil companies that by definition cannot be expropriated. So one should expect the discount rate to be lower after the nationalisation has taken place. Similar ideas have been stated by *Johany* (1980) and *Siebert* (1987a). Another argument for a lower discount rate is that governmental planning is (or should be) long-term oriented whereas private firms are expected to assign a lower weight to the future.

A change in the discount rate has two effects. First, it has an impact on the *Hotelling* rule

$$(3.2.8) \qquad \dot{p}(t) \; = \; r \, (p(t)\text{-}k) \, .$$

The price change decreases if r decreases. Therefore, a lower discount rate implies a slower price increase along the intertemporally optimal path. The other effect is due to the finiteness of resources. If, from an arbitrary point of time, the price increased at a lower rate, the resource would be over-exhausted since in all future periods demand would exceed its prior level. To avoid this, i.e. to achieve an intertemporal demand-supply equilibrium, the initial price must be lower than the price corresponding to the high discount rate. This has been formalised in an elegant way by *Farzin* (1984). A graphical interpretation has been given by *Johany* (1979), p. 76, and *Siebert* (1987a), p. 80. A similar representation will be used here.[111] Figure 3.4. shows the

---

[111] See also *Farzin* (1986), p. 10.

effect of a change in the discount rate. At a lower discount rate, the resource would be "over-exhausted" if the same initial price were chosen. The initial price must be higher, and the two price paths intersect. The initial extraction rate is lower. Thus, the long-run resource production is higher. What has been saved in the first period can be extracted additionally in the second period. This is represented by the shaded areas under the extraction path.

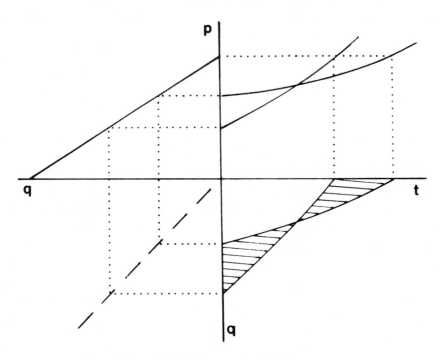

Figure 3.4.: An increase in the discount rate

Now the central idea of this approach is the following one. Resource-exporting countries have a lower time preference rate and, therefore, tend to conserve their wealth in the ground. After the nationalisation of the resources, the resource-exporting countries restrict their production, and this causes the price shock.

There are some shortcomings of the approach. First, it does not explain more than one price shock since property rights have changed only once. Second, it does not explain the periods of decreasing real oil prices after price shocks. And third, it does not consider Saudi-Arabia's measures to reduce production both after the first and the second oil price shock. Another counter-argument is that all attempts to quantify *Hotelling* rents empirically produced estimates which were too low to fill the gap between extraction costs and oil prices.[112] Finally, there is an empirical study by *Griffin* (1985) which tries to identify the impact of property-rights alteration on the level of oil production. The exogenous variable is the government's share in the oil industry. One should expect a negative impact. *Griffin*, however, does not find much support for the property-rights hypothesis.[113]

In spite of these counter-arguments, the change-of-property-rights hypothesis is not useless. A part of the oil shock of 1973/74 might indeed be attributed to the revaluation of reserves which was caused by de-facto nationalisation.

3.3.3. Cartelisation

The commonplace view on oil price shocks is that they have something to do with cartelisation. A purely competitive market changes into a non-competitive market which is dominated by one big producer, the cartel. The monopolist or dominant firm charges a higher price than a competitive producer. This is true not only in the static case but also in the intertemporal optimisation model of extractive industry as has been shown in section 3.2.3. Figure 3.3. may serve as a useful illustration. In this context, a shock that drives the price up can be interpreted as the result of a cartelisation; an oil price collapse can be attributed to cartel instability and cheating.

At a first glance, this seems to be a good explanation for the events on the world petroleum market during the seventies and eighties. The problem that there were two upward shocks can be solved by attributing the first one to the change in the property rights and the second to collusive action of OPEC member countries. This argument, however, neglects the fact that even before the second oil crisis some OPEC countries had reduced their production from time to time to keep prices high. Moreover, the first oil crisis was not induced by atomistic producers who accidently at the same time had the idea of changing their discount rates, but by a joint action of a subset of OPEC who found out that a slight reduction of production yielded tremendous price increases. So there are good arguments for the hypothesis that the cartelisation took place in 1973/74 already.

The collapse of the oil price in 1986 was connected with severe stability problems in the cartel. Almost all member countries produced more than their official quotas and used netback contracts and other spot-related deals to dispose of their excess production. When they colluded

---

[112] *Pakravan* (1983), for instance, estimated user costs of some cents per barrel of crude petroleum. These and other estimates, however, should be interpreted with caution.

[113] It should be noted that *Griffin's* procedure tests the hypothesis of an impact of de-jure nationalisation rather than that of de-facto nationalisation

again at the end of 1986, the price increased again. But it did not increase to its prior level as the cartelisation hypothesis would predict. Finally, this approach does not explain the periods of decreasing real prices that followed the first two oil shocks.

3.3.4. The backstop technology

The price of the exhaustible resource is bounded from above by the price of a perfect substitute. *Nordhaus* (1973) has introduced the term 'backstop technology' for such a substitute. In the case of petroleum, the backstop technology can be coal liquefication or hydrogen energy applications on the basis of nuclear or solar energy. Substitutes of petroleum products are still very expensive, especially those that can be used for transportation services. *Mead* (1986) estimates the costs of the backstop technology of oil to lie in the area of some 90$ per barrel of oil equivalent (boe). If the oil price exceeded this level, no one would buy petroleum products any more but switch to the substitute immediately (provided that the adjustment costs are low enough). The demand function is kinked: when the price reaches its choke-off level, then demand falls to zero.[114] This is shown in Figure 3.5.

The estimated price of a backstop techology has increased considerably during the past fifteen years. The costs of producing the perfect substitute were estimated to lie in a range of 10 to 15 $/boe (in 1981 dollars) before the first oil crisis while the oil price was $2 at that time.[115] The increase of the oil price to its new level should have choked off the demand for crude oil, but nothing like this happened. The estimate was corrected upwards to 30$/boe. The second oil shock again led to a higher price, and the backstop price is now thought to be somewhere between 60 and 100$/boe.[116]

What is the effect of the backstop price on the price of the natural resource? On an equilibrium path, the resource should just then be exhausted when the backstop price is reached and demand is choked off. In the case of an increased backstop price, however, there is still demand for the resource at the former choke-off price. The time path of the resource is given by *Hotelling's* rule and can only be changed by changing the initial price. Therefore, in order to establish the equilibrium again, the initial price should be increased. This is shown in Figure 3.5.

---

[114] One can also assume that the substitution possibilities gradually increase with the price. Then the demand function is smooth and intersects the abscissa at the choke-off price.

[115] See *Roumasset/Fesharaki/Isaak* (1983) and *Mead* (1986).

[116] The reasons for these changes in the price of a backstop technology are discussed by *Weitzman* (1981). He argues that investment behaviour and research-and-development strategies depend on the expected oil price, and this in turn leads to an impact of the size of oil reserves on the backstop price.

The arrows indicate the increase in the backstop price and the corresponding oil price increase. Demand is lowered in all periods before the former exhaustion date, the resource lasts longer, and the area under the extraction path remains unchanged (A = B).

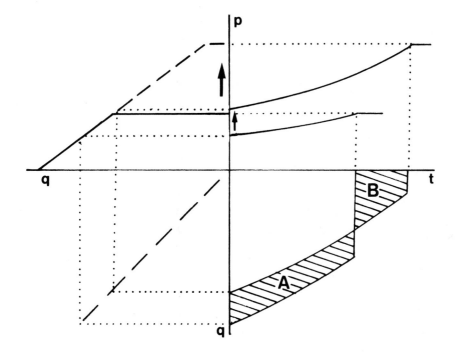

Figure 3.5.: The impact of the backstop price

3.3.5. Additional variables

Besides the size of the resource stock, the cost of the backstop technology, the discount rate, and the market structure, there are still other decisive parameters that affect the price and extraction profiles for natural resoures.

- A shift in tastes moves the demand function. One could argue, for instance, that people in the industrialised countries have increased their concern about environmental problems and tend to prefer a less energy-intensive life-style. This would lower the initial price level, and the depletion date would be deferred.

- Taxation of mineral oil has the same effect. It also shifts the demand function perceived by the producers downwards. At the same price level, less will be sold. The pre-tax price level should be reduced.

- An unpredicted increase in the costs of production reduces the scarcity-rent component of the price. The price path must be flatter, but it starts at a higher level. Initial resource extraction is reduced and the resource lasts longer. Per-period scarcity of the resource, measured by extraction costs, becomes more important compared to intertemporal scarcity.

Extraction costs have indeed increased substantially during the last decade. However, this has been an effect rather than a cause of the oil price shocks. The other arguments concerning the shape of the demand function seem to be more plausible in the explanation of oil price developments. In the long run, changes in the preferences as well as taxation or tariffs can reduce the price of oil.

3.4. Approaches without exhaustibility

While in a lot of publications the intertemporal paradigm has been the dominant tool of analysing oil prices, there are still other approaches which have been used to explain and predict oil prices. A non-intertemporal approach which has already been mentioned is the Ricardian model. But like the *Hotelling* model it has been used predominantly to explain long-run developments rather than short- or medium-term fluctuations. Other models that address the question how the leapfrogging of the oil price over a period of fifteen years can be explained need not necessarily take recourse to concepts of long-term optimality and intertemporal profit maximisation. There is a wide variety of models, and the most important and most intensively discussed approaches will be discussed below.

3.4.1 The impact of GDP fluctuations

Demand for petroleum, like the demand for all other goods, depends on income or the level of economic activity. All other variables remaining unchanged, an increase in income yields an increase in the demand for petroleum products. The demand curve is shifted upwards. Assuming that the supply curve has the usual shape, an increase in demand yields an increase in the price.[117]

The last one-and-a-half decades have not only produced drastic price fluctuations but also substantial fluctuations in the level of economic activity. One might, therefore, argue that part of the oil price fluctuations reflects the impact of the business cycle. This hypothesis has been examined by *Ott/Tatom* (1986). They use statistical causality tests which are based on the

---

[117] This idea, that petroleum demand and prices are driven by economic growth, has been emphasised by *MacAvoy* (1982) in a simulation study and by *Saunders* (1984a) in a more theoretical paper.

hypothesis that causal relations have something to do with the sequence of events: the second event is unlikely to be the cause of the first.[118] The results showed that GDP fluctuations are caused by oil price shocks rather than vice versa. The strong hypothesis of a direct influence has been rejected; nonetheless, there remains some potential for indirect and much weaker feedbacks of GDP fluctuations on oil prices.

3.4.2. The backward-bending supply curve

There are some good arguments in favour of the hypothesis that the supply of petroleum has a backward-bending shape. *Teece* (1982), pp. 66-67 and 86-91, uses a target-revenue model to explain the possibility of such a curve. He assumes that oil-exporting countries have certain development projects that they plan to undertake or that have already been started, e.g. downstream industrialisation and infrastructure investments. In order to finance these expenditures, they need a certain level of oil revenues. Besides these needs, the absorptive capacities of the most important oil producers are limited, at least in the short run. So the short-run supply curve is one of the iso-revenue curves, having a hyperbolic shape in the price-quantity diagram. If there is a price shock for whatever reason, so the argument goes, the oil exporters reduce their supply. This enhances excess demand and causes additional upward pressure on prices. The line of argument is supported by the fact that there also are political motives to restrict supply when the price rises. According to this argument, a too rapid increase in income and purchasing power threatens the stability of traditionalist societies like the Arabian oil exporting countries. High oil revenues bear the danger of corrupting traditional values and, therefore, are avoided by atypical supply behaviour.[119]

There are some counter-arguments that question the target-revenue model. *Adelman* (1982), pp. 44-45, doubts the existence of a constant target revenue, but he argues that needs tend to adjust to increased revenues very quickly. So the backward-bending supply curve may be an important phenomenon only in the very short run.

Extensions of the model have been provided by *Salehi-Isfahani* (1986) and *Rauscher* (1987a) who introduce capital market imperfections into resource models. If capital markets were perfect, it would never be optimal for oil producers to reduce their production during times of increasing prices. But there exists a recycling problem, and oil-exporting countries face difficulties in finding profitable investment opportunities. In this case, not only domestic but also

---

[118] See *Granger* (1969,1980) for a discussion of causality tests.

[119] *Moran* (1981), especially pp. 270-272, and *Niblock* (1985) describe these internal political issues of the Arab Gulf states, in particular the mixing-up of traditional Arab and modern Western values, that, as *Moran* argues, explains a great deal of Saudi-Arabian petropolitics.

international absorption is limited and *Rauscher* (1987a) has shown that the price path can be U-shaped. This indicates the short-term effect of a backward-bending supply curve for petroleum.

Empirical evidence is reported by *Griffin* (1985) who uses government investments as a proxy for target revenues. If the hypothesis holds in its strict version, then production equals investment needs divided by the oil price. *Griffin* uses the logarithms of these variables in regressions for ten OPEC member countries and shows that the strict variant of the model is rejected in all cases. There is only one country, Algeria, for which the parameters are significant and have the correct signs.[120] Thus, the target-revenue model appears to be rejected. There still remains an argument of defence, however. *Griffin's* regressions use annual data and, therefore, do not take short-term effects into account. So this study does not reject the hypothesis that backward-bending supply can be important in the short run, e.g. during the first weeks and months that follow a price shock.

3.4.3. Static monopoly theory

If, as *Pindyck* (1987) has argued, the resource constraint is not so important in the determination of the petroleum price as compared to the effect of cartelisation, then it might be sufficient to deal with the topic in a purely static framework. This can be done by employing a model which is due to *Ruggeri* (1983). The article considers a model in which OPEC is the dominant firm and faces a residual demand curve composed of worldwide petroleum demand and supply coming from the fringe of the cartel. Since extraction costs in the most important member countries are very small, they will be neglected below. This simplifies the analysis considerably.

A slightly modified version of *Ruggeri's* method and different data will be used. Let e_d, e_s, e_o be the elasticities of demand, supply and residual demand for OPEC oil, respectively, and a be OPEC's market share. Then the following condition holds:

$$(3.4.1) \qquad a\,e_o = e_d - (1-a)\,e_s \,.$$

If the revenue function is concave, then the necessary and sufficient condition for OPEC maximising its petroleum profits is

$$(3.4.2) \qquad e_o^* = -1 \,.$$

---

[120] Algeria is just the country to which *Salehi-Isfahani* (1986) applies his model which is implicitly built on the backward-bending supply hypothesis.

Here the assumption of zero production costs is vital. This optimality condition implies that in OPEC's optimum the following condition holds:

(3.4.3) $e_d = -a + (1-a) e_s$.

In Figure 3.6., this locus is depicted by solid lines for the years 1973, 1978 and 1985. In these years OPEC's market shares were 55.5%, 49.3% and 29.1%, respectively. All points below the optimal locus indicate potentials for price increases since in these areas demand for OPEC oil is inelastic. The opposite holds for the areas above the curve.

One can now compare these profit-maximisation loci with the empirical results. *Ruggeri* proposes a simple method starting from the definition of a market share. Let d be demand and s be non-OPEC supply. Then

$$(1-a) = s/d .$$

Let y be income and e_y be the corresponding elasticity. Taking logarithms and differentiating with respect to time, one obtains

(3.4.4) $\widehat{(1-a)} = e_s \hat{p} - e_d \hat{p} - e_y \hat{y}$,

the hat representing the growth rate. Assuming that demand reacts to income changes proportionally, i.e. $e_y = 1$, this reduces to

(3.4.5) $e_s = e_d + (\hat{y} + \widehat{(1-a)}) / \hat{p}$.[121]

The slope of this locus is always unity. One can now determine the intercept by taking data from the records for the variables in question. Growth rates are computed for the periods 1973-78 and 1978-85. These numbers measure reactions to the first two oil crises over the medium-term of five and seven years, respectively. The empirical values of the intercept are 0.195 for 1973-78 and 0.484 for 1978-85.[122] These empirical elasticity schedules are represented by the dashed lines in Figure 3.6.

The following results can be derived: During the first period (1973-78), the empirical line was close to the origin, far below the optimal line which tended to turn left. This indicates

---

[121] *Ruggeri's* original formula (p. 192) looks more complicated, due to the fact that a discrete-time representation is used.

[122] The producion data are taken from the *OPEC Annual Statistical Bulletin 1986*, prices from various issues of the *Petroleum Economist*. They are weighted by the export-price index for manufactured goods from industrial nations *(UN Monthly Bulletin*, various issues). From the same source the index of worldwide industrial production was taken as a proxy for *y*.

that OPEC had not used all its market power and there was potential for further price increases. The second price shock moved the empirical line upwards. Demand reactions following the second oil shock were more vigorous than those after the 1973/74 embargo. From 1978 to 1985, OPEC's market share fell rapidly and the optimal locus turned further left. In 1985 the optimal locus was situated below the empirical locus. This implies that the price had been too high during the preceding years. So *Ruggeri's* model also explains why a drastic price cut, like the one of 1986, was in OPEC's own interest.

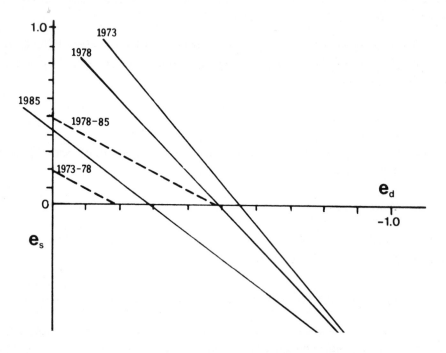

Figure 3.6.: OPEC's market shares and the elasticities
of demand and non-OPEC supply

Due to its simplicity, this approach has some severe limitations. It does not take production costs or even user costs into account. Moreover, the empirical elasticity estimates it uses are very crude and much less reliable than regression results that are based on more data. But it is just the simplicity of the model that allows to use this vivid graphic representation.

3.4.4. Lagged demand reactions

An important aspect in the determination of oil prices is the sluggish nature of demand reactions. Lagged demand adjustments are caused by rigidities and adjustment costs. If the price of petroleum increases, demand will be reduced. On the one hand, this is due to an income effect. Purchasing power is withdrawn, and the budget constraint becomes more restrictive. On the other hand, there is a substitution effect part of which is the attempt to substitute capital and/or labour for oil, for instance to build cars which are more fuel-efficient, to improve the insulation of buildings etc. These measures are expensive and time-consuming, and demand does not adjust to its desired level instantaneously. Similar arguments hold for the supply side. It takes several years until new fields which are profitable at the higher price come on stream.

This aspect has widely been neglected in the literature on the topic.[123] *Pindyck* (1978b) has used this assumption in his exhaustible resources model of the oil market. More recent models have been presented by *Wirl* (1985a,b) and *Rauscher* (1988a). They will, however, not be referred to in the following paragraphs since Chapter 4 uses a similar model and they will be discussed in that context intensively. The basic idea can also be presented by means of *Ruggeri*'s model though it does not use intertemporal arguments explicitly.

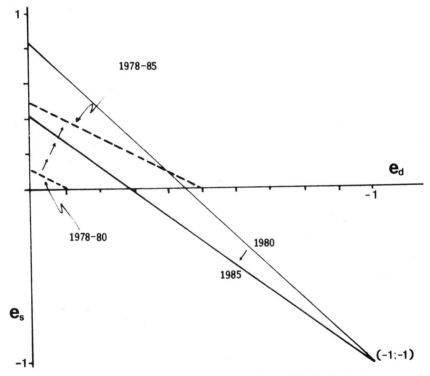

Figure 3.7.: Short and long-term effects of the 1979/80 oil shock

---

[123] *Gately* (1984), p. 1109, for instance, complains about this shortcoming as the major reason for the failure of most of the theoretical approaches. Similar conclusions are drawn by *Fertig* (1986), p. 133-138, from a broad survey of optimisation models of oil price determination.

In order to do this, we use the same graphical representation as in Figure 3.6. The short-term and long-term reactions to the 1979/80 oil shock will be investigated and compared. As a base year, the pre-crisis year 1978 is chosen. Short-run reactions are now defined to extend over a period of two years, while reactions over an interval of seven years are interpreted as long-term reactions. So data for 1980 and 1985 will be analysed. In 1980 OPEC's market share was 44.5%; in 1985 it was down at 29.1%. The corresponding optimal loci are drawn into Figure 3.7. as solid lines. There was a demand reaction that lowered OPEC's market share and turned the optimal locus left. The values of the intercept of the empirical line are 0.119 in 1980 and 0.484 in 1985. If the empirical lines are compared to the optimal loci, the following conclusion can be drawn: in 1980 it seemed as if OPEC had not yet used all its market power, but in 1985 the price turned out to be too high. Since the real oil price was nearly constant during the first half of the eighties, this result must be attributed to the difference between short-run and long-run demand reactions.

The model does not answer the question how a policy taking account of the sluggishness of demand should look like. It only states that the difference between the short and the long run matters a lot. We will go into this deeper in Chapters 4 and 5.

3.4.5. Downstream activities

During the past ten years, oil-exporting countries have devoted much effort to their own industrialisation. Much of this activity went into the downstream sectors of the petroleum industry. Especially the Arab countries made huge investments to build up sophisticated petro-chemical and refining industries. The objective is to export refined petroleum products and basic chemicals like ethylene, urea and methanol instead of the raw material, crude oil.[124] It should also be mentioned that some of the major crude-oil exporters were dependent on imports of refined products to satisfy their domestic needs. The motives for this vertical integration are as follows:[125]

- Many of the oil-exporting countries do not only produce crude oil but also substantial quantities of natural gas which accrues as a by-product of petroleum extraction. In former times this gas has been flared, but now it is used as an input in several downstream processes. The availability of associated gas as an almost free good can constitute a cost advantage and, therefore, a differential rent.

---

[124] For data on the development of capacities see *Siebert/Rauscher* (1985), pp. 212-213.

[125] See again *Siebert/Rauscher* (1985), pp. 213-214, but also *Fesharaki/Isaak* (1983), pp. 86-88, and (1984), pp. 10-11. For a more general discussion of vertical integration see *Blair/Kaserman* (1983) and *Casson* (1984).

- An upstream monopolist has an incentive to move downstream if the downstream industry is competetitive and there are substitutes for the raw material the monopolist produces. In this case, a non-integrated downstream industry would substitute away from the input supplied by the monopolist.

- Vertical integration can lower transaction costs.

- Domestic industrialisation avoids external political risks like freezing of assets and expropriation and, therefore, is superior to other forms of saving that imply holding of foreign bonds and equities.

- Especially for the Arab countries, characterised by low population and high per-capita income, the high capital intensities of petrochemical complexes and refineries have the advantage that not much labour is needed to operate them.

- There is also a psychological motive which *Fesharaki/Isaak* (1983), p. 88, refer to as: *"An opportunity to beat the industrialized nations at their own game is an appealing proposition to almost any Third World government."*

There are, however, also some obstacles to the policy of downstream integration.[126] The petroleum-exporting countries expand their capacities into shrinking markets, and they face disadvantages in transportation and capital costs. An argument which is of much more interest in the context of oil price fluctuations has been forwarded by *Razavi/Fesharaki* (1984). They argue that there is a high correlation between the price of crude oil and the prices of related products (which is not surprising). Thus, exports of refined petroleum products and basic petrochemicals constitute a threat to the cartel price of petroleum. If OPEC member countries act as competitive producers in their downstream markets, they will distract demand for cartelised crude oil. The associated gas contained in these products is a competing substitute of petroleum, but it is not regulated by OPEC's quota systems.[127] So downstream activities provide the opportunity of cheating without violating the cartel's laws. If vertical integration is profitable and if the producers are rational, they will cheat and this will affect the oil price.

The downstream-activity hypothesis might explain part of the oil price collapse of 1986, but other reasons appear to be more important. A counter-argument is the fact that the countries with the most ambitious downstream projects also were the most disciplined cartel members for a long time.

---

[126] See *Fesharaki/Isaak* (1984), pp. 12-26, and *Stournaras* (1985).

[127] *Mossavar-Rahmani/Mossavar-Rahmani* (1986), pp. 79-94, report that OPEC countries have never managed to develop a uniform view on the natural gas issue.

3.4.6. Some empirical models of oil price determination

All the models mentioned above use the assumption that there exists one price to be referred to as the oil price. In reality, the petroleum market has been characterised by segmented prices during the seventies and the most of the eighties. On the one hand, there was OPEC's official price that was negotiated by the cartel. On the other hand, a spot-market price was established by matching supply and demand. The spot price usually reacted first to disequilibrium developments on the quantity side of the market and OPEC's list price followed with a lag. There have been attempts to determine this relation between spot and official prices empirically and - at the same time - to find out how spot prices are fixed. Models of this type have been developed by *Nordhaus* (1980) and *Verleger* (1982).

Nordhaus (1980), 366-371, uses annual data over the period 1972-79 to analyse the process of oil price formation.[128] Let U_t be the utilisation of worlwide petroleum production capacities. Then the relation between the spot price, SP_t, and OPEC's list price, LP_t, is estimated by

$$(3.4.6) \qquad \frac{SP_t}{LP_t} = \begin{cases} 0.977 & \text{for } U_t \leq 0.97 \\ 0.430 + 0.543 \, (5000 \, (U_t - 0.97)^2 + 1) & \text{for } U_t \geq 0.97 \end{cases}$$

Standard errors are reported for two of the coefficients, namely 0.430 and 0.543. Both of them are highly significant. The values of the other parameters have apparently been set. Only two observations (1973 and 1979) satisfy the condition that $U_t > 0.97$. This means that the second equation is used to estimate two parameters from two observations. *Verleger* (1982), p. 41, argues that for this reason the results are not reliable. The model, however, may serve as a first step to model the spot-market price of petroleum as a highly nonlinear function of demand and capacity.[129] The reaction of OPEC's official price to spot price changes is estimated as

$$(3.4.7) \qquad LP_t - LP_{t-1} = 0.37 \, (SP_t - LP_{t-1}) + 5.22 \, Dum74$$

where *Dum74* is a dummy which takes the value one in the year 1974 and zero otherwise. Both coefficients are significant. The value of the first coefficient implies that the list price changes by

---

[128] It is clear that eight observations do not produce very reliable results but this approach was merely meant as an initial step to get some first insights. Meanwhile, time series have become longer and results to be obtained from such an approach may be more satisfying.

[129] *Gately* (1983) and *Baldwin/Prosser* (1988) use a similar equation to model the oil price as a function of capacity utilisation. They, however, do not estimate the parameters econometrically. *Rauscher* (1987b) combines a sluggish demand adjustment process with this type of price equation and obtains oil price cycles.

only 37% of what would be necessary to catch up with the spot price during the same year. It takes five years until the gap is almost (90%) closed. This contradicts empirical observations which indicate that the gap is closed during the year following the price shock. It is obvious that the dummy variable has been introduced to capture this effect.

Similar equations have been estimated by *Verleger* (1982), pp. 46-66. He uses monthly data and looks at short time periods following oil crises. So he obtains 25 observations for 6 periods.[130] Let Q_t be realised and Q^e_t be expected production. Expected production is defined as production of the previous month multiplied by a factor accounting for seasonal effects. The spot price develops according to

$$(3.4.8a) \qquad SP_t - SP_{t-1} = 0.554 \, (Q^e_t - Q_t) \ .$$

$$(3.4.8b) \qquad log \, (SP_t / SP_{t-1}) = 2.06 \, log \, (Q^e_t / Q_t) \ .$$

In both cases the parameters are significant at the 99% level. The parameter estimated by the second equation is a constant elasticity. A 1% cutback in production yields a 2% price increase. The adjustment of the official price is modelled by a simple *Koyck* lag structure on the basis of quarterly data:

$$(3.4.9) \qquad LP_t = 0.757 \, LP_{t-1} - 0.256 \, SP_{t-1} \ .$$

The median lag is 2.5 periods.[131] This means that it takes seven and a half months until half of the adjustment process is completed. Again, this is an underestimation of the true adjustment speed.[132]

Hubbard (1986), pp. 97-100, estimates a modified version of *Verleger's* model for longer time series (lasting to 1984) and reports that the relation between spot and official prices is un-

---

[130] For a definition of these six crises see *Verleger* (1982), pp. 33-38.

[131] If β is the coefficient of the lagged dependent variable, the median lag, n, is given by $\beta^n = 0.5$.

[132] This failure of the econometric models might be caused by the complexity of the true adjustment process which is too complicated to be reflected by a simple geometric lag structure. A more realistic model should perhaps use a variable adjustment speed. During an initial period there is almost no adjustment while in the longer run official oil prices are more flexible.

stable over time. This result is attributed to the fact that the share of spot-related transactions has increased considerably after the second oil shock.[133]

Another model of oil price determination has been presented by *Rampa* (1987). It can be interpreted as an extension of *Verleger's* model. While in *Verleger's* model the explanatory variables, expected and realised production, are exogenous, *Rampa* introduces a price-dependent adjustment function. Let p be the price of oil, $f(p)$ the demand for non-OPEC oil, q be the quantity supplied by non-OPEC countries and a a positive adjustment parameter. Then price is assumed to adjust according to

(3.4.10) $\dot{p} = a\,(f(p) - q\,)$.

He also defines a lagged quantity adjustment process, depending on non-OPEC supply, and by combining these two equations he obtains oil market cycles. The cycles, however, run counter-clockwise in the price-quantity diagram and, thus, counter to the oil market cycle, which is depicted in Figure 2.3. on p. 29. This implies that *Rampa's* model, designed to model non-OPEC supply behaviour, cannot be applied to OPEC behaviour.

The main problem with above-mentioned models is that they answer one question by posing another. For instance, the underlying concept in *Nordhaus'* (1980) and *Gately's* (1983) papers is the existence of a desired level of capacity utilisation. Deviations from this level explain price changes. *Verleger* (1982) uses differences between expected and actual levels of demand. The question that remains open in all these models is how the exogenous variables are determined. Which level of capacity utilisation is desired? How can the deviation of oil production from its expected level be explained? There must be a missing link between these models of price determination and an economic foundation of the behaviour of supply and demand.

3.4.7. Is OPEC a cartel ?

Many of the approaches that have been discussed up to here start from the assumption that OPEC is a cartel and acts as the dominant firm or residual supplier on the market. There have, however, been only a few attempts to test this conjecture empirically. This can be done by

---

[133] He also presents a theoretical model taking these changes into account. The main short-coming of the model is its formulation in differences. If the difference between the prices of two subsequent periods depends on excess demand or supply, then it is possible that a transitory demand or supply shock causes a permanent price increase (*Hubbard* (1986), pp. 93-96). Although ratchet effects had an important impact in the process of oil price formation and transitory shocks indeed influenced long-run price levels, this approach appears to be artificial. The adjustment process produces an algebraic result for which an economic explanation is not given.

means of historical analysis or quantitative methods. The latter approach has been chosen by *Griffin* (1985) and *Loderer* (1985).

Griffin (1985) considers the market-sharing version of the cartel model. It is assumed that the members of the cartel obey to rules of how to share the market. There are several ways of sharing the market the simplest of which is to assign to everyone a constant market share. One can, however, also think of variable market shares depending on joint production and the price. This is the case, for instance, when those who suffer relatively hard from bad times are allowed to produce a bigger share than in good times. *Griffin* chooses the general approach and estimates the equations

$$(3.4.11) \qquad log\, q_i \ = \ a_i \ + \ b_i log\, Q_i \ + \ c_i log\, p$$

where q_i is production of the ith country, Q_i the production of the other countries, p the price and a_i, b_i and c_i the parameters to be estimated. A situation in which $b_i = 1$ and $c_i = 0$ is the constant-market-sharing-model. If only $b_i = 1$ but the other parameter differs from zero, this is referred to as market sharing, and a situation in which b_i is only positive but not unity is partial market sharing. The data used cover the period from the first quarter of 1971 to the third quarter of 1983. The parameter estimates suggest that in all but one cases the constant-market-sharing version is rejected. The less restrictive version is rejected for six out of eleven OPEC countries, and the partial market sharing model cannot be rejected for any of the countries. These results are compared with the estimates of a model of competitive behaviour where prices explain oil production. It is plausible to assume a positive relationship between the price and production. This hypothesis is rejected for five OPEC countries but only for one of the eleven major non-OPEC countries.[134] Estimation of the market-sharing model for non-OPEC countries yielded less support for this hypothesis. *Griffin's* estimates, therefore, suggest that OPEC's behaviour can be described by a sort of market-sharing behaviour whereas the fringe of the cartel rather acts competitively.

An empirical investigation yielding much less support for the cartel hypothesis has been carried out by *Loderer* (1985). The hypothesis is that, if OPEC's decisions on its member conferences do not influence the price of petroleum, then OPEC is not a cartel. So the null hypothesis of the empirical test is that OPEC is unable to influence the price. During the period 1974-83, there were 34 OPEC meetings that brought about pricing decisions of various magnitudes. During the 1974-80 subperiod no evidence can be found that OPEC's decisions systematically affected the spot price of oil products. If the market does not react to what OPEC decides to do, then OPEC cannot have any market power. For the subsequent period, 1981-83, the results are different. It is shown that the outcomes of the OPEC meetings systematically affected the prices for heating-oil futures. From this *Loderer* concludes that, contrary to commonplace thinking,

---

[134] This country was the USA, a result which *Griffin*, p. 960, attributes to price controls.

OPEC's cartel power was substantial during periods of softening prices but not when prices went up drastically.[135] In the times of rising prices, OPEC's official pricing decisions were reactions to market developments rather than their causes. *Loderer's* approach, however, does not test to what extent these market developments were due to unofficial decisions of OPEC countries. The latter hypothesis is supported by the fact that OPEC's market share shrank from 54.9% to 44.9% during the 1974-80 period. This indicates restrictive production policies that are unlikely to occur in competitive markets.[136] Additionally, as *Nordhaus* (1980), *Verleger* (1982), and *Fitzgerald/Pollio* (1984) show, official oil prices have adjusted to free market prices and not vice versa.

Even more difficult than the identification of cartel behaviour is the assessment of its stability, especially if empirical measures of cartel stability are sought. There have been few authors who have addressed this question and the analyses are in a very preliminary state.

Danielsen (1980) defines two indices which he refers to as the reserve-sacrifice ratio and the capacity-sacrifice ratio.[137] They measure the reserve-to-production ratios and the degrees of capacity under-utilisation in single OPEC member countries divided by the corresponding variables aggregated over all OPEC countries. So, for both variables low values (less than one) indicate that the country produces at a relatively high rate compared to the OPEC average. These two indices are used as dependent variables in cross-section regression analyses for different years (1973-78). Explanatory variables are oil wealth, measured by reserves, and population.[138] In all cases the impact of population is negative (though not always significant) and the opposite holds for oil wealth. Poor countries extract relatively rapidly. The fit of the model to the data increases over time and so does the significance of the estimated parameters. *Danielsen* reports increasing willingness to sacrifice reserves or capacity and concludes that cooperation has increased over the time period under consideration. These findings, however, do not exclude competitive behaviour. If poor countries have a high discount rate, then, according to the *Hotelling* model, they extract the resource relatively fast, and one should expect them to be less tolerant to capacity under-utilisation. This is exactly what *Danielsen* finds in his regressions.

---

[135] This view is shared by some other authors, for instance *Mead* (1986), who looks at stylised facts instead of using sophisticated statistical methods.

[136] As mentioned earlier, there were indeed cutbacks of Saudi-Arabian oil production to maintain the price between the two oil crises, especially in summer 1978. Moreover, capacity expansion plans were adjusted downwards substantially.

[137] See also *Danielsen/Kim* (1988).

[138] The concept on which this model is based is similar to *Griffin's* (1985) partial-market-sharing model. In the case of constant market sharing both of *Danielsen's* sacrifice ratios would equal one. They are, however, variable and depend on individual country characteristics. This corresponds to *Griffin's* finding that the parameter estimates of the partial-market-sharing model vary across countries.

Geroski/Ulph/Ulph (1987) also find support for the hypothesis of collusion. They consider a Nash-Cournot model of the oil market and introduce an unobservable variable which measures the weight that single OPEC countries attribute to the long-run profits of the other countries. These weights in turn are specified as functions of other variables and can, therefore, be determined indirectly. Regressions are made for four subgroups of OPEC using quarterly data from 1966(III) to 1983(III). In all cases the estimates of the weights suggest that the willingness to cooperate has increased over time, with substantial jumps in 1973 and 1979. This result (if it is not an artifact of the method) indicates increasing cartel stability.

Although some proxies for cartel stability have been suggested, it remains difficult to predict future stability. The empirical evidence can, however, be used to evaluate historical developments. It is suggested that there has been a cartel or at least cartel-like behaviour in the past. The burdens of collusion, however, have been distributed in an unequal manner among OPEC's member countries, with Saudi-Arabia having the role of the swing producer.[139] The conclusion I would draw is that, no matter how the burdens were shared, OPEC had some monopoly power during the 1970s and 1980s.

3.5. An evaluation

This chapter has been an attempt to give an overview of the economic approaches to the question of oil price formation. There are competing paradigms the most developed of which appears to be the exhaustible-resources model. This model, however, is rejected by the data - at least as far as its simple versions are concerned which do not produce any fluctuations similar to those experienced on the world petroleum market during the seventies and eighties. As a reason, *Pindyck* (1981), p. 135, argues:

> *"It is interesting that most economists feel comfortable attributing perfect dynamic optimization behaviour to producers, even though there is evidence (both anecdotal and statistical) that producers may not optimize at all, that to the extent they do optimize, their time horizons may be very limited, and at the very least, dynamic optimization is often accompanied by large discount rates."*

---

[139] Because of this reason, *Plaut* (1981) prefers to speak of an oligopoly with Saudi Arabia as the dominant firm rather than a cartel. But with the introduction of the quota system in 1983, the sharing of burdens has increased. From 1979 to 1985 OPEC's production has nearly been halved. Of this 15.5 milion barrels per day cutback Saudi-Arabia accounted for 6.4 and the other Arab Gulf states for 2.6 million barrels. The only countries having had no significant reductions were Gabon and Ecuador, together accounting for 3% of OPEC's production in 1985.

Smith/Krutilla (1984) see an additional limitation of these models in their simplicity. *Banks* (1986) emphasises the role of uncertainty.

In contrast, there are a variety of publications by OPEC economists, in which one can usually find intertemporal arguments. *Jaidah* (1983), p. 25, explicitly refers to the economic theory of depletable resources and *Hotelling's* rule. Moreover he defines the present value of oil revenues as the objective variable in OPEC's pricing decisions (pp. 98-99), and elsewhere (p. 92) he states that *"we will never find the answer to the evolution of the oil price over the last 20 years by looking at marginal costs, for example"*. Similar arguments are used by *Al-Chalabi* (1982) and *Al-Chalabi/Al-Janabi* (1982), especially pp. 54-58. Intertemporal thinking has also influenced official OPEC documents. On their 1975 conference in Algier, the OPEC countries passed a declaration which stated:

> *"The price of oil should from now on reflect the scarcity value of this depletable commodity, ..."*[140]

If, on the one hand, the exhaustible-resources model is not supported by the data, but, on the other hand, OPEC speaks about depletability influencing the price, what should a consistent model of the oil market look like?

An answer can be found in the approaches that allow for parameter changes in exhaustible-resources models. It has been shown that these models can produce discrete price changes if plans based on incorrect assumptions about the state of the world are corrected. Critical parameters are the level of reserves, the price of the backstop technology, the shape of the demand function, changes in property rights and in market structure.

The empirical results that have been discussed above support the cartel hypothesis of OPEC behaviour. Therefore, the approach to be used in the following will be a model of a dominant firm or residual supplier. For the theoretical model it does not matter who the dominant firm is. It can be Saudi Arabia; it can be the group of the Arab Gulf states or OPEC as a whole. It is only necessary that there is someone who accepts the role of the residual supplier and bears the burden of keeping production low.

Moreover, it has been shown in a static framework that the differences between short-run and long-run demand matters a lot. Demand reactions are sluggish, and a profit-maximising monopolist (or a welfare-maximising OPEC cartel) should take this into account. The next question then is connected to the impredictability of demand behaviour. Due to little variation of oil prices over nearly two decades (the fifties and the sixties), no one could predict how demand would react to a price shock. How does this impredictability affect prices? These are the major issues the following chapters will tackle.

---

[140] Cited from *Al-Chalabi* (1980), p. 92.

4. An intertemporal model of OPEC's pricing policy

4.1. Basic assumptions

In this section a theoretical model of the world petroleum market will be constructed which will be used to analyse the process of price formation. The following issues will be taken into account:

- OPEC's role as a cartel,

- the role of the fringe of the cartel,

- differences between the short- and long-run elasticities of demand,

- the exhaustibility of petroleum reserves, and

- exogenous demand growth.

We shall follow the approaches of *Aarrestad* (1978,1979), *Dasgupta/Eastwood/Heal* (1978), and *Siebert* (1985) and consider a resource-exporting country that intends to maximise the present value of future utility streams. Utility is derived from consumption of a homogeneous product. The consumption good is imported in exchange for petroleum, which is produced domestically. The resource-exporting country is assumed to be the residual supplier on the world petroleum market, i.e. it faces a demand function which is the difference between global demand for crude oil and competitive supply. Both demand and competitive supply are sticky in the short run and more elastic in the long run. The petroleum reserves of the country are assumed to be finite and non-renewable.

The following notation will be used: A dot above a variable denotes its derivative with respect to time, a subscript (except numbers and the letters i, j, and n) its partial derivative with respect to the variable in question. A prime represents the derivative of a function having only one argument. The subscript zero denotes the initial value of a time-dependent variable. While d in italics stands for the variable 'petroleum demand', the roman d is the differential operator. Subscripts i, j, and n and numbers denote elements of a vector or a matrix.

4.1.1. Consumption, foreign assets, and the resource stock

Let utility, $u(.)$, be a twice continuously differentiable concave function of consumption, $c(t)$, satisfying the following conditions:

(4.1.1) $u' > 0 \ , \ u'' < 0 \ , \ u'(0) = \infty \ , \ u'(\infty) = 0$

Future utility is discounted at a positive and constant rate δ,[141] so that the welfare function turns out to be

(4.1.2) $$\int_{o}^{\infty} u(c(t))\, e^{-\delta t}\, dt\,.$$

The country intends to maximise its welfare subject to several constraints such as its balance-of-payments equation, the demand conditions, and the finiteness of its resource endowment.

Optimisation is carried out over an infinite time horizon. One could, however, postulate that the length of the planning horizon should be determined endogenously. Such a claim would make perfect sense if a private firm were considered. Then it can be part of the optimisation calculus at what time the shop will be closed down. In the case of a country, however, the termination of the program within finite time would imply that the welfare of future generations has no weight at all. Therefore, an infinite time horizon is postulated.[142] Nevertheless, the welfare integral is assumed to be finite. This assumption avoids the problem of comparing infinite target functions that all satisfy the necessary conditions of optimality. It, however, implies an additional restriction on some parameters of the model, which will be discussed later.

The country imports the consumption good and exports its petroleum production, $q(t)$, at a price $p(t)$ measured in units of the consumption good. Let $k(q(t))$ be the costs of petroleum production, also measured in units of the consumption good. Let the cost function be increasing and convex:

(4.1.3) $$k' > 0\,,\ k'' > 0\,.$$

OPEC can accumulate a stock of foreign assets, $V(t)$, yielding a constant and positive rate of interest, r. The initial endowment with foreign assets is exogenously given. Negative values of $V(t)$ denote debt. The balance-of-payments equation turns out to be

(4.1.4) $$\dot{V}(t) + c(t) + k(q(t)) = p(t)q(t) + rV(t)\,.$$

(4.1.5) $$V(0) = V_o\,.$$

---

[141] The legitimacy of discounting the welfare of future generations cannot be discussed here. The reader is referred to *Baumol* (1968), *Dasgupta* (1974, 1978) and *Wenz* (1985).

[142] It can be shown that the endogenously determined time horizon is infinite if marginal utility goes to infinity for zero consumption. See *Rauscher* (1985), p. 13. This means that it does not pay to terminate the program within some finite time T since a marginal unit of consumption transferred to some $t > T$ would yield a non-negligible contribution to the welfare integral.

Towards the end of the program, debt should be repaid:

(4.1.6) $\lim_{t\to\infty} V(t) \geq 0$.

The assumption that OPEC does not produce anything else but petroleum is restrictive. It is made for the sake of simplicity here but an extension of the model into that direction could easily be made. One would obtain the result that the marginal productivity of capital should equal the interest rate along an optimal path.[143] The basic results of the model concerning optimal price policies would, however, remain unchanged.

Petroleum is a non-renewable resource and the initial reserves, R_o, are finite:

(4.1.7) $$\int_{o}^{\infty} q(t)\, dt \geq R_o.$$

OPEC is assumed to be the dominant firm on the world petroleum market: customers first satisfy their needs from non-OPEC sources, and OPEC produces the residual:

(4.1.8) $q(t) = d(t) - s(t)$,

where $d(t)$ is global demand for petroleum and $s(t)$ is non-OPEC supply.

4.1.2. Demand for petroleum

Petroleum cannot be consumed directly. A production process is needed to transform petroleum into useful goods and services such as heating or transportation. Therefore, the demand for petroleum does not only depend on final demand but also on the characteristics of the production process. In particular, it depends on the structure of the capital stock and the stock of durable consumption goods needed to do the transformation. For instance, an economy is endowed with different types of cars using gasoline to produce transportation services. Thus, demand for gasoline is a function not only of demand for transportation services but also of the fuel efficiency of the stock of cars the economy is endowed with. We assume a putty-clay vintage structure of this stock of petroleum-using durable goods: new capital goods that are added to the current capital stock can be adjusted to the prevailing prices, but it is impossible to redesign the

---

[143] See *Dasgupta/Eastwood/Heal* (1978).

whole capital stock at once in order to cope with energy price changes.[144] Different vintages of capital goods have different energy intensities, and substitution proceeds slowly. In the putty-clay model, the structure of capital and durable consumption goods is reflected in the level of current demand for energy. The change in demand then depends on the level of demand and the current price:

- The lower the level demand at a given price, the more likely is it that demand increases. This is due to the fact that for any price level there exists a desired level of demand. If demand is lower than its desired level, there will be an upward adjustment.

- The impact of the price should be negative since a high price induces downward adjustments of the price.

Another influence comes from economic growth. Ceteris paribus, the impact of the level of economic activity on demand should be positive. We now define an adjustment function $f(.,.,.)$ such that

(4.1.9) $\dot{d}(t) = f(d(t),p(t),t)$

with

(4.1.10) $f_d < 0 , f_p < 0 , f_t > 0$

and

(4.1.11) $d(0) = d_o$

The initial demand for petroleum, d_o , is given historically. The impact of t denotes the influence of economic growth. In this model economic growth is exogenous and, in particular, does not depend on the situation prevailing on the petroleum market.[145]

If demand is constant, we obtain an implicit function $f(d^*(t),p(t),t)=0$, and demand, d^*, can be expressed as a function $D(.,.)$ of price and time. $D(.,.)$ can be interpreted as the desired level of demand, given the price of petroleum and the level of economic activity.

---

[144] Energy price changes lead to a revaluation of the existing capital stock. Empirical evidence in favour of this hypothesis has been reported by *Daly/Mayer* (1983) for the used-cars market and *Berndt/Wood* (1984) for capital goods in general. The revaluation shows that there is need for a restructuring of the capital stock and that there are adjustment costs.

[145] To put it correctly: the possibility of an impact of the petroleum price on economic performance is not excluded, but in this model OPEC does not take it into account when planning its optimal pricing strategy. If this relationship were taken into account, another state variable, namely the level of economic activity, would have to be introduced into the model.

(4.1.12) $d^*(t) = D(p(t),t)$

with

(4.1.13) $D_t = -f_t/f_d > 0$ and $D_p = -f_p/f_d < 0$.

      The type of specification of sluggish demand functions introduced here has often been used in empirical analyses of energy demand. See, e.g., *Berndt/Morrison/Watkins* (1981) and *Kouris* (1981,1983).[146] A typical specification is the loglinear demand function in discrete-time formulation:

$$logd(t) - logd(t-1) = \beta_0 + \beta_1 logd(t) + \beta_2 logp(t) + \beta_3 logy(t)$$

where $y(t)$ is the level of economic activity. In this case the long-run demand function turns out to be

$$logd^*(t) = -\beta_0/\beta_1 - \beta_2/\beta_1 logp(t) - \beta_3/\beta_1 logy(t)$$

and $-\beta_2/\beta_1$ and β_2 are the short-run and long-run price elasticities, respectively.

      Let the second derivatives of the adjustment function have the following properties:

(4.1.14a) $f_{pd} \geq 0$.

(4.1.14b) $f_{dd} < 0$, $f_{pp} < 0$, $f_{dd}f_{pp} - f_{pd}^2 \geq 0$.

(4.1.14c) $f(0,p(t),t) \geq 0$.

Inequality (4.1.14a) states that an increase in demand lessens the impact of a price increase. This effect is obtained if, for example, the impacts of demand and price in the adjustment function are

---

[146] This adjustment model, hoever, is only a simplified representation of demand behaviour. A better formulation of the adjustment process would be what *Berndt/Morrison/Watkins* (1981) call third-generation models. Such an approach explicitly models the optimising behaviour on the demand side. There are two reasons why this approach is not chosen here. First, it would fortify the complexity of the model. And second, the problem of dynamic inconsistency would arise since the model would turn into a *Stackelberg*-type differential game. See *Newbery* (1981,1984) and *Kemp/Long* (1984), p. 405-411. The simplifying approach chosen here is not too bad: *Struckmeyer* (1987), p. 321, and *Wirl* (1988) provide some good arguments for approximating the true model by this simpler version.

multiplicative. (4.1.14b) is the condition for $f(.,.,.)$ to be concave in $d(t)$ and $p(t)$.[147] From (4.1.14c) it follows that demand cannot become negative. Negative prices, however, are not excluded. Since demand is rigid in the short run, customers are addicted to the product in the sense that they cannot give up their habits at once. Therefore, in some extreme cases, it can turn out to be optimal to set a negative price in some initial period to increase the level of demand and exploit the rigidities in the long run.[148]

From the second-order conditions (4.1.14a-c), conclusions concerning the shape of the long-run demand curve can be drawn. Partial differentiation of (4.1.13) with respect to $p(t)$ and $d(t)$ yields

$$D_{pp}\mathrm{d}p = -f_d^{-2}\left((f_{pp}f_d - f_{dp}f_p)\,\mathrm{d}p + (f_{dd}f_p - f_{dp}f_d)\mathrm{d}d\right)$$

and

(4.1.15) $$D_{pp} = -f_d^{-1}\left(f_{pp} + f_{dp}D_p + (f_{dd}D_p + f_{dp})D_p\right).$$

It follows from the shape of the function $f(.,.,.)$ that all terms in the brackets on the right-hand side of equation (4.1.15) are negative. Hence, the long-run demand function is concave in p. This implies that there is a finite choke-off price at which demand becomes zero.

4.1.3. Petroleum supply from non-OPEC sources

Similar arguments as for the demand side hold for the petroleum supply of non-OPEC countries. The adjustment process is sluggish too. A price increase provides incentives to explore for new oil-fields and to develop known oil-fields that have not been profitable before. From the price increase it takes several years until a new field comes on stream. Adjustments to sinking prices are much faster, but they are not performed without lags. High-cost fields are the first to be closed down after a price collapse, but bringing them on stream again is very costly so that it can be worthwhile to keep on producing and to find out whether the price drop turns out to be permanent. This happened for some small fields in the US and the North Sea in 1986.

---

[147] It should be noted that in most empirical analyses of energy demand, the adjustment functions are implicitly assumed to be convex instead of concave. As an example, see the loglinear specification above. This has been pointed out by *Wirl* (1985a).

[148] This, however, presupposes the non-existence of sufficient storage facilities on the demand side.

Moreover, there is evidence that oil companies do not only use profitability criteria when making their investment decisions but also take their current cash-flow into account.[149] Thus, exploration and development activities do not only depend on expected but also on current oil prices. This finding strongly supports the hypothesis of adaptive supply adjustments.

Let $s(t)$ be non-OPEC supply and s_o be its initial level which is exogenously given. Then let $g(.,.,.)$ be the adjustment function.[150] It is increasing in the price and decreasing in the supply level. Another influence comes from the exhaustion of reserves. The higher cumulated production, the lower should current production be.[151] For the sake of simplification we introduce a trend having a negative impact:[152]

(4.1.16) $\dot{s}(t) = g\,(s(t),p(t),t)$

with

(4.1.17) $g_s < 0\ ,\ g_p > 0\ ,\ g_t < 0$

and

(4.1.18) $s(0) = s_o.$

The constant-supply locus is a non-stationary function of the price. So $S(p(t),t))$ is the desired level of supply for a given price and a given size of the reserves stock.

(4.1.19) $s^*(t) = S\,(p(t),t)$

---

[149] See *Griffin* (1988).

[150] Like demand behaviour, the adjustment process of non-OPEC supply should better be modelled on the basis of optimising behaviour. This approach was not chosen for the same reasons as above.

[151] There are two effects of cumulated production. On the one hand, there is the depletion effect, but on the other hand a learning effect has to be taken into account. Experience increases the probability of finding new fields and and new techniques allow for a better exploitation of producing fields. These effects of cumulative production have already been mentioned by *Ricardo* (1817), ch. 3. In modern resource economics, they are often taken into account explicitly. See *Pakravan* (1983), p. 37, and *Barrett* (1986), p. 238, for example. Here we assume that the depletion effect dominates.

[152] If the depletion effect were modelled explicitly, it would become part of OPEC's optimisation problem. OPEC would deliberately determine the evolution of the reserves of the rest of the world. This assumption is unrealistic and, therefore, the model is specified such that OPEC just knows that there is a tendency of production to decrease over time.

76

with

(4.1.20) $S_t = -g_t/g_s < 0$ and $S_p = -g_p/g_s > 0.$

Finally, we impose some additional assumptions on the adjustment function:

(4.1.21a) $g_{ps} \geq 0$.

(4.1.21b) $g_{ss} > 0$, $g_{pp} > 0$, $g_{ss}g_{pp} - g_{ps}^2 \geq 0.$

(4.1.21c) $g\,(0,p(t),t) \geq 0.$

Inequality (4.1.21a) states that a decrease in supply lessens the impact of a price increase. (4.1.21b) is the condition for $g(.,.,.)$ to be convex in $s(t)$ and $p(t)$. From (4.1.21c) it follows that supply cannot become negative.

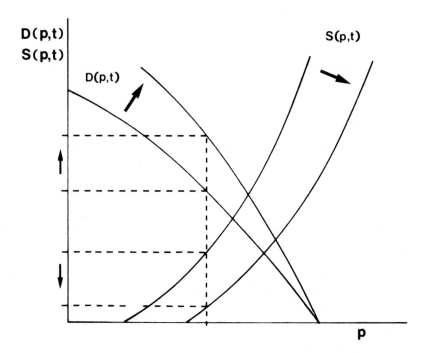

Figure 4.1.: Long-run demand and supply functions

The shape of the long-run demand curve can be obtained by partially differentiating the second equation in (4.1.20) with respect to $p(t)$ and $d(t)$. The result resembles equation (4.1.15):

(4.1.22) $\qquad S_{pp} = -g_s^{-1} (g_{pp} + g_{sp} S_p + (g_{ss} S_p + g_{sp}) S_p)$.

From the shape of the function $g(.,.,.)$ it follows that all terms in the brackets on the right-hand side of equation (4.1.22) are positive. Hence, the long-run supply function is convex in p.

From the concavity of the demand function and the convexity of the supply function it follows that the residual demand for OPEC oil, determined by equation (4.1.8), is concave too. Over time demand is increased by economic growth while the depletion effect reduces non-OPEC supply. The result of the combination of these effects is an increase of demand for OPEC oil. This is shown graphically in Figure 4.1.

4.1.4. The literature on dynamic monopoly models

Models of monopolistic pricing in the presence of demand rigidities have a long tradition in economic theory reaching back to *Evans* (1924). In this article, he investigated the optimal policy of a monopolist who faces a demand function which does not only depend on the price but also on its change. Thus the price is a state variable in a variational problem. In *Evans'* model, the Cournot monopoly price turns out to be a solution which is attained asymptotically.

The models investigated by *Jacquemin* (1972), Section 3, and *Jacquemin/Thisse* (1973) can be interpreted so as to be referring to the dynamic monopoly problem. They consider a profit-maximising firm whose profits depend on a decision variable (e.g. the price) and a state variable (e.g. the quantity sold). The state equation is linear in both variables and the profit function is convex. The solution is a long-run equilibrium which is approached asymptotically. Along the optimal path, the monopolist uses most of her power in the beginning and reduces the effort in the long run. Similar results will be obtained in this chapter, but only for special parameter constellations.

More recent investigations, explicitly concerning the petroleum market were undertaken by *Pindyck* (1978b), *Marshalla* (1979), *Wirl* (1985a,b,1988), and *Rauscher* (1986, 1988a,b).

Pindyck (1978b) uses a model similar to the one presented here. He additionally introduces a Ricardian element, namely stock effects in the cost function. *Pindyck*, however, does not solve the dynamic optimisation model explicitly but carries out simulations with realistic parameters and obtains a U-shaped price profile after the cartelisation. The model is restrictive insofar as most of the functional relations among different variables are assumed to be linear.

Marshalla (1979), ch. 3, investigates a simplified version of *Pindyck*'s model. Demand and non-OPEC supply are aggregated, and the adjustment process as well as the demand funtion are assumed to be linear. Therefore, the Hamiltonian function he obtains is linear in the price, and the solution either is a boundary value of the price or a singular arc. *Marshalla* shows that there is an initial period during which the price is set equal to one of its boundary values, depending on the initial level of demand. In the second period, a so-called balanced demand path is followed: the price level lies between the upper and the lower bound and increases because of the depletion effect. *Marshalla*'s results are compatible with those obtained by *Pindyck*. If initial demand exceeds balanced demand, e.g. after a cartelisation, the first-period price is at the upper bound. This outcome of the model is equivalent to *Pindyck*'s U-shaped price profile. The main criticisms of this model are its restrictive functional relationships and the exogeneity of the price bounds.

Wirl (1985a) allows for more general functional relationships in his model but does not take the scarcity of the resource into account. He obtains an equilibrium with the price exceeding the static monopoly price. *Wirl* uses non-concavities in the adjustment function to explain price volatility. If there are upper and lower bounds for the price, the optimal pricing policy is cyclical, and the price fluctuates between these bounds. The bounds can be explained by the threat of military intervention if the price is increased too much and by the possibility of building up inventories in the case of very low prices. Nonetheless, an explicit model of these bounds would be desirable. The decisive question, however, is whether real-world demand adjustments are characterised by non-concavities. The loglinear specification often used in econometric analyses implies convexity, but it is preferred because of its handliness rather than because of its realism. Whether real-world functions are concave or convex, is an empirical question, and it will be tackled in Chapter 6. Finally, even though oil price fluctuations can be optimal, historical evidence suggests that price shocks, especially the price collapse of 1986, have been a result of a trial-and-error search for the correct price rather than of well-informed planning.

Rauscher (1986) assumes that everything is concave and well-behaved. This assumption can, of course, also be criticised because of its lack of empirical content. Oil price fluctuations are explained by OPEC's wrong expectations on demand behaviour and corrections of the pricing strategy. In another paper (*Rauscher* (1988a)), the monopolist is substituted by a resource-exporting country, and the optimal export strategy is discussed. Moreover, the exhaustibility of petroleum is taken into account, and the resulting price profile is U-shaped if rigidity effects dominate the scarcity effects in the short run.

One of the assumptions of these models which is too restrictive is that demand for OPEC oil is treated as an aggregate. *Rauscher* (1988b) obtains the result that almost anything can be optimal if this assumption is dropped and there are different adjustment processes in demand and non-OPEC supply: cyclical and unstable solutions cannot be excluded. It will be shown in this chapter that some of these results have to be corrected and, in particular, that unstable optimal solutions are not possible. The model analysed by *Rauscher* (1988b) is static in the sense that shifts in the functions, due to GDP growth and exhaustion of reserves are neglected.

The present model, which will be examined in the following sections, is more general and avoids many of the shortcomings that have been mentioned above.

4.2. Necessary conditions of optimality

OPEC's problem is to maximise the present value of its welfare with respect to its balance-of-payments equation (4.1.5), its petroleum reserves restriction (4.1.7), its role as the swing producer (4.1.8), and the reactions of demand (4.1.9) and non-OPEC supply (4.1.16). The initial values of the state variables are given, and foreign debt must be repaid in the long run. OPEC's control variables are its level of consumption and the petroleum price. The price determines the behaviour of demand and non-OPEC supply and, in the long run, the date of exhaustion of the reserves. The choice of the consumption level affects welfare and the accumulation of foreign assets or debt. The problem can be solved by applying *Pontryagin's* maximum principle.[153] In the following, the argument t of time-dependent variables will be omitted for convenience. Then the current-value Hamiltonian turns out to be:

$$(4.2.1) \qquad H = u(c) + y \{p'(d\text{-}s)\text{-}k(d\text{-}s)\text{-}c + rV\} - z \{d\text{-}s\} + v f(d,p,t) + w g(s,p,t),$$

where y, z, v, and w are the costate variables of foreign assets, the resource stock, demand, and non-OPEC supply, respectively. The costate variables, which can also be interpreted as shadow prices, change according to the canonical equations. Omitting the arguments of the functions for convenience, these equations are

$$(4.2.2) \qquad \dot{y} = (\delta - r) y,$$

$$(4.2.3) \qquad \dot{z} = \delta z,$$

$$(4.2.4) \qquad \dot{v} = (\delta - f_d) v - y (p - k') + z,$$

$$(4.2.5) \qquad \dot{w} = (\delta - g_s) w + y (p - k') - z.$$

The Hamiltonian can now be maximised with respect to the price of petroleum, p, and consumption, c:

$$(4.2.6) \qquad y = u',$$

and

$$(4.2.7) \qquad (d - s) y + f_p v + g_p w = 0.$$

---

[153] The appendix contains a short treatise on the method and references to the literature.

Equation (4.2.6) is a variant of *Ramsey's* rule of optimal saving. The shadow price of the store of wealth equals marginal utility. This result was first established by *Ramsey* (1928) in his seminal paper on the optimal accumulation of capital. The interpretation is as follows. If a marginal unit of income is not consumed, it can be used to accelerate asset accumulation. The effect of this marginal unit of additional assets on the present value of future utility flows is measured by the costate variable or shadow price y.[154] On the other hand, a marginal unit of saving causes an instantaneous welfare loss equal to the marginal utility of consumption. In the optimum, this loss must be just as great as the gain from increased accumulation.

Equation (4.2.6) states that, along an optimal path, the net effect of a price variation on the welfare function must be zero. $(d-s)y$ is the effect of the price variation via the process of asset accumulation. $f_p v$ and $g_p w$ are the effects that are induced by demand and supply rigidities, respectively. Since a price increase lowers future demand and hence future income and consumption possibilites, $f_p v$ should be negative. The same proposition holds for $g_p w$ because the price rise increases future supply by non-OPEC countries and, therefore, reduces OPEC's future oil revenues. Hence, one expects the shadow price of demand, v, to be positive and the shadow price of non-cartel supply, w, to be negative.

4.3. The consumption path

Since, in this model, the capital market is perfect in the sense that the rate of interest is constant and unique, *Fisher's* separation theorem holds, and along the optimal path petroleum extraction is not affected by the consumption and savings decisions. Moreover, the conditions for the optimal consumption profile are independent of the extraction path. These separation properties are useful in the analysis of the optimal solution. The Hamiltonian is concave in (c, V) and, therefore, conditions (4.2.2) and (4.2.6) are sufficient for an optimum with respect to consumption, c.[155]

Establishing growth rates in equation (4.2.6) yields

(4.3.1) $\hat{c} = \eta^{-1}(r - \delta)$

where $\eta = -u''c/u'$ is the elasticity of marginal utility. If the discount rate exceeds the interest rate, consumption will decrease since the weight given to the welfare of future

---

[154] See also *Dorfman* (1969), *Feichtinger/Hartl* (1986), p. 28-31, and *Léonard* (1987) for the interpretation of the costate variables.

[155] See Theorem A.3. in the appendix for the second-order conditions.

generations is small. If the interest rate dominates the discount rate, it is optimal to postpone consumption in favour of future generations because of the growth potential of asset income.

The latter case, however, causes mathematical problems, for the welfare integral does not necessarily converge any more. Restricting the analysis to the case of a constant-elasticity utility function, we can derive a condition for convergence. The utility function turns out to be

(4.3.2a) $\qquad u = (1 - \eta)^{-1} c^{1-n}$ $\hspace{4cm}$ for $\eta \neq 1.$

or

(4.3.2b) $\qquad u = log(c)$ $\hspace{4cm}$ for $\eta = 1.$

The argument of the welfare integral, i.e. discounted utility, then is

(4.3.3a) $\qquad e^{-\delta t} u = u_o \, exp \, [(\eta^{-1} (r - \delta)(1 - \eta) - \delta) \, t \,]$ $\hspace{2cm}$ for $\eta \neq 1.$

(4.3.3b) $\qquad e^{-\delta t} u = (u_o + (r - \delta) \, t \,) \, e^{-\delta t}$ $\hspace{3cm}$ for $\eta = 1.$

Hence, the following conclusion can be drawn:

PROPOSITION 4.1

For a constant-elasticity utility function the welfare integral is finite if and only if

(4.3.4) $\qquad r (1 - \eta) < \delta$.

For the remainder of this study, it will be assumed that inequality (4.3.4) holds.

4.4. Accumulation of foreign assets and the existence of an optimal solution

How does a resource-exporting country convert its wealth in the ground into money at the bank? Can it live from capital income when the resource is depleted? Is it possible that a debtor country turns into a creditor by placing its petrodollars in the world capital markets? These questions are of great importance in the economic theory of resource-exporting countries.[156] *Siebert* (1985), p. 78-80, has established a condition for an increase in the stock of

---

[156] *Dasgupta/Eastwood/Heal* (1978), *Aarrestad* (1979) and *Siebert* (1985), ch. 5, have analysed these questions in detail.

foreign assets under the assumption of a competitive market for the resource. Then, the elasticities of demand for the resource and demand for consumption goods by the resource-exporting country play a major part in the accumulation process. It can be shown that accumulation takes place if the *Marshall-Lerner* condition holds.

It is, however, impossible to derive a similar condition here since the model is too complex. What can be done is an analysis of the process of asset accumulation in the long run. From the long-term behaviour, conclusions can be drawn concerning the process of saving during the initial periods of the program. Moreover, the question of the existence of an optimal program will be addressed.

As will be shown later, it is likely that OPEC exhausts its reserves within finite time along the optimal path.[157] Thus, oil revenues are zero after the exhaustion date and the balance-of-payments equation is

$$\dot{V} = rV - c$$

or

(4.4.1) $\qquad \hat{V} = r - c/V .$

Since the terminal condition requires debt to be repaid as t goes to infinity, and consumption is positive, the stock of foreign assets, V, must grow at a rate less than the interest rate.[158]

The time profile of asset accumulation can now be derived from equation (4.4.1). The solution must be a steady-state in which consumption and the stock of foreign assets grow at the same rate. Otherwise, the assets-to-consumption ratio would either go to infinity, which indicates over-accumulation, or the stock of assets would become negative. This would violate the terminal condition. The growth rate of consumption is determined by *Ramsey's* rule, equation (4.3.1). Thus,

(4.4.2) $\qquad \hat{V} = \hat{c} = \eta^{-1} (r - \delta) .$

Inserting this into (4.4.1), one obtains

(4.4.3) $\qquad \dfrac{c}{V} = r - \eta^{-1} (r - \delta) .$

---

[157] See Chapter 4.6. This is not a general result, but it holds for realistic specifications of the demand and non-OPEC supply functions.

[158] *Toussaint* (1985) has established this result by applying a theorem which is due to *Michel* (1982). See also Theorem A.2. in the appendix.

Since both consumption and assets must be positive in the long run, this implies

(4.4.4) $r(1-\eta) < \delta$.

This is exactly the condition that has been derived for the finiteness of the welfare integral.

Figure 4.2. represents a typical profile of V. It is assumed, that the oil-exporting country is indebted initially and that the discount rate is larger than the interest rate such that the economy declines in the long run. In a first period, the debt is repaid. Then a stock of foreign assets is accumulated. As oil revenues decline, an increasing part of consumption is paid from interest income. Finally, when the oil reserves are exhausted, the stock of foreign assets is the only source of income. This is only one scenario - other cases, e.g. with a positive long-run growth rate, can easily be constructed.

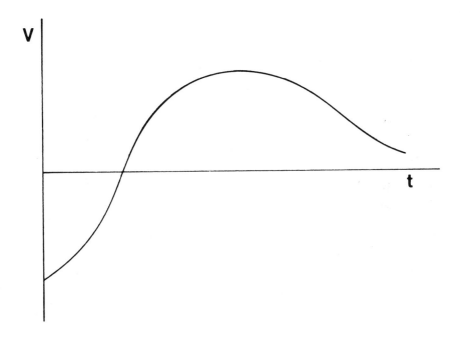

Figure 4.2.: A typical debt cycle

From the preceding arguments, a condition concerning the existence of an optimal program can be derived. An optimal solution does not exist if, given the initial endowment, there is no path that satisfies the terminal conditions (debt repayment and finiteness of the resource base). This can occur if the resource-exporting country is highly indebted in the beginning. If additionally the resource base is small and the resource-exporting country has not much monopoly power, i.e. if demand is elastic and adjusts quickly to price changes, then it might be possible that the country is unable to repay debt. In a more rigorous formulation the existence condition is

$$(4.4.5) \qquad \int_o^\infty p\,q - k(q) + rV\ dt\ +\ V_o\ >\ 0.$$

In the case $V_o \geq 0$, an optimal program exists unless extraction costs are prohibitively high or a minimum level of consumption is introduced into the model.

4.5. The price path

Due to *Fisher*'s separation theorem, the price path can be examined independently of the consumption path. In a first step, an equilibrium will be derived which will be used as a reference point for further analyses. The corresponding equilibrium values of the variables will be indicated by asterisks. Behaviour near the equilibrium is to be investigated, and we will obtain different scenarios depending on the values of certain parameters.

4.5.1. A long-run equilibrium price

The long-run equilibrium is normally derived by setting the changes in the state and co-state variables equal to zero. Here, however, this procedure would be incorrect since it would not take the shadow price of foreign assets, y, into account. In order to show this, the model is simplified by neglecting the trend impact on demand and non-OPEC supply and the exhaustibility of petroleum. Assume that the state variables, demand and non-OPEC supply, have reached their desired levels and are, therefore, constant. An equilibrium in the costate variables implies that the right-hand sides of the canonical equations, (4.2.4.) and (4.2.5), are equal to zero. As *Rauscher* (1988b) has shown, this implies an equilibrium price defined by

$$(4.5.1) \qquad p^* - k' \ = \ \left(\frac{g_s S_p}{g_s - \delta} - \frac{f_d D_p}{f_d - \delta} \right)^{-1} (D - S)\,.$$

If such an equilibrium exists, the price must be constant since there are no time-dependent variables by which it can be shifted.

On the other hand, one can differentiate the optimality condition

$$(4.2.7) \qquad (d\text{-}s)\,y + f_p v + g_p w \ = \ 0$$

with respect to time. In the equilibrium, the state variables d and s and the costate variables v and w are constant. This implies

(4.5.2) $(d-s)\dot{y} + (f_{pp}v + g_{pp}w)\dot{p} = 0.$

According to the canonical equation (4.2.2), y changes by a rate of $(\delta - r)$. Depending on whether the discount rate is greater, equal or less than the interest rate, one obtains an either growing, constant or decreasing equilibrium price, provided that the costate variables have the expected signs. This result obviously contradicts the equilibrium price condition, (4.5.1).

A consistent way of computing the equilibrium is to leave the state variables and the price (instead of the costate variables) constant. Demand and non-OPEC supply are in equilibrium if they equal their desired levels:

(4.5.3) $d^* = D(p,t).$

(4.5.4) $s^* = S(p,t).$

Differentiating the optimality condition (4.2.7) with respect to time and noting that d, s and p are constant and that $\dot{y} = (\delta - r)y$, one obtains

(4.5.5) $(d^* - s^*)(\delta - r)y + f_p\dot{v}^* + g_p\dot{w}^* + f_{pt}v^* + g_{pt}w^* = 0.$

In order to keep matters simple, we assume that the trend impact on f_p and g_p is negligible:[159]

(4.5.6) $f_{pt} = g_{pt} = 0.$

The last two terms on the left-hand side vanish and one can conclude that in the equilibrium the costate variables change according to:

(4.5.7) $\dot{v}^* = (\delta - r)v^*,$

(4.5.8) $\dot{w}^* = (\delta - r)w^*.$

If these conditions hold, then (4.5.5) satisfies the optimality condition. This can be seen by inserting v^* and w^* into (4.5.5) and dividing by $(\delta - r)$.

---

[159] In the next chapter, that will investigate a simplified version of this model, the influence of the trend on the equilibrium solution will be analysed in greater detail.

Instead of an equilibrium with constant shadow prices, we obtain a steady state with the shadow prices y, v and w growing at the same rate. If the system is not in the steady state, the shadow prices change according to their canonical equations:

(4.2.4) $\qquad \dot{v} = (\delta - f_d) v - y (p - k') + z ,$

(4.2.5) $\qquad \dot{w} = (\delta - g_s) w + y (p - k') - z .$

Equilibrium conditions can be obtained by setting the right-hand sides of these equations equal to the right-hand sides of (4.5.7) and (4.5.8):

(4.5.9) $\qquad v^* = (r - f_d)^{-1} (y (p-k') - z) .$

(4.5.10) $\qquad w^* = - (r - g_s)^{-1} (y (p-k') - z) .$

It follows that, if $(y(p - k') - z)$ is positive, then v^* is positive and w^* is negative. This result is in accordance with the conjectures made at the end of Chapter 4.2.

Equations (4.5.9) and (4.5.10) can now be combined with the optimality condition (4.2.7) such that the costate variables, v^* and w^*, are eliminated. This yields

(4.5.11) $\qquad (d^*-s^*) y + f_p (r - f_d)^{-1} (y (p^*-k') - z) - g_p (r - g_s)^{-1} (y (p^*-k') - z) = 0.$

Dividing by y and rearranging terms yields

(4.5.12) $\qquad d^* - s^* + [f_p (r - f_d)^{-1} - g_p (r - g_s)^{-1}] (p^* - k' - z/y) = 0.$

Now, (4.5.3) and (4.5.4) can be inserted into (4.5.12). In addition, note that the slopes of the long-run demand and supply curves are $D_p = - f_p / f_d$ and $S_p = - g_p / g_s$, respectively. Using this, the following proposition can be stated:

PROPOSITION 4.2

The state variables and the control variable are in equilibrium if

(4.5.13) $\qquad p^* - k' - z/y = \left(\dfrac{g_s S_p}{g_s - r} - \dfrac{f_d D_p}{f_d - r} \right)^{-1} (D - S) .$

For $z/y=0$, this equilibrium price is constant. Thus, this result is consistent with the optimality condition since all the shadow prices increase at the same rate, namely $(\delta - r)$. Given the signs of the derivatives of the functions, equation (4.5.13) implies:

PROPOSITION 4.3

If $(D-S)$ is positive, i.e. if OPEC is a net exporter of petroleum, then $(p^*-k'-z/y)$ is positive too. Thus the shadow price of demand, v, is positive and the shadow price of non-OPEC supply, w, is negative in a close neighbourhood of the equilibrium.

Condition (4.5.13) has the following interpretation. The left-hand side contains price minus marginal production cost minus the fraction of the shadow prices z and y. Using (4.2.2) and (4.2.3), z/y can be rewritten as

$$(4.5.14) \qquad z/y = e^{rt} z_o/y_o.$$

Thus, z/y is the *Hotelling* element in the process of price formation. It is the user cost of extracting a non-renewable resource. As Proposition 4.3 states, the price exceeds the sum extraction and user costs.

The right-hand side of (4.5.13) contains the elements of the price which are due to monopoly power and rigidities. Let either r go to zero or f_d and g_s go to minus infinity. The first case affects the rate by which future profits are discounted; in the second case, the adjustment speeds are infinite so that the adjustment processes from an actual to a desired level of demand or non-OPEC supply take place instantaneously. This implies:

PROPOSITION 4.4

$$(4.5.15) \qquad p^* - k' - z/y = -(D-S)/(D_p-S_p) \qquad \text{if } r=0 \text{ or } f_d = g_s = -\infty.$$

The left-hand side of (4.5.15) is just the price over the elasticity of demand for OPEC oil. So this is the conventional monopoly result: marginal revenue equals marginal costs which include the user cost of the resource.[160]

---

[160] See *Stiglitz* (1976), p. 658, or *Dasgupta/Heal* (1979), p. 324.

4.5.2. The effects of parameter changes

The introduction of rigidities leads to a price different from the monopoly price. Conclusions concerning the direction of this change can be drawn by differentiating the equilibrium price with respect to r, f_d, and g_s. First (4.5.13) can be rewritten such that

(4.5.16) $D - S + (D_p f_d (f_d - r)^{-1} - S_p g_s (g_s - r)^{-1}) \, (p^* - k' - z/y) = 0.$

Total differentiation yields

(4.5.17) $[\, (p^* - k' - z/y) \, (D_p f_d (f_d - r)^{-2} - S_p g_s (g_s - r)^{-2}) \,] \, dr$

$+ \, [\, -r D_p \, (p^* - k' - z/y) \, (f_d - r)^{-2} \,] \, df_d$

$+ \, [\, r S_p \, (p^* - k' - z/y) \, (g_s - r)^{-2} \,] \, dg_s$

$+ \, [\, D_p - S_p + (D_p f_d (f_d - r)^{-1} - S_p g_s (g_s - r)^{-1}) \, (1 - k'' (D_p - S_p)) +$

$\quad (p^* - k' - z/y) \, ((f_d - r)^{-2} (D_{pp} f_d (f_d - r) - r D_p (f_{dp} + f_{dd} D_p)) -$

$\quad (g_s - r)^{-2} (S_{pp} g_s (g_s - r) - r S_p (g_{sp} + g_{ss} S_p)) \,] \, dp^*$

$= 0.$

From the signs of the functions and their derivatives it follows that the factors by which the differentials dr, df_d and dg_s are multiplied are all positive. The first terms of the multiplier of dp^* are negative but the impact of

$$(f_d - r)^{-2} (D_{pp} f_d (f_d - r) - r D_p f_{dp} + f_{dd} D_p)$$
$$- (g_s - r)^{-2} (S_{pp} g_s (g_s - r) - r S_p (g_{sp} + g_{ss} S_p))$$

is ambiguous. The sign of this term can be checked by substituting for D_{pp} and S_{pp} from equations (4.1.15) and (4.1.22). Substituting for D_{pp} yields

$$D_{pp} f_d (f_d - r) - r D_p f_{dp} + f_{dd} D_p$$
$$= - (f_{pp} + f_{dp} D_p + (f_{dd} D_p + f_{dp}) D_p) \, (f_d - r) - r D_p (f_{dp} + f_{dd} D_p)$$
$$= - (f_{pp} + f_{dp} D_p) \, (f_d - r) - f_d D_p (f_{dd} D_p + f_{dp}) < 0.$$

Correspondingly,

$$- S_{pp} g_s (g_s - r) - r S_p g_{sp} + g_{ss} S_p$$
$$= (g_{pp} + g_{sp} S_p) (g_s - r) + g_s S_p (g_{ss} S_p + g_{sp}) < 0.$$

Therefore, the long term in square brackets in front of dp^* is unambiguously negative. It follows that all three parameters, r, f_d and g_s, have positive impacts on the equilibrium price. f_d and g_s are negative by definition. For given price and quantities, their absolute values are measures of the adjustment speeds of demand and non-OPEC supply, respectively. This implies:

PROPOSITION 4.5

The more slowly the adjustments of demand and non-OPEC supply take place and the higher the interest rate is, the higher is the long-run equilibrium price.

This in turn implies:

PROPOSITION 4.6

There is a rigidity rent in addition to the conventional monopoly rent. The long-run equilibrium price turns out to be

$$price = marg.\,cost + user\,cost + marg.\,monopoly\,rent$$
$$+ marg.\,rigidity\,rent\,.[161]$$

4.5.3. Second-order conditions

Before we proceed to a deeper investigation of OPEC's optimal pricing policy, particularly the question of stability of the equilibrium described above, it is necessary to find out

---

[161] *Evans* (1924), *Jacquemin* (1972) and *Jacquemin/Thisse* (1973) did not discover this rigidity rent since profits were not discounted in their models. As *Helmedag* (1986) managed to show, this result can also be derived from a static model in which long-run and short-run profits are weighted according to the time prefences of the monopolist.

whether the solution derived by setting the derivatives of the Hamiltonian with respect to the control variables equal to zero is really a welfare-maximising optimum.

This can be done by investigating the properties of the second-order derivatives of the Hamiltonian. It is shown in the appendix that conditions (4.2.2) to (4.2.7) are sufficient for an optimum if the maximised Hamiltonian is concave in the state variables. Due to *Fisher's* separation theorem and the fact that the stock of petroleum reserves does not occur in the Hamiltonian, the analysis can be restricted to concavity in *(d,s)*.

A function is concave if its Hessian is negative semidefinite.[162] In order to compute the Hessian, the optimal Hamiltonian has to be determined first. This requires the price variable to be eliminated. The optimal price can be expressed as a function of the state and costate variables due to the optimality condition

$$(4.2.7) \qquad (d\text{-}s)\,y + f_p v + g_p w \; = \; 0.$$

Applying the implicit function theorem to (4.2.7) yields

$$(4.5.18) \qquad (y + vf_{dp})\,\mathrm{d}d - (y - wg_{sp})\,\mathrm{d}s + f_p\,\mathrm{d}v + g_p\mathrm{d}w \; = \; -\,(vf_{pp} + wg_{pp})\,\mathrm{d}p.$$

The price now is a function of the other variables, and the signs of the partial derivatives are unambiguously determined:

$$(4.5.19) \qquad p = m(d,s,v,w).$$

with the partial derivatives

$$(4.5.19a) \qquad m_d \; = \; \partial p/\partial d \; = \; -\,(y + vf_{dp})/H_{pp},$$

$$(4.5.19b) \qquad m_s \; = \; \partial p/\partial s \; = \; (y - wg_{sp})/H_{pp},$$

$$(4.5.19c) \qquad m_v \; = \; \partial p/\partial v \; = \; -f_p/H_{pp},$$

$$(4.5.19d) \qquad m_w \; = \; \partial p/\partial w \; = \; -g_p/H_{pp},$$

and

$$(4.5.19e) \qquad H_{pp} \; = \; vf_{pp} + wg_{pp}.$$

---

[162] See *Takayama* (1985), pp. 125-126.

Noting that $H_p = 0$, the first derivatives of H with respect to (d,s) turn out to be

(4.5.20) $\qquad H_{(d,s)} = [y\,(p\text{-}k') - z + vf_d \;, \;\; -y\,(p\text{-}k') + z + wg_s]^T,$

the superscript T denoting the transpose. Differentiating this again and using (4.5.19a-d) yields the Hessian

(4.5.21) $\qquad H_{(d,s)(d,s)} = \begin{bmatrix} vf_{dd} - yk" - (y + vf_{dp})^2/H_{pp} & yk" - (y + vf_{dp})(y\text{-}wg_{sp})/H_{pp} \\ yk" - (y + vf_{dp})(y\text{-}wg_{sp})/H_{pp} & wg_{ss} - yk" - (y\text{-}wg_{sp})^2/H_{pp} \end{bmatrix}.$

The matrix is not necessarily negative definite. For instance, the first element of the Hessian can be rewritten by substituting for H_{pp}:

(4.5.22) $\qquad vf_{dd} - yk" - (y + vf_{dp})^2/H_{pp}$

$$= \frac{v^2\,(f_{dd}f_{pp} - f_{dp}^2) + vwf_{dd}g_{pp} - yk"\,(vf_{pp} + wg_{pp}) - y^2 - 2\,y\,v\,f_{dp}}{vf_{pp} + wg_{pp}}.$$

Due to the concavity of the adjustment functions, the denominator is negative and the first terms in the numerator are positive. The last two terms, however, exhibit the 'wrong' sign. A similar result would occur if we expressed the second-row second-column element of the Hessian in this way. The ambiguity is caused by the non-concavity of the profit function, $p(d\text{-}s)\text{-}k'$, whose Hessian with respect to (p,d,s) is

$$\begin{bmatrix} 0 & 1 & -1 \\ 1 & -k" & k" \\ -1 & k" & -k" \end{bmatrix}.$$

Two of the second-order principal minors of this matrix are negative, namely -1. Because of these non-concavities in the profit function, the terms ym_d and ym_s occur in the Hessian of the Hamiltonian and produce terms having 'wrong' signs. In the following, it will be assumed that the concavity of the adjustment function and the convexity of the cost function dominate these effects and that, therefore, the Hamiltonian is concave in (d,s).

4.5.4. Behaviour near the equilibrium

The equilibrium price determines long-run levels of demand and non-OPEC supply. The initial levels of these variables do not, however, generally equal their equilibrium values. Thus, the question arises whether the optimal path is stable. Does it approach the equilibrium from any initial state? If not, the equilibrium cannot be used as a reference point for the behaviour of optimal paths.

The adjustment functions have been specified such that, for a given price, demand and non-OPEC supply asymptotically approach their equilibrium or desired levels. In other words: the system is stable if no control is exerted. It is, however, not clear whether it is in OPEC's interest to leave the system stable. Does OPEC have the capability to destabilise the oil market? If this is possible, does OPEC have an interest in such a pricing policy, and what are the decisive parameters in favour of such a decision? These are the questions which will be addressed below.

In order to do this, the dynamic behaviour of the linearised state-costate system will be investigated. The linearisation is a good approximation to the original system in a close neighbourhood of the equilibrium.

The Hamiltonian system consists of four differential equations, two in the state and two in the costate variables:

(4.1.9) $\qquad \dot{d} = f(d,p,t)$

(4.1.16) $\qquad \dot{s} = g(s,p,t)$

(4.2.4) $\qquad \dot{v} = (\delta - f_d)v - y(p - k') + z,$

(4.2.5) $\qquad \dot{w} = (\delta - g_s)w + y(p - k') - z.$

Taking account of the fact that the price along the optimal path can be expressed as a function of the state and costate variables,

(4.5.19) $\qquad p = m(d,s,v,w),$

the system of differential equations can be linearised in the equilibrium by computing partial derivatives. The costate variables v and w are, however, not constant in the equilibrium. In order to obtain a stationary equilibrium, they are transformed by dividing them by y:

(4.5.23) $\qquad v^y = v/y$ and $w^y = w/y$.

Using this transformation, the system can be written as

$$(4.5.24) \qquad \dot{d} = [f_d + f_p m_d] (d-d^*) + f_p m_s (s-s^*) + y f_p m_v (v^y - v^{y*}) + y f_p m_w (w^y - w^{y*}) ,$$

$$(4.5.25) \qquad \dot{s} = g_p m_d (d-d^*) + [g_s + g_p m_s] (s-s^*) + y g_p m_v (v^y - v^{y*}) + y g_p m_w (w^y - w^{y*}) ,$$

$$(4.5.26) \qquad \dot{v}^y = -[v^y (f_{dd} + f_{dp} m_d) + m_d - k''] (d-d^*) - [v^y f_{dp} m_s + m_s + k''] (s-s^*)$$
$$+ [r f_d - (v f_{dp} + y) m_v] (v^y - v^{y*}) - [(v f_{dp} + y) m_w] (w^y - w^{y*}) ,$$

$$(4.5.27) \qquad \dot{w}^y = -[w^y g_{sp} m_d - m_d + k'')] (d-d^*) - [w^y (g_{ss} + g_{sp} m_s) - m_s + k'')] (s-s^*)$$
$$+ [(y - w g_{sp}) m_v] (v^y - v^{y*}) + [r - g_s - (y - w g_{sp}) m_w] (w^y - w^{y*}) .$$

m_d, m_s, m_v, and m_w can be substituted from the equations (4.5.19a-d). Then the system, now written in matrix form, turns out to be

$$(4.5.28) \qquad \begin{bmatrix} \dot{d} \\ \dot{s} \\ \dot{v}^y \\ \dot{w}^y \end{bmatrix} = \begin{bmatrix} A & B \\ C & rI - A^T \end{bmatrix} \begin{bmatrix} d-d^* \\ s-s^* \\ v^y - v^{y*} \\ w^y - w^{y*} \end{bmatrix}$$

with

$$(4.5.29) \qquad A = \begin{bmatrix} f_d - f_p(y + vf_{dp})/H_{pp} & f_p(y - wg_{sp})/H_{pp} \\ -g_p(y + vf_{dp})/H_{pp} & g_s + g_p(y - wg_{sp})/H_{pp} \end{bmatrix} ,$$

$$(4.5.30) \qquad B = \begin{bmatrix} -y(f_p)^2/H_{pp} & -yf_p g_p/H_{pp} \\ -yf_p g_p/H_{pp} & -y(g_p)^2/H_{pp} \end{bmatrix} ,$$

$$(4.5.31) \qquad C = -\begin{bmatrix} v^y f_{dd} - k'' - (1 + v^y f_{dp})^2/H_{pp} & k'' + (1 + v^y f_{dp})(1 - w^y g_{sp})/H_{pp} \\ k'' + (1 + v^y f_{dp})(1 - w^y g_{sp})/H_{pp} & w^y g_{ss} - k'' - (1 - w^y g_{sp})^2/H_{pp} \end{bmatrix} .$$

Let J be the Jacobian matrix that contains the partial derivatives of the linearised system:

$$(4.5.32) \qquad J \; = \; \begin{bmatrix} A & B \\ C & rI\text{-}A^T \end{bmatrix} .$$

The submatrices A, B, and C have some special properties which can later be used to derive some further results. B is symmetric. It can easily be verified that its diagonal elements are positive and the determinant is zero. Therefore, B, i.e. the Hessian of H with respect to (v,w), is positive semidefinite.[163] B is a constant matrix.

The matrix C is positive definite since it equals $-y^{-1}H_{(d,s)(d,s)}$, which has been assumed to be negative definite. Moreover, C is a constant matrix since the factor y^{-1} just offsets the change in the Hessian.

A is not a symmetric matrix. Its diagonal elements are negative. The determinant turns out to be

$$(4.5.33) \qquad det\,A = f_d g_s - f_p g_s (y + vf_{dp})/H_{pp} + f_d g_p (y - wg_{sp})/H_{pp} > 0.$$

The eigenvalues of a $(2x2)$ matrix, e_1 and e_2, are given by

$$(4.5.34) \qquad e_{1,2} = \tfrac{1}{2}tr\,A \pm \sqrt{\tfrac{1}{4}(tr\,A)^2 - det\,A} .$$

Since the trace is negative and the determinant is positive, both eigenvalues have negative real parts and A is a stability matrix.

The properties of the matrices A, B and C are summarised in the following proposition:

PROPOSITION 4.7

A has negative diagonal elements and a positive determinant and, therefore, is a stability matrix. B is the Hessian of H with respect to (v,w). It is positive semidefinite. C has the same properties as the negative Hessian of H with respect to (d,s). It is positive definite.

It should be noted, that the equilibrium values of the costate variables are not constant in this model. The following stability analysis will, therefore, deal with the question whether the

---

[163] It is shown in the appendix (Corollary A.1.) that the Hessian of the Hamiltonian function with respect to the costate variables is always positive semidefinite if the number of state variables exceeds the number of control variables.

shadow prices asymptotically approach their steady state path rather than a constant equilibrium. Another difference compared to other optimal control models is that the Jacobian matrix, J, contains the submatrix $(rI\text{-}A^T)$ instead of $(\delta I - A^T)$. Nevertheless, the theorems known from the usual discounted multi-dimensional control problem can be applied since the structure of J remains unchanged.

The theorem on conditional stability (Theorem A.4. in the appendix) can be applied in order to investigate the behaviour of the system near the equilibrium. It states that a system consisting of n differential equations posesses a k-dimensional stable manifold if k of the n eigenvalues of the system matrix have negative real parts. Since, in this case, we have a four-dimensional system and two of the initial values, namely d_o and s_o, are given exogenously, there remain two degrees of freedom. Thus there should be two eigenvalues having negative real parts in order to guarantee stability of the optimal solution. Then it is possible to choose the initial values of the control variable and, thereby, the initial values of the costate variables such that the optimal path starts on the stable manifold.

For the sake of tractability the analysis will be restricted to the simplest case: the time effects on the adjustment functions are assumed to be zero, and we obtain a standard Hamiltonian-Jacobian system with the interest rate, r, as the discount parameter. For this case, the standard theory can be applied.

It can be shown that the eigenvalues of the Jacobian, J, are symmetric around $r/2$.[164] This means that instability cannot be excluded since three or all four eigenvalues can have non-negative real parts. Sufficient conditions for the stability of systems having more than one state variable have been established by *Rockafellar* (1976), *Brock/Scheinkman* (1977) and *Magill* (1977), based on *Liapunov* functions. Their conditions, however, are too restrictive for practical use in many cases.[165] Conditions that are necessary <u>and</u> sufficient are connected with the eigenvalues of the Jacobian. *Dockner* (1985) has derived a relatively simple formula for the eigenvalues of the two-state-variable problem. The theorem as well as an extension which will be useful here are stated in the appendix. See Theorem A.11., Theorem A.12. and Corollary A.3.

The stability of the system depends on the determinant of the Jacobian, *det J*, and a variable which is the sum of the determinants of three particular submatrices of *J*. Corollary A.3. states that, if the Hessian matrices B and C are positive definite or semidefinite and A is a stability matrix, then the following propositions can be made:

---

[164] See *Levhari/Liviatan* (1972), p. 90, and Remark A.13. in the appendix.

[165] For instance, the theorem by *Brock/Scheinkman* (1977) requires B to be of full rank which is not satisfied in this model. See the appendix for the application of *Liapunov* functions on stability problems in optimal-control theory and for further discussions of this approach.

- If and only if $det\,J$ is negative, there is one negative eigenvalue and three eigenvalues have positive real parts. The optimal solution is unstable.

- If and only if $det\,J$ is positive, two of the eigenvalues have negative real parts and there exists a two-dimensional stable manifold. This is the conventional result of saddle-point stability. The eigenvalues can, however, turn out to be complex, especially if $det\,J$ is large. Then the optimal path is cyclical.

The determinant of the Jacobian matrix can be computed and it turns out to be

$$
(4.5.35) \qquad det\,J = f_d g_s\, det(rI - A^T) \;+\; (r - f_d)(r - g_s)(f_d g_p (1 - w^y g_{sp}) - g_s f_p (1 + v^y f_{dp}))/H_{pp}
$$

$$
+\; f_p g_p (1 + v^y f_{dp})(1 - w^y g_{sp})(r(f_d + g_s) - 2f_d g_s)\,/H_{pp}{}^2
$$

$$
+\; k''(f_p g_s - g_p f_d)(f_p (r - g_s) - g_p (r - f_d))/H_{pp}
$$

$$
+\; f_p{}^2 g_s (g_s - r)\, v^y f_{dd}/H_{pp} \;+\; g_p{}^2 f_d (f_d - r)\, w^y g_{ss}/H_{pp}\; .
$$

All terms in (4.5.35) are positive and so is the determinant. This implies:

PROPOSITION 4.8

The optimal solution is stable in the saddle-point sense.

Thus, the optimal paths approaches the equilibrium asymptotically.[166] The optimal path is a two-dimensional manifold in the four-dimensional state-costate phase space. Whether cyclical solutions are possible, remains an open question.[167]

---

[166] This corrects the results derived in a similar model, *Rauscher* (1988b), by means of numerical examples. In that paper, unstable solutions seemed to be possible. However, the examples were constructed by neglecting some of the particular relations among the elements of the Jacobian matrix J. I am indebted to Franz Wirl for pointing out this error.

[167] In principle, a condition for the occurrence of cycles can be derived by applying *Dockner's* formulae, (A.22) and (A.23), to this model. See also Corollary A.3. The structure of the problem, however, is so complex that an unambiguous result can hardly be derived. Numerical simulations did not produce any evidence in favour of cyclical behaviour. Therefore, the cyclical paths appear to be rather unlikely but their occurrence cannot be excluded.

4.5.5. A numerical example

In order to get an impression of how the optimal path looks like, a numerical example will be constructed that allows to represent the solution graphically in a price-quantity space. This procedure involves the concept of the algebraic *Riccati* equation, which is discussed in detail in the appendix. Here we only present a sketch of what the meaning of the *Riccati* equation is in this context. Suppose the optimal path is characterised by a two-dimensional stable or unstable manifold in the four-dimensional state-costate space. Further assume that along the optimal path the costate variables are a linear function of the state variables. So we introduce a *(2x2)* matrix W such that

$$(4.5.36) \qquad \begin{bmatrix} v^y - v^{y*} \\ w^y - w^{y*} \end{bmatrix} = W \begin{bmatrix} d-d^* \\ s-s^* \end{bmatrix} .$$

This relation can be used to eliminate the costate variables from the linearised Hamiltonian system, equation (4.5.28). This procedure and some simple algebraic transformations that are carried out in the proof of Theorem A.7. in the appendix yield the following condition for W:

$$(4.5.37) \qquad WBW + A^T W + WA - C - rW = 0.$$

This is the algebraic *Riccati* equation. Since it is a quadratic matrix equation, two solutions exist one of which is negative definite.[168] If W is this negative definite solution, the optimal paths of demand and non-OPEC supply of petroleum are given by

$$(4.5.38) \qquad \begin{bmatrix} \dot{d} \\ \dot{s} \end{bmatrix} = (A + BW) \begin{bmatrix} d-d^* \\ s-s^* \end{bmatrix} .$$

---

[168] The existence of a negative definite solution of the algebraic *Riccati* equation requires $(A-(r/2)I,B)$ to be controllable. See Theorem A.7. in the appendix. According to Definition A.3., this condition is satisfied if

$$rank\,[\,B \;\; AB-(r/2)B\,] = 2.$$

In general, this matrix has full rank. The second-row elements of B equal (f_p/g_p) times the corresponding first-row elements. This is not true for AB, except for some special matrices A, e.g. if A were a diagonal matrix. Thus, one can claim that the ordered pair $(A-(r/2)I,B)$ is controllable and the algebraic *Riccati* equation has a negative definite solution.

The price path can be determined by using (4.5.36) in (4.5.18). This yields[169]

$$(4.5.39) \qquad p - p^* \; = \; (\, [m_d \; m_s] + [m_v \; m_w] \; W \,) \begin{bmatrix} d - d^* \\ s - s^* \end{bmatrix} .$$

The example can now be constructed by assigning numerical values to the elements of the matrices A, B, and C and then computing W. Since the *Riccati* equation is difficult to solve for W, it turns out to be more convenient to start with A, B, and W and solve the *Riccati* equation for C. This is done in the following.

Assume that $f_p = f_d = -1$, $g_p = 1$, $g_s = -6$, $(1 + v^y f_{dp}) = 5$, $(1 - w^y g_{sp}) = 2$, and $H_{pp} = -1$. Then

$$(4.5.40) \qquad B = \begin{bmatrix} 1 & -1 \\ -1 & 1 \end{bmatrix} \quad \text{and} \quad A = \begin{bmatrix} -6 & 2 \\ 5 & -8 \end{bmatrix}$$

If

$$(4.5.41) \qquad W = \begin{bmatrix} -1 & 0 \\ 0 & -1 \end{bmatrix} \quad \text{and} \quad r = 1 \,,$$

then

$$(4.5.42) \qquad C = \begin{bmatrix} 14 & -8 \\ -8 & 18 \end{bmatrix} .$$

This implies that $k'' = 18$, $v^y f_{dd} = -21$, and $w^y g_{ss} = -4$. Thus, the numerical values are in accordance with the assumptions about the derivatives of the adjustment functions. The optimal path is characterised by:

$$(4.5.43) \qquad \begin{bmatrix} \dot{d} \\ \dot{s} \end{bmatrix} = \begin{bmatrix} -7 & 3 \\ 6 & -9 \end{bmatrix} \begin{bmatrix} d - d^* \\ s - s^* \end{bmatrix}$$

and

$$(4.5.44) \qquad p - p^* = 6\,(d - d^*) - 3\,(s - s^*)$$

---

[169] See also Corollary A.2. in the appendix.

The first of these equations decribes the dynamic behaviour of the state variables in the linearised system. The transition matrix is, of course, stable. The second equation represents the price path. It shows the plausible result that the initial price is an increasing function of the initial level of demand for OPEC oil and a decreasing function of initial supply of non-OPEC oil.

Before a graphical representation of the optimal path is given in the price quantity diagram, a further result can be established. In the one-state-variable version of this model (see *Wirl* (1985a), *Rauscher* (1986,1988a) and the next chapter of this study), the price is either monotonously increasing or monotonously decreasing over time, depending on wether the initial price is above or below the long-run equilibrium price. This result, however, does not hold in the two-state-variables case. In order to show this, assume that the initial levels of demand, d_o, and non-OPEC supply, s_o, are such that the initial price equals the equilibrium price $(p_o = p^*)$. This implies $(s_o - s^*) = 2(d_o - d^*)$. Differentiating (4.5.44) with respect to time, using (4.5.43), and substituting $2(d_o - d^*)$ for $(s_o - s^*)$ yields

(4.5.45) $\qquad \dot{p} = 30 (d_o - d^*) \quad$ for $\quad p_o = p^* .$

The price change can be positive or negative depending on the initial level of demand, d_o. Thus, if the price equals its equilibrium level initially and then increases or decreases, there must be some point where the price path reverses its direction to return to the equilbrium price level. This locus is given by the following condition which can be derived from (4.5.43) and (4.5.44).

(4.5.46) $\qquad 3 (s - s^*) = 4 (d - d^*)$

Similar conditions can in principle also be derived for the general model, though the arithmetics of such a procedure would turn out to be puzzling. In order to show that the possibility of price path reversals exists, it is, however, sufficient to construct a numerical example which exhibits the desired properties.

PROPOSITION 4.9.

Along the optimal path, the price path may change its direction. It can increase or decrease in an initial period and then reverse its direction.

Using the information available in equations (4.5.43) and (4.5.44), one can now draw optimal paths into a price-demand or into a price-non-OPEC-supply diagram. The paths are characterised by

(4.5.47) $\dot{d} = -(d - d^*) - (p - p^*)$

(4.5.48) $\dot{p} = 30 \, (d - d^*) - 15 \, (p - p^*)$

for the (p,d) diagram and

(4.5.49) $\dot{s} = -6 \, (s - s^*) + p - p^*$

(4.5.50) $\dot{p} = 15 \, (s - s^*) - 10 \, (p - p^*)$

for the (p,s) diagram. This can be used to draw the $(\dot{p}=0)$, $(\dot{d}=0)$ and $(\dot{s}=0)$ loci into the phase diagrams. They are depicted in Figure 4.3. In both diagrams, the equilibria are stable nodes. It can be seen that the optimal paths can intersect the $(\dot{p}=0)$, $(\dot{d}=0)$ and $(\dot{s}=0)$ loci. There are only four linear paths.

All paths in Figure 4.3. can be optimal. It depends on the initial values of demand and non-OPEC supply which one will be chosen. This path can be determined graphically by drawing d_0 and s_0 into the diagrams and then selecting those paths for which the initial price is the same in both diagrams. There is only one solution, namely

(4.5.44') $p_0 - p^* = 6 \, (d_0 - d^*) - 3 \, (s_0 - s^*)$

Non-monotonous price paths are possible if demand and non-OPEC supply are both either above or below their equilibrium levels. Then the price is driven by two opposing forces: a high initial level of demand requires a high price, but a high level of non-OPEC supply requires a low price. These interactions of demand and supply effects can lead to pricing strategies which are more complex than in the simple one-state-variable version of the model: OPEC might find it optimal to increase the price during an initial period and lower it in the long run or vice versa. The historical situation at the time of the first oil crisis, however, was characterised by a high level of demand and a low level of non-OPEC supply, both induced by more than a decade of low prices. At least for this numerical example, the corresponding price path is monotonous.[170]

---

[170] Given the complexity of the theoretical model, the question whether this result can be generalised must remain without answer.

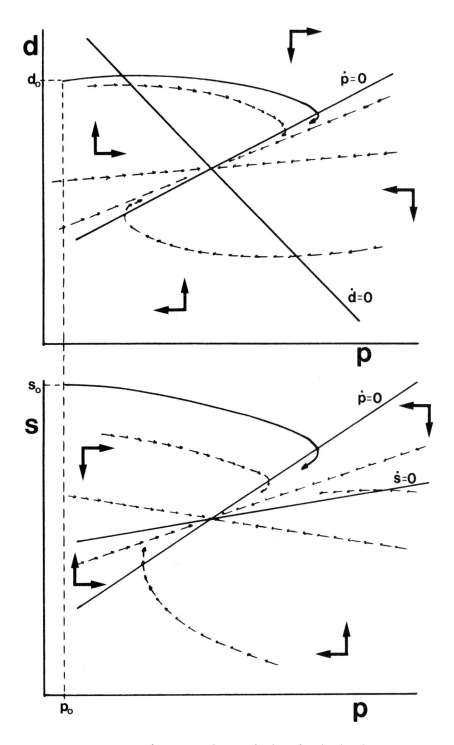

Figure 4.3.: Characterisation of optimal paths

4.6. The equilibrium in the long run

In the preceding sections, conditions for an equilibrium have been derived and its stability properties have been analysed. The long-run dynamics of the equilibrium itself, however, have not been investigated so far. In the equilibrium the price is given by

$$(4.5.13) \qquad p^*-k'-z/y \; = \left(\frac{g_s S_p}{g_s - r} \; - \; \frac{f_d D_p}{f_d - r} \right)^{-1} (D - S).$$

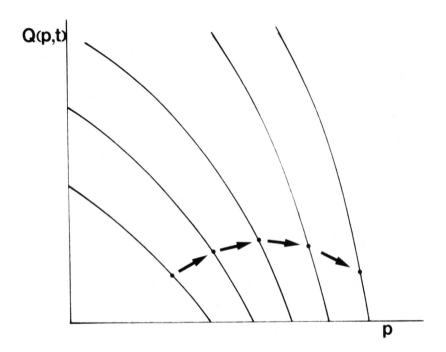

Figure 4.4.: The shifting equilibrium

In such an equilibrium, there are no incentives to change demand and supply, and OPEC does not intend to change the price. But this does not imply that the equilibrium itself is constant. There are two effects that cause its location in the price-quantity space to change. The user costs of the resource, z/y, increase over time and drive the price up. Moreover, both the long-run demand function and the non-OPEC supply curve are changing their locations over time. Demand is driven up by economic growth, and depletion of non-OPEC reserves drives the supply of the fringe down. The first effect has been modelled explicitly by taking the finiteness of OPEC's petroleum reserves into account; the other effects have been considered by simply introducing exogenous trends in the demand and non-OPEC supply functions. The interaction of these effects is shown in Figure 4.4. $Q(p,t)$ is the long-run demand for OPEC oil, i.e. the difference beween worldwide demand and non-OPEC supply:

(4.6.1) $Q(p,t) = D(p,t) - S(p,t).$

This curve is shifted outwards in the price-quantity diagram. At the same time, due to increasing user costs, the equilibrium point moves downwards along the long-run demand curve. It can be seen that the price increases over time. The direction of change of demand is ambiguous, at least during some initial periods: the scarcity effect may be dominated by the exogenous expansion of demand. In the very long run, however, demand must go to zero since the resource is finite and the reserves constraint has to be satisfied.

What does "in the long run" mean in this context? Is the extraction period finite or infinite? Using the result that that the equilibrium given by (4.5.10) is stable and shifts along the long-run demand curve, one can establish the following condition for oil production to go to zero within finite time:

(4.6.2) $\dot{D} - \dot{S} < 0$ for $D - S = 0.$

Equality in (4.6.2.) would imply that production goes to zero only approximately. Total differentiation yields:

(4.6.3) $\dot{p} > - \dfrac{D_t - S_t}{D_p - S_p}$ for $D - S = 0.$

One can now eliminate $\dot{p}$ by differentiating (4.5.13) with respect to time. The complicated term by which $(D - S)$ is multiplied will be substituted by α for convenience. (4.5.13) can be rewritten as

$p^* - k' - z/y = \alpha\,(D - S)$, $\alpha > 0.$

Differentiating with respect to time yields

(4.6.4) $\dot{p}\,(1 - (k'' + \alpha)(D_p - S_p)) = (k'' + \alpha)(D_t - S_t) + rz/y$ for $D - S = 0.$

This result can be used in (4.6.3), and by rearranging terms one obtains the following proposition:

PROPOSITION 4.10.

Provided that adjustments towards the equilibrium are sufficiently fast, the extraction period is finite if

$$(4.6.5) \qquad r\,y/z > - \frac{D_t - S_t}{D_p - S_p} \qquad\qquad for \quad D - S = 0.$$

Condition (4.6.5) states that the scarcity effect must dominate the exogenous time impact in the long run. Whether it is satisfied, depends on the shapes of the long-run demand and non-OPEC supply functions. Assume, for instance that non-OPEC supply goes to zero within finite time. This is in accordance with the results of the theory of exhaustible resources presented in Chapter 3. If OPEC's resources last longer than those of the fringe of the cartel (otherwise the extraction period would be finite anyway), then condition (4.6.5) changes into $r y/z > - D_t/D_p$. If, moreover, the exogenous growth of demand is exponential such that $D(p,t) = e^{\sigma t}D(p,0)$, then $D_t/D_p = \sigma D/D_p$. This goes to zero when D goes to zero. Thus, since $r y/z$ is positive, condition (4.6.5) is always satisfied for this case and the extraction period is finite.

These propositions hold under the proviso that the adjustment process towards the long-run equilibrium is sufficiently fast. Otherwise, it would not make much sense to analyse the long-run behaviour of the equilibrium alone. The interactions of shifts of the equilibrium and adjustments towards the equilibrium would have to be considered. This will be done in the next chapter for a simplified version of this model which is easier to handle and can be represented in a two-dimensional space.

4.7. An evaluation of the model and its results

A model that interpretes OPEC as a dominant firm on the supply side of the international petroleum market has been used to investigate OPEC's optimal pricing strategies. An equilibrium has been derived which is characterised by the fact that the price exceeds the static *Cournot* monopoly price by a rigidity mark-up. This confirms the results of earlier investigations by *Wirl* (1985a) and *Rauscher* (1986). The slower the adjustments of demand and non-OPEC supply and the higher the rate of discount, the higher is this rigidity rent and, hence, the price. Some hints concerning the true optimal policy can be obtained by comparing the simulation figures with historical data.

The historical data, plotted in Figure 2.3. on p. 29, seem to support the hypothesis of a price path which reverses its direction or a cyclical pricing policy. It is, however, questionable whether the historical price path represents the optimal solution of OPEC's intertemporal maximisation problem. The paths derived from the theoretical model are all smooth while in reality there have been drastic jumps in the variables, in particular the price. In my view, there is not much evidence that OPEC - be it deliberately, be it by accident - has followed an optimal price and production policy during the last one and a half decades. Neither the true model nor the necessary information was available, and OPEC's policy should be described as a trial-and-error search rather than by rational optimising behaviour. This hypothesis will be the object of the next chapter.

The results of this chapter may, however, explain why non-monotonous pricing policies can be optimum even if the world is described by nicely behaved functions. The price path chosen by OPEC might turn out to be not so far from an optimal as many economists have thought.

5. A simplified version of the model

5.1. The assumptions

In this chapter, a simpler approach to the question of how oil prices are determined will be followed. Demand for OPEC oil will be treated as an aggregate, i.e. there will be no distinction any more between adjustment processes on the demand side and adjustments by the fringe of the cartel. This simplification yields a much simpler structure of the model, and some of the features that have been neglected in Chapter 4 will now be analysed in more detail. This applies to the long-run dynamics of the model, to the effects of parameter variations, and to the economic interpretation of some results.

Again, OPEC is assumed to maximise the present value of future utility streams,

(5.1.1)
$$\int_{o}^{\infty} u(c) \, e^{-\delta t} \, dt \, ,$$

subject to the state equations

(5.1.2) $\quad \dot{V} = pq - k(q) - c + rV \, ,$

(5.1.3) $\quad \dot{R} = -q \, ,$

(5.1.4) $\quad \dot{q} = \beta h \, (q,p,t)$

with respect to the control variables, consumption, c, and petroleum production, q, given the initial values of the state variables, V_o, R_o, and q_o. The notation remains unchanged besides some minor alterations. q is the demand for OPEC oil, i.e. the difference between worldwide demand and the supply coming from outside the cartel. The adjustment function is now denoted by $\beta h(.,.,.)$. The time impact includes exogenous growth of demand as well as depletion effects on the supply side. β is a constant parameter measuring the speed of the adjustment process. The parameter β will be used later when the influence of parameter changes on the optimal path will be investigated. The terminal conditions again are the debt repayment restriction and the finiteness of OPEC's petroleum reserves:

(5.1.5) $\quad \lim_{t \to \infty} V \geq 0 \, .$

(5.1.6) $\lim_{t \to \infty} R \geq 0 .$

The shapes of the functions are assumed to be as follows:

(5.1.7) $u' > 0 , u'' < 0 , u'(0) = \infty , u'(\infty) = 0.$

(5.1.8) $k' > 0 , k'' > 0 .$

(5.1.9) $h_q < 0 , h_p < 0 , h_t > 0$

(5.1.10.) $\dfrac{h_{pq}q}{h_p} < 1 ,$

(5.1.11) $h_{qq} < 0 , h_{pp} < 0 , h_{qq}h_{pp} - h_{pq}^2 \geq 0 .$

(5.1.12) $h\,(0,p,t) \geq 0 .$

With one exception the derivatives have the same signs as those of the global demand function that has been introduced in Chapter 4. The only difference occurs in the assumption about the cross derivative of the adjustment function. The new condition is less restrictive than the old one. Inequality (5.1.10) states that an increase in demand yields a less than proportional increase in the reaction to a price change. Due to the simpler structure of the model, this weaker condition suffices to derive the desired results.

An additional assumption is imposed on the time impact. We assume that h_p is logarithmically separable in (p,q) and t. This implies that

(5.1.13) $h_{pt} < 0 .$

Since h_p is negative, this means that the trend increases the reactions of demand to price changes. Moreover, separability implies

$$h_{pp}h_{pt} = h_{ppt}h_p \quad \text{and} \quad h_{pq}h_{pt} = h_{pqt}h_p .$$

It follows that

$$(5.1.14a) \qquad \frac{d \, (h_{pt}/h_p)}{dp} = 0 \; .$$

$$(5.1.14b) \qquad \frac{d \, (h_{pt}/h_p)}{dq} = 0 \; .$$

So (h_{pt}/h_p) is a function of time only. This assumption is a simplification that will help to derive some unambiguous results in the following sections. It is, however, less artificial than it looks, and one can show that it is satisfied for a broad class of demand functions.[171]

If demand for OPEC oil is constant, we obtain an implicit function, $h(q,p,t) = 0$, and demand can be expressed as a function $Q(.,.)$ of price and time. Again, the constant-demand locus is a non-stationary function of the price. $Q(.,.)$ is the desired or long-run level of demand for OPEC oil, given the price of petroleum and the level of economic activity.

$$(5.1.15) \qquad q^*(t) = Q\,(p(t),t)$$

with

$$(5.1.16) \qquad Q_t = - h_t/h_q > 0 \; \text{ and } \; Q_p = - h_p/h_q < 0.$$

$$(5.1.17) \qquad Q_{pp} = - h_q^{-1} \, (h_{pp} + h_{qp} Q_p + (h_{qq} Q_p + h_{qp}) \, Q_p).$$

It follows from the shape of the $h(.,.,.)$ function that all terms in the brackets on the right-hand side of equation (5.1.16) are negative. Hence, the long-run demand for OPEC oil is a concave function of the price.

---

[171] Let, for instance, a be an exogenous rate of demand growth. Then a demand function that satisfies (5.1.14a) and (5.1.14b) may have the following shape

$$q = a_1 q + a_2 q^2 + (a_3 + a_4 p + a_5 p^2 + a_6 pq) \, e^{at}$$

where a_1 to a_6 are the other parameters of the model. A similar specification will be used in the next chapter for the empirical analyses. Of course, more conventional types of specification like the linear or loglinear demand function also satisfy the conditions.

5.2. Optimality conditions

OPEC intends to maximise its welfare subject to the contraints (5.1.2) to (5.1.4). The control variables are again the oil price and the level of consumption. The current-value Hamiltonian turns out to be:

(5.2.1) $\qquad H = u(c) + x\beta h(q,p,t) + y(pq-k(q)-c+rV) - zq,$

where x, y and z are the costate variables of demand for OPEC oil, foreign assets, and the resource stock. The costate variables or shadow prices change according to the canonical equations. Omitting the arguments of the functions for convenience, these equations are

(5.2.2) $\qquad \dot{x} = (\delta - \beta h_q)x - y(p-k') + z,$

(5.2.3) $\qquad \dot{y} = (\delta - r)y,$

(5.2.4) $\qquad \dot{z} = \delta z.$

Setting the derivatives of the Hamiltonian with respect to the control variables, H_c and H_p, equal to zero, one obtains necessary conditions for an optimum:

(5.2.5) $\qquad y = u'$

and

(5.2.6) $\qquad qy + \beta h_p x = 0.$

It follows that the shadow price of foreign assets is positive since marginal utility is positive. This is not surprising because an increase in OPEC's initial endowment with assets enlarges future consumption possibilities and, therefore, is welfare-improving. The same argument holds for the shadow price of demand. An increase in initial demand increases future revenues since, given a finite resource stock, higher prices can be charged to drive demand down to zero.

The first-order optimality conditions characterise a local extremum which is not necessarily an optimum. A sufficient condition for an optimum is that the Hessian of the Hamiltonian function with respect to the state and control variables is negative definite. Due to the separation properties of the Hamiltonian the consumption and foreign-assets paths can be treated independently of the production and price paths. The Hamiltonian is concave in c, linear in V and there are no cross partial derivatives. So the second-order condition is satisfied for the consumption path. The Hessian of H with respect to (p,q) turns out to be

$$(5.2.7) \qquad H_{(p,q)(p,q)} = x\beta \begin{bmatrix} h_{pp} & h_{pq} - h_p/q \\ h_{pq} - h_p/q & h_{qq} + k''h_p/q \end{bmatrix}.$$

The diagonal elements are unambiguously negative and the determinant is:

$$(5.2.8) \qquad \det H_{(p,q)(p,q)}$$

$$= (\,(h_{pp}h_{qq} - h_{pq}^2) + h_p h_{pp} k''/q - (h_p/q)^2 (1 - 2h_{pq}q/h_p)\,) \, x\beta.$$

The first term in brackets is positive as it has been assumed in (5.1.11). The next term is positive too, but the third term may have the 'wrong' sign. Thus, the Hessian is not necessarily negative definite. Again, the result is due to the non-concavity of the profit function.[172] In order to make matters simpler, it will be assumed in the following sections that these non-concavities are dominated by the concavity of the cost function and the adjustment function. A sufficient condition would be

$$\frac{h_{pq}q}{h_p} > 1/2 \,.$$

From equation (5.2.5), the optimal consumption path can easily be derived, and it is possible to draw conclusions concerning the accumulation of foreign assets. Again, this can be done independently from the investigation of the extraction profile. So the results that have been established for the original model in Chapter 4.3. also hold for its simplified version and do not have to be discussed again.

5.3. The optimal pricing policy

In contrast to the original model, the simplified version allows for deriving the optimal pricing policy directly without taking the long way via the shadow prices and their deviations from steady states. This is due to the fact that only one state variable has to be considered in the simplified model. Therefore, there is also only one shadow price which has to be taken into account, and the price path can directly be determined. This can be done by establishing growth rates in the optimality condition (5.2.6), inserting the canonical equations, (5.2.2) and (5.2.3), and using the optimality condition again to eliminate x. One obtains a differential equation describing the evolution of the price along an optimal path:

---

[172] The profit function is linear in p and contains the term pq. Therefore, the determinant of its Hessian with respect to (p,q) is -1.

(5.3.1) $\quad \dfrac{h_{pp}}{h_p} \dot{p} = -r - h_{pt}/h_p + \beta h_q + (1 - h_{pq} q/h_p) \beta h/q - (p-k'-z/y) \beta h_p/q .$

The factor by which $\dot{p}$ is multiplied is unambiguously positive. So the direction of the price change along the optimal path is given by the right-hand-side of equation (5.3.1). A similar result has been derived by *Rauscher* (1988a). An addition to that result is the term h_{pt}/h_p which is due to the trend impact on demand. At a first glance, $\dot{p}$ seems to be a decreasing function of the interest rate, r, an abnormal result for an exhaustible resource. The interest rate, however, also occurs in the term z/y, which is the *Hotelling* rent element of price formation:

(4.5.14) $\quad z/y = e^{rt} z_0/y_0 .$

Thus, differentiating (5.3.1) with respect to r yields

$$\frac{\partial \dot{p}}{\partial r} = \frac{h_p (t\, e^{rt} z_0/y_0 - 1)}{h_{pp}}$$

It follows that $\dot{p}$ is can be a decreasing function of r only in the short run, i.e. for small t. In the long run, the user-cost effect dominates and the price as well as its time derivative will increase.

5.3.1. The long-run equilibrium

The usual procedure would now be to set $\dot{p}=0$ and analyse the shapes of the loci of constant prices and quantities in the (p,q) plane. Since the derivatives of $\dot{p}$ with respect to p and q contain several terms whose signs are not known, especially some third derivatives of the adjustment function, the analysis will be restricted to the neighbourhood of an equilibrium.

We therefore assume that there exists an equilibrium point where changes in prices and quantities do not take place. This implies $\dot{p} = 0$, $h = 0$, $q = Q(p)$, and $h_q = -h_p/Q'$. Using this in equation (5.3.1) yields

PROPOSITION 5.1.

An equilibrium in which demand is constant and OPEC does not have any incentive to change the oil price is characterised by

(5.3.2) $\quad p^* = k' + z/y - Q/Q_p - \dfrac{Q}{\beta h_p}(r + h_{pt}/h_p) .$

In contrast to the two-state-variable version of the model, the elements of price formation turn out to be additive and, therefore, can easily be identified and interpreted. Five effects can be distinguished from one another:

- k' is the marginal cost of production.

- z/y is the scarcity-rent element of price formation or the user cost of the resource, which increases at the rate of interest.

- $- Q/Q_p$ equals the price over the elasticity of demand. It is the monopolist's mark-up that shifts the price above the competitive level.

- $- rQ/(\beta h_p)$ is due to discounting and the rigidity of demand. It measures the present value of the difference between long-run and short-run demand. This element of price formation constitutes a rigitity rent. It vanishes if either the interest rate is zero or the adjustment speed goes to infinity.

- $- h_{pt} Q/(\beta h_p^2)$ is due to the rigidity of demand and to the exogenous effect that shifts the demand function over time. If h_{pt} is negative (as it should be expected), then the trend effect tends to increase the equilibrium price. This is a combined effect of rigidity and exogenous demand growth. It vanishes if the trend does not affect the reactions on price changes, i.e. $h_{pt} = 0$, or if β, the speed of adjustment, goes to infinity.

All these effects have positive signs. Therefore, it appears to be reasonable to assume that an increase in rigidity yields an increase in the equlilibrium price. This reasoning, however, neglects the indirect effects of such a change. If a change in one of the decisive parameters affects the equilibrium price level, then it also affects the equilibrium quantity and the derivatives of the adjustment function, the cost function and the long-run demand schedule. The overall effect becomes ambiguous.

These indirect effects can be handled by total differentiation of the equilibrium condition. Here the assumption that (h_{pt}/h_p) is independent of p and q proves to be very useful. Total differentiation of (5.3.2) yields:

(5.3.3)
$$\left\{ 2 - k''Q' - \frac{Q_{pp}Q}{Q_p^2} + \frac{(r + h_{pt}/h_p) Q_p}{\beta h_p} \left(1 - \frac{Qh_{pq}}{h_p} - \frac{h_{pp}Q}{h_p Q_p} \right) \right\} dp^*$$

$$= d[z/y] - \frac{Q}{\beta h_p} d\left[r + \frac{h_{pt}}{h_p} \right] + \frac{Q}{\beta^2 h_p} \left(r + \frac{h_{pt}}{h_p} \right) d\beta .$$

The assumptions made on the shape of the adjustment function imply that the long term in brackets on the left-hand side of (5.3.3) is unambiguously positive. So the following conclusions can be drawn:

- An increase in user costs leads to an increase in the price. Since, along an optimal extraction path, user costs increase at the interest rate, the equilibrium price tends to rise over time.

- An increase in the interest rate also implies an increase of the equilibrium price. The higher the discount rate is, the higher the incentive to exploit the short-run rigidity of demand.

- The stronger the trend impact, the higher the price. One can argue that exogenous demand growth constitutes an element of future inflexibility. In an intertemporal framework this is reflected by a higher level of the equilibrium price.

- The adjustment speed, β, measures the short-run flexibility of demand. It has a negative impact on the price.

If all of these effects vanish, the equilibrium price equals the well-known *Cournot* monopoly price:

PROPOSITION 5.2.

If the adjustment speed of demand goes to infinity or the interest rate and exogenous demand growth go to zero, marginal cost equals marginal revenue as it does in the static monopoly model:

$$(5.3.4) \qquad \lim_{\beta \to \infty} p^* \quad = \quad \lim_{\substack{r \to 0 \\ h_{pt} \to 0}} p^* \ = \ k' + z/y - Q/Q_p \ .$$

It follows from (5.3.3.) that in the presence of demand rigidities the price p^* always exceeds the static monopoly price. This implies:

PROPOSITION 5.3.

Given a finite speed of demand adjustment and a positive discount rate or exogenous demand growth, there exits a positive rigidity rent in addition to the monopoly rent.

Due to demand growth, the equilibrium demand curve along which actual demand equals desired demand is not constant. It shifts away from the equilibrium since, given a certain price level, desired petroleum consumption increases over time. Moreover, it has been shown above that user costs and exogenous demand growth have a positive impact on the price. This is equivalent to a movement of the equilibrium along the demand schedule. The combination of these effects has already been studied in Chapter 4 (Figure 4.4.). The price will increase over time. In the long run, production declines because of the reserves constraint, but during some initial periods demand growth may lead to increasing production.

5.3.2. Behaviour near the equilibrium

In order derive conditions for the stability of the equilibrium, one has to look at the dynamic behaviour of prices and quantities in the phase space. Since we have a one-state-variable problem now,[173] this can be done directly without analysing the state-costate system first. In the following stability analysis it is assumed that adjustments of the variables near the equilibrium are relatively fast compared to the movement of the equilibrium itself. So the location of the equilibrium will be treated as being fixed. As usual we will consider adjustments in a close neighbourhood of the equilibrium where the linearised system serves as a good approximation of the original system.

Along the optimal path production and the price develop according to

(5.1.4) $\qquad \dot{q} = \beta h(q,p,t)$,

(5.3.1) $\qquad \dfrac{h_{pp}}{h_p} \dot{p} = -r - h_{pt}/h_p + \beta h_q + (1 - h_{pq} q/h_p) \beta h/q - (p - k' - z/y) \beta h_p /q$.

By linearising this system in the equilibrium one obatins

(5.3.5) $\qquad \dot{q} = \beta h_q (q - q^*) + \beta h_p (p - p^*)$,

(5.3.6) $\qquad \dot{p} = \partial \dot{p}/\partial q \, (q - q^*) + (r + h_{pt}/h_p - \beta h_q)(p - p^*)$.

with

---

[173] Because of *Fisher's* separation theorem, production is independent of consumption and savings. The third state variable, the resource stock, does not occur in the Hamiltonian.

$$(5.3.7) \qquad \frac{\partial \dot{p}}{\partial q} = \frac{\beta h_p}{q h_{pp}} [q h_{qq} + h_p k'' + (2h_q - (r + h_{pt}/h_p)/\beta) (1 - h_{pq} q/h_p)]$$

From the assumptions made about the shape of the demand function, it follows that $\dot{p}$ is a decreasing function of q. Since the derivative with respect to p is positive, the slope of the line of constant prices in the price-quantity space must be positive. For high values of q, or above the $(\dot{p}=0)$ line, price changes must be negative. The locus of constant quantities is the long-run demand function. Excess demand induces adjustments towards the long-run or desired level.

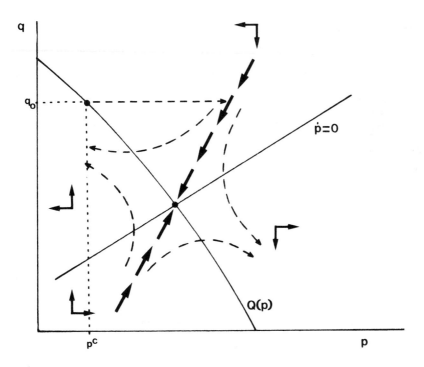

Figure 5.1.: Optimal pricing policies for a constant equilibrium

This is represented by Figure 5.1. It can be seen that the optimal solution exhibits saddle-point stability. Given an initial level of demand, q_o, one can choose a price p_o on the saddle path and then the optimal pricing policy approaches the equilibrium asymptotically.[174]

---

[174] At a first glance, there is no reason why the optimum should be identical to the saddle path since all the other paths also satisfy the optimality condition. Since we have assumed that the Hamiltonian is concave in (p,q) and the saddle path satisfies the transversality condition of

The optimal path is positively sloped.[175] This result has a very intuitive interpretation. If initial demand is greater than the equilibrium level, then it is profitable for OPEC as the residual supplier to set a high initial price and then gradually lower it as demand approaches the equilibrium. Such a scenario may be caused by cartelisation. Let p^c be the competitive price and let demand be at its desired level. Cartelisation causes a price shock and the new price is located on the saddle path that leads to the equilibrium. As demand adjusts, OPEC reduces the price until the long run equilibrium is reached. This strategy allows to exploit the short-run inelasticity of demand. If, on the other hand, initial demand is lower than equilibrium demand, then the cartel chooses low prices in the first periods in order to restrain competitors from exploration and make consumers invest in petroleum-intensive capital goods. In the extreme, this can even require a negative price to promote demand during an initial period. If the desired degree of dependency is reached, the cartel increases the price and exploits the rigidity of demand.[176] This scenario can describe the behaviour of the multinational oil companies, who charged very low prices during the fifties and sixties and showed remarkably little resistance towards OPEC's price increasing policies during the oil crises.[177] Another application is the situation after the 1986 oil price collapse: in order to accelerate demand, prices had to be low.

Behaviour near the equilibrium can also be studied by computing the eigenvalues of the Jacobian matrix of partial derivatives. The elements of this matrix are the coefficients of the linearised price-quantity system, (5.3.5) - (5.3.6). The eigenvalues, $e_{1,2}$, turn out to be

$$(5.3.8) \qquad e_{1,2} = \tfrac{1}{2} (r + h_{pt}/h_p)$$
$$\pm \sqrt{\tfrac{1}{4} (r + h_{pt}/h_p)^2 - \beta h_q (r + h_{pt}/h_p - \beta h_q) + 4 \beta h_q \, \partial \dot{p}/\partial q} \ .$$

Since the last two terms in the argument of the square root are positive, we obtain two real eigenvalues, one of which is positive and the other is negative. Using the conditional-stability theorem (Theorem A.4. in the appendix), one can conclude that the equilibrium is a saddle point.

The slope of the saddle path can now be determined via the algebraic *Riccati* equation corresponding to the dynamic price-quantity system represented by equations (5.3.5) and (5.3.6). In contrast to Chapter 4, where the *Riccati* equation was a matrix equation, it now is a simple quadratic equation that can easily be solved. Assume that W is the slope of the saddle path. Then

---

Theorem A.3. in the Appendix, the saddle path is optimal. See also *Feichtinger/Hartl* (1986), pp. 91-92, for this line of arguing.

[175] The same result has been derived by *Wirl* (1985a) and *Rauscher* (1986,1988a).

[176] At this point it becomes obvious that this model can also be applied to addictive drugs or, in general, to situations where experience with a good is habit-forming.

[177] *Raffer* (1987), p. 173, for instance, argues that "*if OPEC had not already existed Big Oil* [the multinational oil companies, MR] *might have wanted to create it*".

$$p - p^* = W(q - q^*),$$

and the linearised system can be rewritten such that

(5.3.9) $\qquad \dot{W}q = \beta h_q W(q - q^*) + \beta h_p W^2 (q - q^*),$

(5.3.10) $\qquad \dot{W}q = \partial \dot{p}/\partial q \,(q - q^*) + (r + h_{pt}/h_p - \beta h_q) \, W(q - q^*).$

The factors by which $(q - q^*)$ is multiplied must be the same in both equations. This implies that

(5.3.11) $\qquad \beta h_p W^2 + (2\beta h_q - r - h_{pt}/h_p) \, W - \partial \dot{p}/\partial q = 0.$

Solving this equation yields

(5.3.12) $\qquad 2 W_{1,2} = (\beta h_p)^{-1} (r + h_{pt}/h_p - 2\beta h_q)$

$$\pm \, [\, (\beta h_p)^{-2} (r + h_{pt}/h_p - 2\beta h_q)^2 + 4 \, (q \, h_{pp})^{-1}$$

$$[q \, h_{qq} + h_p k'' + (2 h_q - (r + h_{pt}/h_p)/\beta) \, (1 - h_{pq} q/h_p) \,] \,]^{1/2}.$$

From this follows that both solutions are real. The positive solution is the slope of the saddle path, the negative solution is the slope of the unstable manifold that all the other paths approach asymptotically.

PROPOSITION 5.4.

The equilibrium is stable in the saddle-point sense. The saddle path is positively sloped.

It is, however, not possible to determine the effects of parameter changes on the slope of the saddle path. This is due to the fact that they do not only affect the slope but also the location of the equilibrium. This implies that all the derivatives of the adjustment function that occur in equation (5.3.12) are also affected. Therefore, the determination of the effects of parameter changes requires knowledge of third-order derivatives of the adjustment function. Some hints concerning the true effects of parameter variations may be obtained if the location of the equilibrium is kept constant. Derivation of W with respect to β and r yields the following results.

- An increase in β lowers W. The saddle path in Figure 5.1. becomes steeper. This means that an increase in the adjustment speed reduces the initial overshooting of the price. The initial price is closer to the equilibrium price.

- The opposite holds for an increase of the interest rate. W is increasing in r. The saddle path becomes flatter. An increase in the rate of discount amplifies the initial overshooting effect.

5.3.3. The long-run optimal path

In order to derive Figure 5.1., we have assumed that the change in the equilibrium is negligible compared to the adjustment processes of prices and quantities. If the movement of the equilibrium is considered, results change slightly. Two effects are responsible for the shift of the equilibrium. On the one hand, there is exogenous growth of demand that changes the location of the long-run demand curve; on the other hand, increasing user costs cause a downward shift of the equilibrium along the long-run demand schedule.

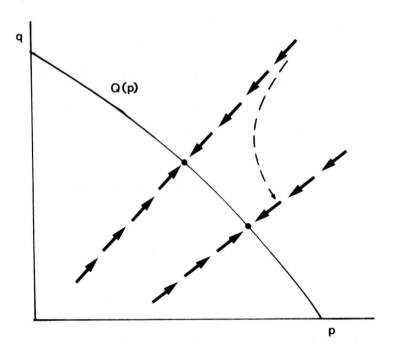

Figure 5.2.: A discrete change in the cost function

The effect of the exhaustibility of petroleum has been shown by *Rauscher* (1988a). The argument goes as follows. The continuous shift of the equilibrium along the desired demand curve is divided into discrete steps. These steps are anticipated since the increase in user costs is part of OPEC's optimal price strategy.[178] If there is one anticipated change in the cost function at a known date, the saddle path leading to the final equilibrium must be reached exactly at this date. Since, according to the optimality condition (5.3.1), a discrete change in costs only affects the growth rate of the price but not its level, the price path must be continuous in this point. Therefore, in order to get there, the optimal path has to start on one of the unstable trajectories of the initial phase diagram. This is shown in Figure 5.2.

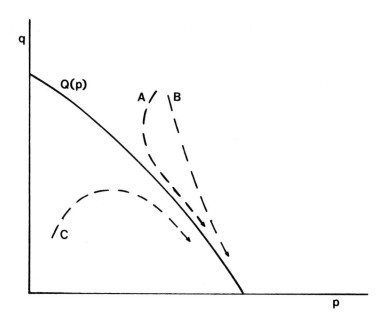

Figure 5.3.: Optimal paths with depletability

The effects of anticipated shifts of the equilibrium are different from those of unanticipated shifts. While the latter cause jumps in the control variables, the former lead to continuous strategies. Continuity can be explained by the fact that an optimal path must satisfy an in-difference condition across time periods. Algebraically, this is reflected by the continuity of the costate variables of the maximum priciple (compare Theorem A.1. in the appendix).

A continuous shift in the cost function can be obtained by dividing the discrete change discussed above into many small steps and letting the number of these steps go to infinity.[179] Such a continuous shift is depicted in Figure 5.3. Three scenarios are shown:[180]

- Path A corresponds to a situation characterised by a high level of initial demand and by demand adjustments that are relatively fast compared to the increase in user costs. The optimal path starts close to the initial saddle path. During an initial period, the rigidity effect dominates and the price decreases. In the long run, when demand has almost adjusted to its equilibrium level, the scarcity effect dominates and the price increases again. This is the U-shaped price profile *Pindyck* (1978) has derived.

- Path B represents a situation in which demand adjusts slowly. Due to the slowliness of demand adjustments, the exhaustibility effect dominates from the beginning and the price grows monotonously.

- Path C will be chosen if initial demand is low and demand adjustments are fast. A low initial price accelerates demand. In the long run, demand has to fall again because of the finiteness of the resource base. If demand reacted more slowly, one would obtain a scenario with demand decreasing monotonously along the whole optimal path.

Similar arguments can be used to derive paths that take the exogenous growth of demand into account. Demand growth implies that the long-run demand schedule is shifted outwards. It is, however, not possible to show how the location of the equilibrium is affected since the trend impact has been specified very vaguely.

If demand growth has a multiplicative effect, then some conclusions can be drawn. The equilibrium price is given by

$$(5.3.2) \qquad p^* = k' + z/y - Q/Q_p - \frac{Q}{\beta h_p}(r + h_{pt}/h_p) \; .$$

First of all, it turns out that h_{pt}/h_p is constant. Moreover, Q/Q_p and Q/h_p are constant. If, finally, the cost function is nearly linear, then the optimal equilibrium price is not affected by exogenous demand growth. Figure 5.4. shows the effect of a discrete change in the demand function for this scenario. Since the change is anticipated, the optimal path starts to the right-hand side of the initial saddle path. In contrast to intuition, the price must be lower than in the case of a constant demand function. This can be explained as follows. The type of demand growth considered in this diagram leaves the elasticity of desired demand unaffected. If the monopolist did not lower

---

[179] For a more detailed exposition of this procedure, see *Rauscher* (1988a), pp. 69-70.

[180] See also *Rauscher* (1988a), p. 70-71, and *Wirl* (1988), p. 19.

the initial price, she would reach the high level of sales which is feasible due to exogenous demand growth too late and thereby renounce an important part of her future profits.

This scenario is based on some special assumptions on the character of demand growth. Since the growth of demand for OPEC oil is composed of (at least) two elements, first worldwide economic growth, that drives demand up, and second depletion of reserves, that reduces non-OPEC supply, the assumption of a constant growth rate is not very realistic. The combination of these effects leads to an increase of the choke-off price and, therefore, the elasticity of demand should decrease over time. This in turn implies higher equilibrium prices and, in contrast to the representation given in Figure 5.4., might cause the initial price to rise rather than to fall. So the effect of demand growth on the shape of optimal paths indeed remains ambiguous.

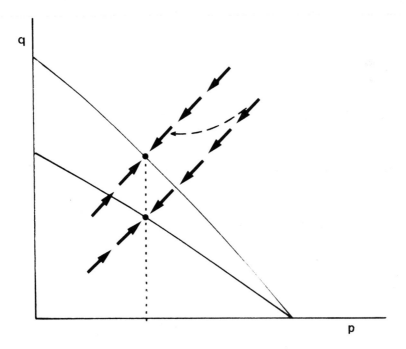

Figure 5.4.: An exogenous shift in the demand function

5.4. Imperfect information and the occurrence of price shocks

The preceding sections have been devoted to the analysis of optimal paths. This is related to the question what OPEC *should do* in order to maximise its welfare. The question still to be answered is what OPEC *really did* and what the model discussed here adds to an understanding of oil price formation and, in particular, the occurrence of price shocks.

Optimisation models usually claim that the planner has perfect information about the state of the world. This assumption seldom holds in reality, and especially for the world petroleum market it is apparently misleading. In the following passages the assumption will be dropped, and we will explore what happens if information or beliefs (used as a substitute if no information is available) about the state of the world are incorrect. It will be shown that price shocks occur when the planner becomes aware of the incorrectness of her former decisions and tries to correct them.

It will be assumed that for the time period under consideration (five to ten years) demand growth and the rise in user costs are negligible. Then saddle paths like the one represented in Figure 5.1. can be used to approximate the true optimal path. Some of the results to be presented in what follows have already been stated in *Rauscher* (1988a). In some respects, these results will be extended here.

5.4.1. The first and second oil shocks

The first oil price shock was a result of the embargo launched by the Arab oil-exporting countries during the Yom-Kippur War at the end of 1973. The price increased sixfold and remained at its new level for five years until the revolution in Iran caused another price shock, that again led to permanent price increases. The first oil shock is often attributed to cartelisation or to the change in property rights that took place in the early seventies. The explanation preferred here is the cartel hypothesis.[181] It will now be shown how a second price increase can be derived from the use of this monopoly power.

The time prior to the first oil price shock was characterised by low prices and only slight price variation. So one can argue that OPEC did not have much information on how demand would react to a massive price increase. There is evidence that at that time the elasticity of demand was estimated to be rather high. For instance, the price of petroleum substitutes, e.g. oil shale, coal liquification, solar energy etc., was believed to be slightly above 10$ per barrel oil equivalent. So the new price of crude oil in 1974 was at a level that should have made alternative

---

[181] A good argument in favour of this is the fact that OPEC countries, in particular Saudi-Arabia, restricted their output already in the seventies to maintain the price level. See Chapter 2.

energy sources competitive.[182] But this did not happen. After a short-term drawback in demand, oil consumption increased again and exceeded the pre-crisis level two years after the shock. In 1979, worldwide demand for crude oil reached a new record level, more than ten percent above the pre-crisis level.

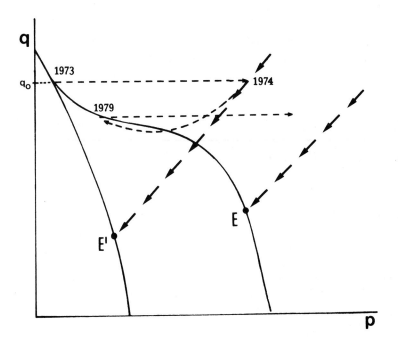

Figure 5.5.: The world petroleum market 1973-1979

So it turned out that the flexibility of demand had been overestimated. Demand was less elastic than it had been expected and OPEC's market power allowed for a second price increase. An explanation of the events following the first oil crisis is given in Figure 5.5. The true backstop price was much higher and the true demand function less elastic than expected. Starting from a low pre-crisis level (1973) the oil price increased towards its new level (1974). Along the expected optimal path, the expected equilibrium, E', should have been approached with demand adjusting downwards and the real price decreasing slowly. The latter was achieved by keeping the nominal price of crude oil constant: the real price was reduced by inflation. The inelasticity of demand, however, would have required an even more drastic price shock. The optimal price level

---

[182] During the middle of the seventies OPEC itself claimed to follow a strategy of keeping the oil price close to the costs of substitutes. See *Al-Chalabi* (1980), p. 92 and *Jaidah* (1983), p. 26. Establishing a new price level above 10$ per barrel was a first step into this direction.

would have been located on the saddle path leading to the equilibrium E. Since the price was too low, demand adjustments turned out to be slower than expected, and finally even an increase in the demand for OPEC oil was in sight. Having experienced this, OPEC could use its market power for another drastic price increase in 1979/80.

5.4.2. Declining oil prices in the eighties

Although the price had increased by a factor of six, demand reactions following the first oil crises were relatively moderate. This can be attributed to two reasons. On the one hand, quite a few people did not expect the new price level to be permanent.[183] On the other hand, the implementation of substitution processes and the development of new oil fields are characterised by long gestation lags. So many of the adjustments induced by the first oil shock had not yet been completed when prices rose a second time in 1979.[184]

Four reasons contributed to the fast decline of demand after the second oil shock. First, this price shock coincided with the completion of oil-saving measures and new extraction capacities. Second, the new price increase induced intensified efforts to reduce demand. Now (almost) everyone believed that the new price level would become permanent. Third, the oil shock induced stagflationary tendencies worldwide. There was no growth that could have induced an increase in demand. Finally, as far as there was economic growth, its impact on demand was less than in former times. This argument is based on the thesis of a decoupling of energy demand from economic growth.

In the framework of the dominant-firm model considered here, these effects can be translated into parameter changes:

- The scale of demand reduction is represented by the long-run demand elasticity.

- The unexpectedly fast reaction to the price shock corresponds to an increase in the adjustment speed parameter β. The higher the speed of adjustment, the lower is the price.

---

[183] Cartels are inherently unstable, and prior to OPEC there have been only a few resources cartels that have been successful over a period longer than four or five years. See *Eckbo* (1976), pp. 25-46.

[184] This can be illustrated by production figures of Mexico and the United Kingdom. In both countries large-scale oil production started in 1977, three years after the price shock. When the build-up of capacities was almost completed in 1982, production had increased by a factor of three and a half in Mexico and by a factor of nine in the British part of the North Sea, compared to the 1976 levels. Most of these increases must be attributed to the first oil price shock.

- Income growth affects the movement of the long-run demand function and a change in the growth rate additionally affects the location of the equilibrium on the long-run demand curve via the term h_{pt}/h_p. Reduced income growth lowers this term, and this in turn implies a lower price.

- Decoupling of income and demand affects the location of the equilibrium in the same way as a reduction of the growth rate.

It has been shown above that the effect of the income-induced movement of the demand curve on the price is ambiguous. Therefore, it will not be considered here. So three parameter changes have to be discussed. An underestimation of the elasticity of demand, an underestimation of the adjustment speed and an overestimation of the trend impact. Since, from an algebraic point of view, the latter two produce the same result, they will be considered together.

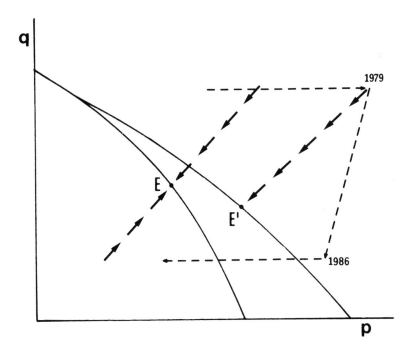

Figure 5.6.: Underestimation of the demand elasticity

Figure 5.6. represents a situation in which the elasticity of demand is underestimated. Again, let E be the true equilibrium and let E' be the expected equilibrium. The argument goes as follows. Having experienced very moderate demand responses after the first oil crisis, OPEC expects a relatively flat long-run demand curve. So the new price is chosen such that the saddle path is attained (1979). Again the real price of petroleum is reduced by keeping the nominal price constant. Since the distance of actual demand from the true long-run level of demand is greater than from the expected long-run level, the actual reaction must be more rapid than the expected reaction. This implies that the realised path is steeper than the saddle path. As OPEC becomes aware of the massive decrease of demand and the suboptimality of its strategy, the price has to be corrected downwards. Since the slight reductions of the official price in 1983 and 1985 did not help, the price had to be lowered considerably. This happened in 1986. According to the model, the equilibrium E is now approached from below.

Similar arguments apply to a situation in which the adjustment speed of demand is underestimated. (Figure 5.7.) The expected equilibrium price is higher than the true price and the corresponding saddle path is flatter. So the cartel sets a high initial price which is slightly reduced in the following periods. Demand, however, decreases very quickly. The realised path is steeper than the saddle path, and demand adjusts to a level below the equilibrium level. If the adjustment of the price is not made in time, a drastic price reduction is necessary to attain the true optimal path.

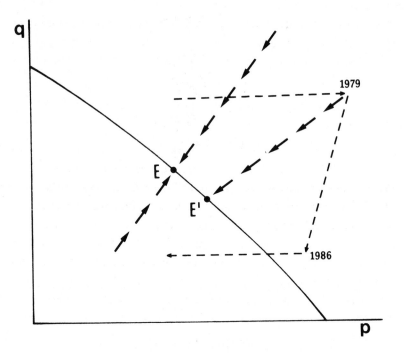

Figure 5.7.: Underestimation of the adjustment speed of demand

With respect to their graphical representation, these scenarios are not very different from each other. In the first case, there is a change in long-run demand; in the second case, we consider a variation of short-term demand and keep long-term demand constant. What has been neglected here is the problem of cartel stability that arose in 1986 when Saudi-Arabia gave up its role as the swing producer. So the historical oil price of 1986 be can expected to be lower than the optimal price.

5.4.3. Heterogeneity of OPEC and endogenous price cycles

Up to here OPEC has been modelled as a monolithic block following well-defined targets and trying to act in a way to achieve these targets. In reality, however, OPEC is a group of heterogeneous countries differing in their resource endowments, the stages of economic development, their population sizes and preferences. This leads to a distinction between high and low absorbers which has already been discussed above. It can be shown that this heterogeneity can create endogenous oil price cycles if country-specific interest rates are taken into account.

As shown above, the interest rate is a decisive parameter in the determination of the optimal price level. Up to now, it has been assumed to be constant and unique. This is a restrictive assumption. On the one hand, there have been substantial exogenous interest-rate fluctuations during the time period considered here. On the other hand, interest rates vary with risk. So one can argue that rich countries (low absorbers) are able to get credit at better conditions than poor countries (high absorbers) with a higher risk of default.

In the framework of this model, this constitutes a conflict of interests within OPEC. It has been shown in Chapter 5.3., that the higher the interest rate the higher is the price. Thus, high absorbers tend to prefer higher prices than low absorbers.

The influence of different countries on OPEC's pricing policies is not constant. It varies over time and depends on the conditions prevailing on the world petroleum market. If the market is tight, even small producers can increase the price by means of a restrictive production policy since demand is inelastic in the short run. And since their discount rate is relatively high, they have an incentive to do so. This happened after the second oil shock when the 'hawks' (Algeria and others) were successful in driving the price up and the 'doves' (especially Saudia-Arabia) did not manage to keep the price at moderate levels. If, on the other hand, there is a glut, the largest producers bear most of the burden of keeping production low and, therefore, have more market power. In the middle of the eighties Saudi-Arabia served as OPEC's swing producer, and by giving up this role it caused the price collapse of 1986.

If this is taken into account, the following scenario becomes conceivable (Figure 5.8.). The optimal path desired by the low absorbers lies above the high absorbers' optimal path. Given a high initial level of demand, the high absorbers accomplish the price policy they desire (point *A*). As demand approaches the equilibrium (point *B*), the low absorbers become stronger and manage to reduce the price to their saddle-path level (point *C*). This in turn causes demand to increase towards the low absorbers' desired long-run equilibrium (point *D*). The market gets tighter and the high absorbers become more powerful. This closes the oil price cycle (point *E*).

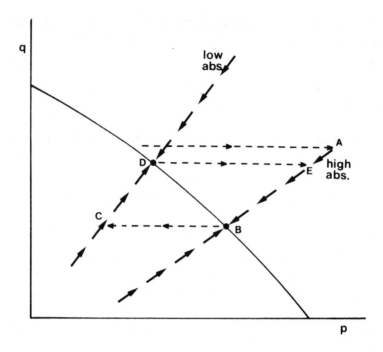

Figure 5.8.: The impact of segmented interest rates

It may be true that the conflict of interest within OPEC had an influence on the development of the oil prices during the second oil price shock and afterwards. This in particular applies to the high overshooting of the price. It might, however, be too far-fetched to attribute future oil price fluctuations to this hypothesis. First, the impact of different interest or discount rates is only one effect (and probably a small one) among many others, and second, it is possible that in the long run a price somewhere between the two equilibrium prices will be achieved.

5.5. Theoretical results and the empirical oil price cycle: a comparison

In the preceding sections, the dominant firm-model of the world petroleum market has been used to explain price shocks as the result of incorrect expectations about the flexibility of demand. This view, however, neglects the political background of the oil crises. The crises were triggered by political events in both cases. In 1973/74 it was the Middle East War and the Arab oil embargo, in 1979 it was the Iranian revolution. These events explain why the oil price went up. But they do not explain why prices did not go down again to their pre-crisis levels at the end of the supply interruptions. Had the price increases been only reactions to these political events and the corresponding shortages, they would have been transitory. The new price levels, however, turned out to be permanent and this can indeed be explained on the basis of economic motives.

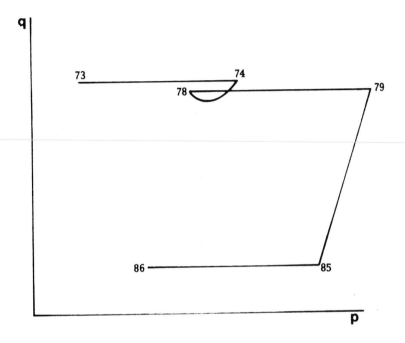

Figure 5.9.: The oil-price cycle in the theoretical model

In the next chapter, the implications of the theoretical model will be tested econometrically. Before this will be done, the predictions of the theoretical model will be compared to historical developments by graphical means. Figure 5.9. is a combination of the price paths derived in Figures 5.5. to 5.7. It shows the development of the oil price over the period 1973-1986 according to the theoretical model. The historical oil price cycle is depicted in Figure 2.3. on p. 29. The resemblance is striking. An exact test of the theoretical approach, however, can only be carried out by means of multivariate methods. This is the subject of the following sections.

6. An econometric model of the world petroleum market

6.1. Objectives of the investigation

In the preceding chapters we have considered theoretical models of OPEC behaviour in the presence of lagged demand reactions. It was shown that the optimal solution is characterised by a long-run equilibrium with a price consisting of four components, related to per-period extraction costs, user costs of the resource, monopoly rent and rigidity rent. This equilibrium itself is shifting over time due to exhaustion of reserves and exogenous demand growth. If demand for OPEC oil is modelled as an aggregate, the optimal path is a saddle path having the usual properties. If, however, demand is disaggregated by considering global demand and non-OPEC supply explicitly, the solution can look more complex. Saddle paths along which the price reverses its direction are possible. But such price changes can also be caused by incorrect expectations about demand behaviour. A great deal of the empirical analysis will be devoted to the identification of parameters critical for both the optimal and the actual paths. The following questions will be tackled:

- Is the theoretical model correctly specified? The theoretical model, even in its disaggregated version, represents a simplified view of the real world, and one should examine to what extent this is an over-simplification. This implies the question which extensions are to be made to yield a better approximation to reality.

- Are the real-world adjustment functions concave? Much of the theoretical analysis has built on the assumption that everything is nicely behaved, but if this is not true, then some of the implications of the model, especially those concerning the shapes of optimal paths, have to be modified.[185]

- Is OPEC a cartel? The model has used the hypothesis that OPEC acts as the dominant firm on the market. Therefore, optimising behaviour based on the estimated demand and non-OPEC supply functions should lead to prices that are in the same ranges as historical prices. This is another test of the cartel hypothesis.

- How can OPEC's behaviour be described? We have argued that incorrect expectations have been of major importance in OPEC's pricing policy. The problem for an empirical analysis is to specify these expectations which are not observable. An important question in this respect is related to OPEC's desired long-run level of production, a concept which has been central to the theoretical analysis.

---

[185] It can, however, be argued that even if the world is characterised by non-convavities, people act as if everything were concave since this corresponds to the commonplace view of economic relationships.

- Is there evidence in favour of the exhaustibility hypothesis? This this would imply that there are some long-run price trends which are hidden by the veil of drastic price fluctuations during the seventies and eighties.

- What can we expect for the future? Given the estimates of decisive parameters, is it possible to advance some cautious forecasts of future oil prices?

These questions will be addressed in the following passages. In order to do this, an econometric model of the world petroleum market will be constructed. The analysis will be concentrated on the period following the first oil shock 1973/74. This is the period for which OPEC is postulated to have exhibited cartel behaviour. The estimations of the demand and non-OPEC supply functions, however, will also use data from earlier periods.

6.2. OPEC and oil price fluctuations

One of the central problems in the process of building an econometric model of the world petroleum market is the specification of OPEC's behaviour. It has been mentioned above that expectations, which are central to the process of price formation, are unobservable. This implies that the expected long-run equilibrium is not known. So the saddle path that defines OPEC's pricing policy cannot be determined. It is, therefore, necessary to construct a model of OPEC's actual behaviour that builds on the optimisation model investigated in the preceding sections but requires less information than the original model. Moreover, it is of major interest how such a pricing rule interacts with the behaviour of the demand side. Are there destabilising effects, arising from the interaction of demand, adjusting sluggishly to some desired level, and OPEC's attempt to adjust the price such as to attain its long-run optimal level of production?

6.2.1. A rule-of-the-thumb approach to determining the oil price

The graphical interpretations of the oil-price shocks presented at the end of Chapter 5 can be used to derive some relationships between OPEC's actual and desired levels of oil production and the changes in the price level. Although these diagrams look very different at a first sight, they exhibit some systematic features. This can be seen if the the pre-crisis situations in Figures 5.5. to 5.7. are compared:

- Just before the 1979 crisis, OPEC production was above the expected equilibrium level and it tended to increase.

- Just before the 1986 oil price collapse, OPEC's production was far below the expected equilibrium level and it tended to decrease further.

In both periods, OPEC followed a pricing policy which was expected to be optimal: the real price of oil fell slowly. Since pricing behaviour was the same in both cases, it is reasonable to argue that it could not be responsible for the drastic price increase of 1979 as well as for the drastic price collapse seven years later. The decisive variable must be the quantity. But not only the level of demand for oil matters; also the direction of change of demand might have an impact. So it appears to be reasonable to model a rule-of-the-thumb price equation in the following way:

- Other things equal, a high level of production should induce a price increase. This is due to the fact that increasing prices reduce demand towards OPEC's desired degree of capacity utilisation.

- Everything else kept constant, an upward tendency in demand should yield a price increase since this increase reverses the tendency.

During the past fifteen years there have been periods of smooth price changes and periods of drastic price shocks. This calls for a nonlinear specification of the price adjustment function. One can argue that close to the equilibrium the changes in the price are small whereas, if demand is far from the equilibrium and tends to move even farther away, the price goes up or down drastically. The adjustment function should, therefore, give a greater weight to situations far from the equilibrium.

Let q be the quantity of oil produced by OPEC, $\dot{q}$ its change and let p be the price (time indices omitted). Then there exists a function $l(.,.)$ increasing in both arguments such that

$$(6.2.1) \qquad \dot{p} = l(\dot{q}, q).$$

Since

$$(6.2.2) \qquad \dot{q} = h(p, q, t),$$

defined as in Chapter 5, the price adjustment function can be rewritten as

$$(6.2.3) \qquad \dot{p} = l(h(p,q,t), q)$$

with

$$(6.2.4) \qquad l_h > 0, \ l_q > 0.$$

The price does not change for certain combinations of $\dot{q}$ and q. Since the partial derivatives are positive, the locus of constant prices is characterised by a inverse relationship between $\dot{q}$ and q. One of the points on this locus is OPEC's desired long-run equilibrium, q^* :

$$l(0, q^*) = 0.$$

Stock-effects, i.e. the exhaustion of resources, are neglected here since the following analysis addresses medium-term rather than long-term price developments. Resource depletion can be taken into account by making $q*$ depend on time: according to the theory of exhaustible resources, $q*$ should then decline over time.

For the following analysis, it turns out to be useful to determine the slope of the $(\dot{p}=0)$ line in the (p,q) plane. Let

$$(6.2.5) \qquad p* \; = \; P(q)$$

be the locus of constant prices, then its slope is given by

$$(6.2.6) \qquad P' \; = \; - h_q/h_p - l_q/(h_p l_h).$$

The first term on the right-hand side is negative while the second is positive. Thus, the $(\dot{p}=0)$ line can be increasing or decreasing.

The locus of constant prices represents OPEC's desired petroleum supply function. Along this curve, the actual level of petroleum production is in accordance with desired production or capacity utilisation. This means that we have identified a further possibility for a backward-bending oil supply curve. An interpretation of this effect can be given by looking at the components of P'. If l_q is small and l_h and the absolute value of h_q are large, then P' is likely to be negative. This is: the indirect effect of production via the demand adjustment process must dominate the direct effect on the price adjustment. One can, however, conjecture that in real-world applications the indirect effect is weaker and that the supply function has the conventional shape.

The supply function derived here is a generalisation of the concepts that have been used by *Nordhaus* (1980), *Verleger* (1982), *Gately* (1983), and *Rauscher* (1987b). In these publications the speed of price adjustment only depends on the deviation of production from its desired level - be it the desired level of capacity utilisation, be it the expected level of production. Since these adjustment processes do not depend on the price, they imply an inelastic long-run supply function: whatever the price level is, supply remains unchanged. The approach chosen here introduces more variability into the model. It also shows that these concepts of price formation, though seemingly ad-hoc at a first glance, can be given a theoretical foundation.[186]

---

[186] No question, it would have been better to introduce an explicit model of expectation formation rather than to use this simple rule-of-the-thumb approach.

6.2.2. The interaction of supply and demand

Before we turn to the empirical part of the analysis, some implications of the model of price formation will be studied. Especially the interaction of supply and demand and the stability of a market equilibrium will be studied. In order to do this, we will use the aggregated version of the model, a simplification which proves to be useful for the stability analysis. The model consists of the two equations

(6.2.2) $\qquad \dot{q} = h(p, q, t),$

(6.2.3) $\qquad \dot{p} = l(h(p,q,t), q)$

In order to make matters simpler, the time impact will be neglected. The slopes of the loci of constant price and quantity are given by

(6.2.7) $\qquad dq/dp = Q' = -h_p/h_q$ $\qquad\qquad$ for $\dot{q} = 0$

and

(6.2.8) $\qquad dq/dp = P^{r1} = -h_p l_h /(h_q l_h + l_q)$ $\qquad\qquad$ for $\dot{p} = 0.$

It follows that, if the $(\dot{p}=0)$ line is negatively sloped, then it is always steeper than the $(\dot{q}=0)$ line. Therefore, if an equilibrium exists, it is unique. If demand and supply are not in equilibrium, then price and quantity adjust in the following way:

- For all levels of demand lying above the desired level at a given price, demand is adjusted downwards.

- If, at a certain level of supply, the price is higher than its equilibrium level, then it will be reduced. This unambiguous result is due to the fact that a high price leads to rapid demand reductions and these demand reductions, ceteris paribus, drive the price down, or algebraically expressed : $h_p l_h < 0.$

The phase diagrams for an increasing and a decreasing supply function are plotted into Figures 6.1. and 6.2., respectively. It can be seen that with a decreasing supply function the equilibrium is a stable node. If, however, the supply function is normally shaped, then price cycles become possible. It should be noted that, in constrast to *Rampa's* (1987) model which has been discussed on p. 64, this model produces a clockwise oil price cycle. This suggests that oil price adjustments are dependent on the behaviour of OPEC supply rather than that of demand for OPEC oil.

In order to identify the parameters which affect the stability properties of this model, its dynamic behaviour will be investigated by determining the eigenvalues of its Jacobian matrix. Let equilibrium values be characterised by asterisks. Then the linearised oil market model is

(6.2.9) $\qquad \dot{q} = h_q(q-q^*) + h_p(p-p^*),$

(6.2.10) $\qquad \dot{p} = (l_h h_q + l_q)(q-q^*) + l_h h_p(p-p^*).$

The Jacobian matrix of this system is

(6.2.11) $\qquad J = \begin{bmatrix} h_q & h_p \\ l_h h_q + l_q & l_h h_p \end{bmatrix}$

Its eigenvalues are

(6.2.12) $\qquad e_{1,2} = \frac{1}{2}(h_q + l_h h_p) \pm \sqrt{\frac{1}{4}(h_q + l_h h_p)^2 + h_p l_q}$

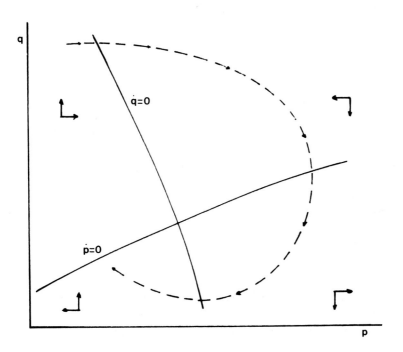

Figure 6.1.: Oil market adjustments with normal supply

136

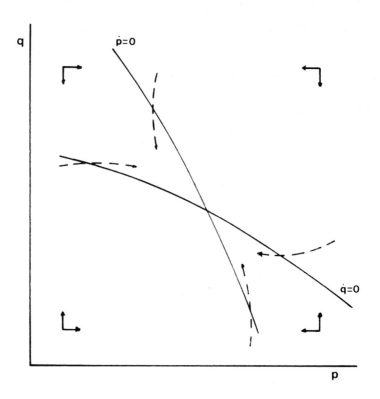

Figure 6.2.: Oil market adjustments with backward-bending supply

Since the terms in front of the square root are negative and $h_p l_q$ is also negative, the eigenvalues have negative real parts. Therefore the system is stable.[187] If the argument of the square root is negative, then the adjustment process is cyclical. This is possible for large values of l_q or h_q and for small values of l_h. In more detail, the impacts of the parameters are as follows:[188]

---

[187] It should be noted that the validity of this analysis is restricted to a close neighbourhood of the equilibrium. Due to non-linearities in the adjustment functions, the true processes are much more complex and the model need not be stable if the starting point is far enough from the equilibrium.

[188] Similar reasoning applies to the corresponding parameters of the generalised version of this model in which the adjustment processes of demand and non-OPEC supply can be distinguished. Then it is, however, not possible to determine the eigenvalues explicitly since they are roots of a cubic equation. It is intuitive, however, that parameters that measure the response of a variable to its own deviation from the equilibrium have a stabilising impact whereas parameters measuring the reaction to deviations of other variables from the equilibrium are pro-cyclical.

- If h_q is small, then the adjustment speed of demand is low. It is intuitive that slow adjustments promote cyclical behaviour.

- The same reasoning applies to l_h. If l_h is small, then the price reacts slowly to changes in demand which in turn are inversely related to the price itself. So l_h measures the sensitivity of the price to deviations from its own equilibrium value.

- l_q is the price response to deviations from the equilibrium demand level. If this reaction is vigorous, it destabilises the adjustment of the price towards its own equilibrium level.

- The effect of h_p is ambiguous since, on the one hand, it measures the impact of disequilibrium prices on demand and in this respect it is destabilising; on the other hand, $l_h h_p$ is the corresponding price reaction that stabilises the system.

In the long run, the equilibrium changes its location. Economic growth and depletion of reserves in non-OPEC countries shift the demand curve away from the origin. At the same time, OPEC supply at given prices decreases due to depletion effects. The combination of supply and demand changes will result in an increasing price.

6.3. Empirical results

In order to empirically quantify parameters, a discrete-time version of the model was estimated by econometric methods. During some preliminary analyses it turned out that the simplified version of the model had to be rejected. The adjustment processes of demand and non-OPEC supply are too different to be aggregated. Therefore, three equations were estimated: a price adjustment equation, demand and non-OPEC supply.

$$\dot{p} = h(\dot{q}, q).$$

$$\dot{d} = f(p, d, t).$$

$$\dot{s} = g(p, s, t).$$

In most cases it appeared to be appropriate to specify nonlinear equations. So it was necessary to use NLLS (nonlinear least squares) methods.[189] The regressions were carried out by means of the RATS (regression analysis for time series) package by *Doan/Litterman* (1984).

In the following passages, the notation will be subjected to some changes. Lower-case variables will denote parameters, except t which is the time index. Furthermore, let upper-case

---

[189] See *Goldfeld/Quandt* (1972) and *Gallant* (1987).

letters be time-dependent variables and a subscript specify the date. For instance P_{t-1} is the price at the date *t-1*. The following variables will be used:

- P_t, the real price of petroleum: the spot price of Saudi-Arabian Light crude oil divided by the exports price index for manufactured goods from industrial countries (1980 = 1.00). For 1986 and 1987, the price of Dubai Fateh crude was used as a proxy since Saudi-Arabian crude was not dealt on the spot market during most of this period. Sources: *Petroleum Economist, Petroleum Intelligence Weekly* and *OPEC Bulletin* (various issues) for prices, and *UN Monthly Bulletin* (various issues) for the price index.

- D_t, worldwide demand for petroleum including natural gas liquids measured in million barrels per day. Sources: *BP Statistical Review of World Energy* (various issues) and, for data prior to 1966, *Jenkins* (1985), p. 79. For some investigations demand was disaggregated into three groups of countries: OECD countries, centrally planned economies (CPEs) , and developing countries (LDCs).

- O_t, OPEC supply of crude oil including natural gas liquids measured in million barrels per day, OPEC consisting of the thirteen states that have been members since 1975. Sources: for 1966-1986 *BP Statistical Review of World Energy* (various issues), prior to 1966 *OPEC Annual Statistical Bulletin* (various issues). 1987 values were estimated on the basis of data published in the 1987 year-end issue of the *Oil and Gas Journal.*

- S_t, non-OPEC supply of crude oil including natural gas liquids (same sources as above).

- Y_t, the level of economic activity for the three country groups (OECD, CPEs, LDCs) and the world as a whole, approximated by the index of industrial production. Source: *UN Monthly Bulletin* (various issues). In the following passages Y_t will sometimes be referred to as 'income' rather than 'level of economic activity'.

It should be noted that supply measured by crude oil production does not generally equal demand which is measured by crude oil consumption. This is due to transportation lags and other biases in the data. Therefore, it is not true that $O_t = D_t - S_t$, as it would be in the theoretical model. For this reason, single-equation methods have been used to estimate the three-equations system.[190]

For the purpose of being able to neglect the substantial seasonal components in demand, industrial production and prices, all regressions were carried out on the basis of annual data - of course at the expense of a sometimes very small number of degrees of freedom. The small number of degrees of freedom is an additional reason for why single-equation methods have been preferred to simultaneous-equations estimations.

---

[190] Moreover, single-equation methods have the advantage that mis-specifaction of one equation does not affect the parameter estimates of the other equations.

6.3.1. Specification of equations

6.3.1.1. Demand

According to the theoretical model, changes in demand depend on three variables: the price, the level of economic activity and demand itself. It is convenient to start from the long-run level of demand, i.e. the level desired at a given price and given GDP, and then model an adjustment process. Two types of specifications are imaginable. The first and more common one leads to a model which is linear in the logarithms of the variables. It has the advantage of being estimable by ordinary least squares and providing direct estimates of short-run and long-run demand elasticities. But it also has a major disadvantage: it implies that the adjustment function is convex in the price and, in this respect, contradicts the assumptions made for the theoretical model. Therefore, most of the regressions were carried out with a partially linear model. The corresponding long-run demand functions can be specified as follows:

$$(6.3.1) \qquad logD_t^* = a_2 + a_3 logP_t + a\, logY_t$$

and

$$(6.3.1') \qquad D_t^* = (a_2 + a_3 P_t)\, Y_t^a\,.$$

In both cases, a is the constant income elasticity of demand. For the specification in logarithms, a_3 denotes the long-run price elasticity of demand.

There are also different options for the specification of the adjustment process. Besides different functional forms, a distinction can be made with respect to the influence of changes in the level of economic activity or income.[191] If, on the one hand, demand adjustments to income changes as well as to price changes are lagged, matters are quite simple. In discrete-time formulation the adjustment processes are specified as follows:

$$(6.3.2) \qquad logD_t - logD_{t-1} = a_1 (logD_t^* - logD_{t-1})$$

and

$$(6.3.2') \qquad D_t - D_{t-1} = a_1 (D_t^* - D_{t-1})\,.$$

This implies

$$(6.3.3) \qquad logD_t = (1-a_1)\, logD_{t-1} + a_1 a_2 + a_1 a_3 logP_t + a_1 a\, logY_t$$

---

[191] For an analysis these different adjustments to income changes see *Kouris* (1981).

and

(6.3.3') $D_t = (1-a_1) D_{t-1} + (a_1 a_2 + a_1 a_3 P_t) Y_t^a$.

Of course a_1 should be in the interval [0,1] in order to produce a stable adjustment. In the logarithmic model, $a_1 a_3$ and $a_1 a$ measure the short-run elasticities of demand with respect to the price and income, respectively.

Matters become more complicated if, on the other hand, reactions to income changes take place instantaneously. One can argue that adjustments to income changes are easier to make than adjustments to price changes. The degree of utilisation of oil-using capital goods will be increased or reduced at once. In contrast, a change in prices implies a longer period of adjustment since the design of oil-using goods has to be changed. In this case, a price change does not affect demand itself but demand corrected for the income effect. If we again assume a constant income elasticity, corrected demand, D_t^c, can be written as

(6.3.4) $D_t^c = D_t Y_t^{-a}$

Long-run corrected demand is in equilibrium if

(6.3.5) $logD_t^{c*} = (logD_t - a\, logY_t)^* = a_2 + a_3 logP_t$

and

(6.3.5') $D_t^{c*} = (D_t Y_t^{-a})^* = a_2 + a_3 P_t$,

respectively. Assuming that again a_1 is the adjustment parameter - now for corrected demand - one obtains the following demand equations

(6.3.6) $logD_t = (1-a_1)\, logD_{t-1} + a_1 a_2 + a_1 a_3 logP_t + a\, logY_t + (a_1 - 1)\, a\, logY_{t-1}$

and

(6.3.6') $D_t = Y_t^a ((1-a_1) D_{t-1} Y_{t-1}^{-a} + a_1 a_2 + a_1 a_3 P_t)$.

In this case, the long-run equilibrium level of demand can be determined by setting the right-hand sides of (6.3.6) and (6.3.6') equal to $logD_{t-1}$ and D_{t-1}, respectively, then solving for these variables and setting $D_{t-1} = D_t$:

(6.3.7) $logD_t^* = a_2 + a_3 logP_t + a/a_1 (logY_t - logY_{t-1}) + a\, logY_{t-1}$

and

(6.3.7') $D_t^* = (1 - (1-a_1)(Y_t/Y_{t-1})^a)^{-1} a_1 Y_t^a (a_2 + a_3 P_t)$.

It is obvious that the specification based on instantaneous adjustments to income changes leads to more complicated results than the lagged-adjustments assumption. But the model not only becomes more complex, it can also become sensitive to variables that do not play any role in the first formulation. If the adjustment speed, measured by the parameter a_1, is close to zero, then the growth rate of income can have a substantial influence on the equilibrium level of demand. For instance, let a and a_1 take the values 1 and 0.1, respectively. In the logarithmic model, a 5% income growth rate increases equilibrium demand by a factor of $e^{0.5}$ or by 65%. In the other model this effect is even stronger, and if the speed of adjustment to price changes is slow enough, non-existence of a positive long-run demand level becomes possible.

At a first glance, this importance of the income growth rate is surprising, but it can easily be explained. We start from a situation with positive economic growth and corrected demand being in equilibrium. Then uncorrected demand grows too, with a rate depending on the income growth rate.[192] Demand could be constant if the price were higher. The magnitude of this price increase necessary to bring demand into equilibrium also depends on the income growth rate. If the adjustment speed is low, a large price increase is necessary to reduce demand growth to zero. If it is large, demand reactions are more sensitive and the required price increase is smaller. The slower demand adjustments and the higher the income growth rate, the higher is the price at a given level of equilibrium demand or - to turn the argument around - the higher is the equilibrium level of demand at a higher price.

This sensitivity of demand with respect to income changes can cause severe problems in the interpretation of empirical results. They indeed arose in the computation of equilibrium levels of demand and non-OPEC supply, especially for the late sixties and early seventies when economic growth was high. For some of these years and low estimated adjustment parameters, the partially linear model turned out to produce negative long-run demand levels.

Another question raised in the preceding chapters is the problem of concavity: Is the adjustment process concave in prices and quantities? For instance, the logarithmic specification is always convex in the price, at least as long as the coefficient is negative. To test this, several procedures are possible.

- One can estimate a linear version of the model and then carry out statistical test such as the procedure developed by *Harvey/Collier* (1977). But this test is based on recursive residuals and, therefore, is appropriate only for univariate regression models. In multivariate models,

---

[192] The growth rate of demand is just a times the income growth rate.

the effects caused by different variables can overlap and the power of the test must be expected to be low.[193]

- The other approach is to specify a model which is nonlinear in the variables and look at the signs of the parameters. This approach has widely been discussed in the literature in the context of flexible functional forms like translog or generalised *Leontief* demand and production functions.[194]

The method to be chosen here is a simplified version of the second approach. We specify an adjustment function which is quadratic in the variables. This is done by introducing additional quadratic and interaction terms into (6.3.6) and (6.3.7). Due to the impact of the income variable which enters in a multiplicative fashion, these equations have to be estimated by nonlinear regression methods. If adjustments to income changes are not lagged, matters are relatively simple:

$$(6.3.8) \qquad D_t = (1 - a_1) D_{t-1} + a_1 (a_2 + a_3 P_t + a_4 P_t^2) Y_t^a + a_1 a_5 P_t D_{t-1} Y_t^a$$
$$+ a_1 a_6 D_{t-1}^2 .$$

It has again been assumed that income enters the equation in a constant-elasticity fashion. The interaction term in this equation, $a_5 P_t D_{t-1} Y_t^a$, can be specified with or without an income influence. If demand reactions with respect to income changes are not sluggish, this amibiguitiy vanishes. The adjustment process is given by

$$D_t Y_t^{-a} - D_{t-1} Y_{t-1}^{-a} = a_1 (a_2 + a_3 P_t + a_4 P_t^2 - D_{t-1} Y_{t-1}^{-a}$$
$$+ a_5 P_t D_{t-1} Y_{t-1}^{-a} + a_6 D_{t-1}^2 Y_{t-1}^{-2a}) .$$

This can be rearranged such that

$$(6.3.9) \qquad D_t = Y_t^a \{ (1 - a_1) D_{t-1} Y_{t-1}^{-a} + a_1 (a_2 + a_3 P_t + a_4 P_t^2)$$
$$+ a_1 a_5 P_t D_{t-1} Y_{t-1}^{-a} + a_1 a_6 D_{t-1}^2 Y_{t-1}^{-2a} \} .$$

For both equations, (6.3.8) and (6.3.9), the coefficients $a_1 a_4$ and $a_1 a_6$ are negative if the adjustment process is concave in (P_t, D_t).

---

[193] See *Krämer/Sonnberger* (1987), p. 82. They also dicuss some other procedures that test for the functional form. However, none of them explicitly addresses the question of convexity/concavity.

[194] See *Morey* (1986) and *Diewert/Wales* (1987), for instance.

6.3.1.2. Non-OPEC supply

Supply of petroleum primarily is a function of the price but some other effects also have to be considered. According to the economic theory of exhaustible resources, there are inter-temporal relationships that govern the supply of a depletable resource. The central result of this theory, *Hotelling's* rule, states that there is a gap between the price and marginal extraction costs. This gap increases over time and constitutes a scarcity rent which is appropriated by the owners of the resource.[195] If the price were constant, marginal extraction costs should decrease. Given the conventional assumption about the shape of cost functions, this implies that the rate of extraction decreases over time. In a multivariate analysis of supply behaviour one should, therefore, find a negative impact of a trend variable or of cumulated production.

This effect can be offset by other factors, for instance by technological progress that reduces extraction costs or by discovery of new cheap oil fields. This reduces the scarcity rent and, therefore, also tends to lower the price. One can conjecture that the latter effect was dominant during the sixties when supply increased at tremendous rates of 6-7% per annum in spite of decreasing prices.

The adjustment process is assumed to take the usual form. Linear as well as loglinear specifications are tested. The long-run supply function is given as

$$(6.3.10) \qquad logS_t^* = b_2 + b_3 logP_{t-i} + b\,t^2$$

and

$$(6.3.10') \qquad S_t^* = (b_2 + b_3 P_{t-i})\, exp(bt^2) \;.$$

Extending the demand function by a quadratic price impact did not improve the estimation results. Therefore, this variable was omitted. The quadratic trend was introduced to cover the increase in supply during the sixties and the early seventies. Since t was chosen to be zero for the year 1980, the trend impact almost vanishes for the late seventies and the early eighties given that the estimate of b is sufficienty small. A specification involving a linear trend impact was also tested but rejected since it did not produce any significant parameter estimates.

Finally, it proved to be necessary to introduce the price in a lagged fashion. This has the following reason: if the conventional adjustment process is chosen, the change in supply is an increasing function of the distance between the desired and the actual levels of supply. This adjustment mechanism has no memory, i.e. it does not matter when the price shock causing the deviation has occurred. Moreover, it implies that most of the adjustment takes place during the first period and that the following adjustments are declining geometrically. In reality, however, adjustment processes are not timeless in this sense. In the petroleum market, the first-period

---

[195] For a more detailed exposition see Chapter 3.

reaction has been relatively small compared to those of the second, third and fourth year. This lag has its origin in some pecularities of the process of exploration and development. There is a strong correlation between the price and capital investments in the upstream sector of the petroleum industry.[196] Price-induced exploration and development efforts, however, do not yield an at-once increase in production. Normally it takes several years until new fields come on stream or production from existing fields is increased by introducing costly advanced recovery techniques. In order to model this effect, the price to which demand reacts was introduced with a lag.[197] It should be noted that this is a substantial deviation from the theoretical model in which the adjustment of non-OPEC supply depends on the current rather than the lagged price level. The effects of this modification will be discussed in one of the following sections.

One might claim that these arguments hold for times of rising prices only. It should be relatively easy to close an oil field after a substantial price decrease. Therefore, the reactions to sinking oil prices should take place without this lag. This argument, however, neglects the fact that there are high fixed costs of stopping production from an oil field. Since it is costly or impossible to re-activate such a field, considerable opportunity costs have to be taken into account. So it depends on expectations about future price developments rather than current prices whether or not production is stopped. Some first experiences after the 1986 oil price collapse seem to indicate that closures of wells indeed are of minor importance. Sharp drawbacks in exploration and development expenditures have been much more significant.[198] The latter, of course, have only a long-term effect on supply. So there is evidence that also in times of falling prices supply of petroleum is characterised by considerable lags.

---

[196] A regression of the official OPEC list price of Arabian Light crude oil, OP_t, on worldwide nominal capital expenditure in the upstream sector, INV_t, (annual data from 1968 to 1984 from *Behling/Dobias/Anderson* (1985)) led to the following result:

$$logINV_t = 2.511 + 0.476 \, log \, OP_t + 0.054 \, (t - 1980) \, , \quad R^2_{adj} = 0.974 \, .$$
$$\quad\quad\quad (13.23) \quad (7.60) \quad\quad\quad (4.45)$$

Numbers in brackets are *t*-values. The result shows that upstream investments in the petroleum industry are indeed closely related to the price. See also *Griffin* (1988).

[197] As an alternative specification, a model in which the adjustment was made nonlinear function of the difference between desired and actual supply was tested. Small and large deviations produced slow adjustments whereas medium-size distances were assumed to induce larger changes. This model provided a good fit to the data since there is an empirical correlation between the deviation from desired demand and the time that has passed after the price shocks. The model was rejected since it exploits a more or less accidental correlation rather than building on theoretically well-grounded reasoning.

[198] See *World Oil* (1987), especially the table on drilling activities on p. 21. US figures are presented by *West* (1988).

The adjustment process takes the conventional form

(6.3.11) $logS_t - logS_{t-1} = b_1 (logS_t^* - logS_{t-1})$

and

(6.3.11') $S_t - S_{t-1} = b_1 (S_t^* - S_{t-1})$.

Combining this with equations (6.3.10) and (6.3.10') yields

(6.3.12) $logS_t = (1-b_1) logS_{t-1} + b_1 b_2 + b_1 b_3 logP_{t-i} + b_1 b t^2$

and

(6.3.12') $S_t = (1-b_1) S_{t-1} + b_1 (b_2 + b_3 P_{t-i}) exp(bt^2)$.

In order to test for convexity, again a quadratic function was specified:

(6.3.13) $S_t = (1-b_1) S_{t-1} + b_1 (b_2 + b_3 P_{t-i} + b_4 P_{t-i}^2 + b_5 P_{t-i} S_{t-1}) exp(bt^2)$

$$+ b_1 b_6 S_{t-1}^2 .$$

Convexity implies that the parameters $b_1 b_4$ and $b_1 b_6$ are positive.

6.3.1.3. The price of petroleum

It has been argued above that the process of oil price formation can be modelled by a rule-of-the-thumb approach which incorporates two explanatory variables. First it is assumed that there exists an (unobservable) level of desired petroleum production by OPEC countries. Other things equal, a high level of production should induce a price increase. On the other hand, there is an impact by the direction of previous demand movements. An upward tendency in demand should yield a price increase since a price increase reverses this tendency. Moreover, one can argue that the adjustment of prices is a highly nonlinear function of these variables. If demand is close to the desired level and does not change very much, then price changes are moderate. Drastic price shocks occur in situations far from the equilibrium.[199] Such an adjustment function is illustrated in Figure 6.3.

---

[199] Nonlinear functions of this type have also been used by *Nordhaus* (1980) and *Gately* (1983).

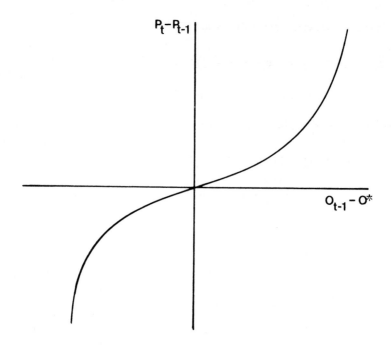

Figure 6.3.: Nonlinear price adjustments

Regression analyses were carried out for the period during which OPEC is postulated to have behaved as a cartel, i.e. the years 1974 to 1987. OPEC's desired levels of production are, of course, unobservable. The theoretical model presented in Chapter 5 presents some good arguments in favour of the hypothesis that three different levels were desired during the period in question. After the first oil shock, demand was believed to be rather elastic. This implies a high level of production. Between the oil price shocks the flexibility of demand was underestimated. Therefore, the desired level of production should have been lower during this period. For the period following the oil price collapse, the desired oil price should lie in between the two previous levels. These desired levels were estimated by three dummies, $D74_t$, $D79_t$ and $D86_t$, defined as follows

- $D74_t$: unity for 1974-1979 and zero otherwise,

- $D79_t$: unity for 1979-1985 and zero otherwise,

- $D86_t$: unity for 1986-1987 and zero otherwise.

The corresponding parameters measure OPEC's desired production levels during these periods.

The equations to be estimated are specified as

(6.3.14) $\quad P_t - P_{t-1} = \{ c_1 (O_t - c_2 D74_t - c_3 D79_t - c_4 D86_t + c_5 (O_t - O_{t-1})) \}^n$

with $n = 1,3,5,7,9....$.

Odd values of n produce price adjustment processes like the one depicted in Figure 6.3. Instead of doing the regression analyses with given values of n, one can also endogenise n and estimate it as a parameter of the model. The problem arising here is that the argument of the power function, denoted by the term in brackets, is not always positive. It can be avoided by the following procedure. Define

(6.3.15) $\quad Z_t = c_1 (O_t - c_2 D74_t - c_3 D79_t - c_4 D86_t + c_5 (O_t - O_{t-1}))$.

Then n can be determined by estimating the equation

(6.3.16) $\quad P_t - P_{t-1} = Z_t (Z_t^2)^{(n-1)/2}$.

This equation was estimated in addition to (6.3.14). The estimates obtained from (6.3.14) provided good starting values for (6.3.16) so that problems of convergence turned out to be less severe than they first seemed to be.

6.3.2. Estimation results

The equations were estimated by nonlinear least squares. Besides the estimates themselves, the following statistics are reported. t-values are given in brackets under the corresponding parameter values.[200] R^2_{adj} denotes the multiple correlation coefficient adjusted for the degrees of freedom (times 100). DW is the *Durbin-Watson* test statistic. Since some of the models contain lagged endogenous variables, it is necessary to use *Durbin's* h-statistic (denoted by Dh) to test for autocorrelation.[201] This statistic is computed by an approximation suggested in *Johnston* (1984), p. 318, which is based on the *Durbin-Watson* test statistic:

(6.3.17) $\quad Dh = (1 - DW/2) (T / (1 - T Var(\beta_1)))^{1/2}$

---

[200] Note that in the case of nonlinear regressions these statistics only approximately follow a t-distribution. See *Gallant* (1987), pp. 16-19.

[201] This test was suggested by *Durbin* (1970).

where T is the number of observations and $Var(\beta_1)$ is the estimated sampling variance of β_1, the coefficient of the lagged endogenous variable.

6.3.2.1. Concavity and convexity

In order to provide empirical evidence concerning the concavity of OPEC's optimisation problem, the equations (6.3.8), (6.3.9) and (6.3.13) were estimated. Two observation periods were chosen, the complete sample and a subsample using only recent information since 1976. The choice of the latter period involves a serious loss of degrees of freedom since seven parameters have to be estimated. Since only some of the estimates are significantly different from zero, numerical values are not reported in Tables 6.1. and 6.2. Significance of a parameter at the 5% level is denoted by an asterisk. The observations last until 1986 for the demand equations and until 1987 for supply.

The results for the longer time period do not allow conclusions concerning the issue of concavity or convexity. None of the parameters that measure the impact of the squared variables is significantly different from zero. For one of the estimated demand functions, a significant impact can be identified for the interaction term. This information alone, however, does not imply anything for the shape of the adjustment function.

Table 6.1.: Concavity and convexity of the adjustment functions (1961/3-1986/7)

	demand, reactions to income changes lagged	demand, reactions to income changes not lagged	non-OPEC supply
P	+	-	-
P^2	-	-	-
D, S	+	+ *	+ *
D^2, S^2	-	+	+
PD, PS	-	-*	+

For the shorter time period, some significant parameters can be reported. Negative impacts of D^2 in the demand function and P^2 in the supply function hint at concavity with respect to demand and price. In the first case, the result is in accordance with the theoretical model, in the second case, it is a contradiction to the postulate of a convex supply function. Given the fact that the numbers of degrees of freedom are only four and five for these equations, this result should be interpreted - if at all - only very cautiously.

Table 6.2.: Concavity and convexity of the adjustment functions (1976-1986/7)

	demand, reactions to income changes lagged	demand, reactions to income changes not lagged	non-OPEC supply
P	+	+	-
P^2	-	-	-*
D, S	+*	+	+*
D^2, S^2	-*	-	-
PD, PS	+	-	+

One can summarise that the procedure adopted here has not produced substantial evidence against or in favour of convexity or concavity of the functions in question. This confirms the results obtained by *Wirl* (1988), pp. 28-29, in an analysis of aggregate demand for OPEC oil.[202] What are the implications of this finding? Depending on the shape of the functions, especially their second derivatives, two conclusions are possible:

- If the functions do not satisfy the second-order conditions, then the optimisation problem of the theoretical model is not concave. This implies the optimality of boundary solutions. *Wirl* (1985a) has shown that, given upper and lower bounds of the oil price, a cyclical pricing policy is optimal. The price switches from the upper to the lower bound and vice versa.

- On the other hand, if all functions are nicely behaved, there may be changes in the direction of the price path, but price shocks cannot be optimal. This has been shown in Chapter 4. Price shocks have to be explained by unexpected parameter changes.

Since the empirical results do not allow to discriminate between these two hypotheses, one is left with intuition in the explanation of oil price fluctuations. An argument in favour of the second hypothesis is that, in the absense of perfect information, people tend to choose a plausible rule-of-the-thumb strategy. And given lagged adjustments of demand, it is plausible to exploit the rigidity of demand by setting a high price if demand is high or, if initial demand is low, to set a low price to increase the long-run dependency on petroleum rather than to chose a sophisticated cyclical pricing strategy. Moreover, recent experience, especially the 1986 oil price collapse,

---

[202] *Wirl* only considers the impact of the squared price.

indicates that drastic price fluctuations are not part of a long-term oriented oil policy deliberately chosen by a cartel of oil-producing countries.

6.3.2.2. Demand for petroleum

Regressions were run for four different types of specifications (linear vs. loglinear, income lagged vs. income not lagged), for different country groups (OECD, LDCs, CPEs and the world as a whole), and for different subperiods of the period 1961-1986. The specifications are the following.

$$(6.3.18) \qquad logD_t = (1-a_1) \, logD_{t-1} + a_1 a_2 + a_1 a_3 logP_{t-1} + a_1 a \, logY_t \, ,$$

$$(6.3.18') \qquad D_t = (1-a_1) \, D_{t-1} + a_1 (a_2 + a_3 P_{t-1}) \, Y_t^a \, ,$$

$$(6.3.19) \qquad logD_t = (1-a_1) logD_{t-1} + a_1 a_2 + a_1 a_3 logP_{t-1} + a \, logY_t + (a_1 - 1)a \, logY_{t-1}$$

$$(6.3.19') \qquad D_t = Y_t^a \, (\, (1-a_1) \, D_{t-1} Y_{t-1}^{-a} + a_1 (a_2 + a_3 P_{t-1}) \,),$$

The first pair assumes lagged adjustments to income changes, and the second pair implies instantaneous adjustments. Note that the original specifications (equations (6.3.3) and (6.3.6)) have been modified slightly by lagging the price.[203] This was necessary since specifications with P_t tended to produce estimates of the adjustment speed, a_1, that were not significantly different from zero or even negative. A quadratic price impact did not yield significant estimates and, therefore, was omitted. Disaggregation of demand into different groups shows the heterogeneity of demand behaviour. Finally, regressions were run for subperiods in order to show that there has been considerable variability of the parameters over time.

Results for the different country groups and different assumptions about reactions to income changes for the linear-demand model are listed in Table 6.3. The column indicated "Y lag" contains the estimates of the version of the model, in which demand reactions to income changes are lagged. In the column "Y n.lag" are assumed to be completed instantaneously. In most cases, the parameters are significant and of the expected magnitude. P^{max} is the maximum price, at

---

[203] With this modification, demand adjustments are assumed to be caused by the deviation of last year's demand from desired level of demand corresponding to last year's rather than to current prices. Compared to the three-periods lag in the supply function, this is only a minor modification of the original model.

which demand is choked off. It has been computed by dividing the constant, $a_1 a_2$, by the coefficient of the price, $a_1 a_3$.

- It turns out that the assumption of instantaneous adjustments of the price to income changes systematically affects the estimates of the adjustment speed and the income elasticity. Both parameters are estimated to be smaller than in the model with lagged reactions to income changes. With the exception of the developing countries, the fit tends to be slightly better for the instantaneous-adjustment model.

- There are significant differences between country groups. Most surprising are the positive price coefficients for the group of the developing countries. For the centrally planned economies, the adjustment speed is estimated to be very close to zero, in the instantaneous-adjustment model it is even negative. The only group that produces results in accordance with standard economic theory are the industrialised countries.

- The choke-off price is estimated to be in an area of 65 to 95$ per barrel. The slope of the long-run demand function of the world, a_3, is 0.9 for the lagged-adjustment model and 1.3 for the instantaneous-adjustment model. For the industrialised countries the slope is 0.7 in both cases.

Table 6.3.: Demand for crude oil by country groups 1961-1986 (linear specification)

	WORLD		OECD		LDCs		CPEs	
	Y lag	Y n.lag	Y lag	Y n.lag	Y lag	Y n.lag	Y lag	Y n.lag
a	1.036	0.634	1.150	0.722	0.967	0.884	0.888	0.374
	(11.21)	(5.04)	(9.30)	(5.38)	(8.74)	(10.77)	(6.09)	(0.374)
$(1-a_1)$	0.771	0.938	0.718	0.885	0.550	0.346	0.995	1.046
	(12.15)	(3.15)	(11.45)	(19.17)	(3.41)	(2.59)	(23.79)	(43.85)
$a_1 a_2$	19.901	5.207	15.518	5.607	4.050	5.156	1.354	0.232
	(4.49)	(2.36)	(5.08)	(3.04)	(3.42)	(4.63)	(2.26)	(1.56)
$a_1 a_3$	-0.209	-.0812	-0.195	-.0790	0.0402	0.0754	-.0373	-.0288
	(-5.62)	(-4.58)	(-5.48)	(-5.02)	(1.81)	(4.71)	(-8.2)	(-5.41)
R^2_{adj}	99.40	99.53	98.55	98.77	98.71	98.50	99.91	99.92
DW	1.94	2.08	1.81	1.77	2.52	2.00	1.74	1.85
Dh	0.15	-0.22	0.50	0.62	-2.23	0.01	0.68	0.38
P^{max}	95.22	65.09	79.40	70.95	-	-	36.25	n.s.

The results have been re-estimated for different subperiods of 1961-86. The results are represented in Table 6.4. Asterisks denote parameters significant at the 5% level. Due to the logarithmic specification used here, elasticities are constant and can easily be compared.

The first period, 1961-1973, covers the information available prior to the first oil crises. Table 6.4. shows that the price impact is insignificant for all country groups. The second subsample includes the years following the first oil shock. For the OECD countries the long-run price elasticity becomes significant. The third sample covers the whole period 1961-1986, and the last contains data of the latest eleven years available. Again the developing countries and the centrally planned economies do not behave normally in the sense of economic theory. The price coefficients of the developing countries exhibit 'wrong' signs and the socialist countries do not show significant price impacts at all. A negative, though insignificant, adjustment parameter occurs for the period 1981-86.

The results for OECD and global demand are again very similar to one another. It turns out that the income elasticity has been reduced over time: there is a divergence of economic growth and oil consumption. The price elasticity has increased. The development of the adjustment speed estimates is a bit dubious. For the complete sample it is estimated to be lower than for any subsample.

Table 6.4.: Long-run demand elasticities for different countries (loglinear specification, income reactions lagged)

	1961 -1973	1961 -1979	1961 -1986	1976 -1986
WORLD adj. speed price income	0.301 -0.067 1.178*	0.412* -0.074* 1.111*	0.169* -0.255* 1.037*	0.456* -0.179* 0.233*
OECD adj. speed price income	0.374* -0.080 1.318*	0.405* -0.094* 1.218*	0.187* -0.296* 1.078*	0.471* -0.323* 0.133
LDCs adj. speed price income	0.954* -0.023 0.963*	0.943* 0.074 1.005*	0.564* 0.111* 1.013*	0.289* 0.158* 0.518*
CPEs adj. speed price income	0.332 0.013 1.048*	0.189 -0.157 1.009*	-0.030 1.325 1.054*	0.234* -0.138 0.104

In Table 6.5., specifications with and without a price lag are compared. It can be seen that, with the exception of 1961-79, adjustment speeds are estimated to be higher in the lagged-price model. This is just the subsample for which the model without a price lag produces a better fit. In Table 6.5. it has been assumed that reactions to income changes are sluggish. The instant-aneous-adjustment model with no price lag (P_t) was tested too, but the results are not documented here. It turned out that the estimated adjustment parameters became even smaller and were not significantly different from zero any more.

Table 6.5.: Worldwide demand for crude oil (linear specification)

	price lagged (P_{t-1})				price not lagged (P_t)			
	61-73	61-79	61-86	76-86	61-73	61-79	61-86	76-86
a	1.186 (23.38)	1.061 (12.68)	1.036 (11.21)	0.218 (3.26)	1.120 (24.80)	1.170 (27.75)	0.831 (3.46)	-0.384 (-0.88)
$(1-a_1)$	0.648 (3.54)	0.626 (3.78)	0.771 (12.15)	0.547 11.66	0.690 (4.00)	0.493 (4.43)	0.956 (15.69)	0.809 (5.53)
$a_1 a_2$	30.971 (2.29)	29.070 (2.61)	19.901 (4.49)	33.042 (11.40)	28.180 (2.24)	40.140 (5.24)	7.403 (1.92)	15.600 (1.86)
$a_1 a_3$	-0.444 (-0.71)	-0.171 -(2.08)	-0.210 (-4.49)	-0.198 (-11.71)	-0.144 (-0.40)	-0.239 (-5.35)	-0.164 (-5.33)	-0.138 (-3.48)
R^2_{adj}	99.79	99.31	99.40	96.83	99.78	99.70	99.34	75.64
DW	2.56	1.81	1.94	2.32	2.56	2.30	2.15	2.16
Dh	-1.34	0.58	0.15	-0.54	-1.28	-0.75	-0.39	-0.29
P^{max}	n.s.	169.91	95.22	167.06	n.s.	167.54	45.15	113.00

Table 6.6. contains the final versions of the demand functions some of which will be used for simulation purposes later.

Table 6.6.: Worldwide demand for crude oil (linear specification)

	income reactions lagged				income reactions not lagged			
	61-73	61-79	61-86	76-86	61-73	61-79	61-86	76-86
a	1.186 (23.38)	1.061 (12.68)	1.036 (11.21)	0.218 (3.26)	1.136 (19.69)	0.667 (3.48)	0.634 (5.04)	0.059 (2.96)
$(1-a_1)$	0.648 (3.54)	0.626 (3.78)	0.771 (12.15)	0.547 (11.66)	0.392 (1.43)	0.934 (13.48)	0.938 (23.15)	0.580 (10.89)
$a_1 a_2$	30.971 (2.29)	29.070 (2.61)	19.901 (4.49)	33.042 (11.40)	49.934 (2.48)	5.387 (1.49)	5.207 (2.36)	30.272 (9.07)
$a_1 a_3$	-0.444 (-0.71)	-0.171 (-2.08)	-0.209 (-5.62)	-0.198 (-11.71)	-1.505 (-2.00)	-.0619 (-1.02)	-.0812 (-4.59)	-0.175 (-11.91)
R^2_{adj}	99.79	99.31	99.40	96.83	99.59	99.48	99.53	96.64
DW	2.56	1.81	1.94	2.32	2.14	2.19	2.08	2.00
Dh	-1.34	0.58	0.15	-0.54	-1.60	-0.43	-0.22	-0.01
P^{max}	n.s.	169.91	95.22	167.06	n.s.	n.s.	65.09	173.46

For two of the four chosen observation periods, the instantaneous-adjustment model fits the data better than the lagged-adjustment model. High values of *Durbin's h* indicate negative serial correlation for the 1961-1973 subperiod. Besides these findings, Table 6.6 in principle confirms the results of the loglinear model.

- For the 1961-73 sample, which contains the information available at the time of the first oil crisis, some of the parameter estimates are insignificant.

- There is strong evidence in favour of decreasing income elasticities for both types of specification.

- The findings concerning the magnitude of the adjustment-speed, a_1, are again ambiguous. The complete sample, 1961-1986, produces the smallest estimates of this parameter.

- Long-run price elasticities have been computed for the lagged-adjustment model. Given the linear shape of the long-run demand curve, elasticities vary with the price. For a price of 20$ per barrel the estimated elasticities are 0.133, 0.267, and 0.136 for the periods 1961-79, 1961-86 and 1976-86, respectively. Elasticities at a price of 30$ are 0.214, 0.462, and 0.219. The evidence in favour of an increase in the elasticities is weaker than in the loglinear model.

To summarise, one can state that the variability of demand has increased over time. The difficulty occurring here is the fact that the estimations for the 1961-86 period indicate an increase of the price elasticity at the expense of a loss of adjustment speed whereas the 1976-86 period suggests an increase in the adjustment parameter but no substantial change of the long-run price elasticity.

For further analyses like the simulation of long-run optimal price paths, the results of the lagged-adjustments model will be used. Certainly, the other approch yielded slightly better estimates for some of the subperiods, but in these cases the estimated adjustment speeds turned out to be very low. This in turn implies problems in determining long-run equilibria since the instantaneous-adjustment model tends to overemphasise the influence of the income growth rate (as shown in Chapter 6.3.1.2). The information available at the time of the second oil price shock is represented by the parameter estimates of the 1961-1979 sample. The update of the informations can be obtained from one of the samples extending to 1986:

$$D_t = 0.626\, D_{t-1} + (\, 29.07 - 0.171\, P_{t-1}\,)\, Y_t^{1.061} \qquad \text{(1961-1979).}$$

$$D_t = 0.771\, D_{t-1} + (\, 19.90 - 0.210\, P_{t-1}\,)\, Y_t^{1.036} \qquad \text{(1961-1986).}$$

$$D_t = 0.547\, D_{t-1} + (\, 33.02 - 0.198\, P_{t-1}\,)\, Y_t^{0.218} \qquad \text{(1976-1986).}$$

6.3.2.3. Non-OPEC supply of petroleum

Non-OPEC supply was estimated for a linear and loglinear specification. The observation period extends to 1987. The estimated equations are

(6.3.12) $\qquad logS_t = (1-b_1)\, logS_{t-1} + b_1 b_2 + b_1 b_3 logP_{t-i} + b_1 b\, t^2$

and

(6.3.12') $\qquad S_t = (1-b_1)\, S_{t-1} + b_1 (b_2 + b_3 P_{t-i})\, exp(bt^2)\,.$

The impact of the choice of lags in the price variable is shown in Tables 6.7. and 6.8. The period under consideration covers the time following the Teheran and Tripolis meetings of OPEC when the first price increases after a long period of declining prices became effective. During further analyses it turned out that the choice of the observation period did not affect the result substantially, at least as far as the choice of the price lag is concerned. For the period under consideration here, the trend variable did not produce a significant influence for this sample and was, therefore, omitted.

Table 6.7.: Non-OPEC supply of petroleum: different price lags (linear specification)

	P_t	P_{t-1}	P_{t-2}	P_{t-3}	P_{t-4}	P_{t-5}
$(1-b_1)$	0.964	0.964	0.860	0.838	0.929	1.047
	(27.30)	(21.49)	(14.03)	(11.65)	(10.47)	(12.92)
$b_1 b_2$	1.757	1.866	4.250	4.960	2.826	-0.070
	(1.79)	(1.60)	(2.84)	(2.78)	(1.25)	(-0.03)
$b_1 b_3$	0.018	0.013	0.062	0.070	0.026	-0.030
	(1.02)	(0.62)	(2.24)	(2.22)	(0.67)	(-0.81)
R^2_{adj}	98.70	98.83	98.97	98.96	98.64	98.66
DW	1.36	1.39	1.22	1.51	1.26	1.44
Dh	1.33	1.28	1.65	1.06	1.65	1.22

Table 6.8.: Non-OPEC supply of petroleum: different price lags (loglinear specification)

	P_t	P_{t-1}	P_{t-2}	P_{t-3}	P_{t-4}	P_{t-5}
$(1-b_1)$	0.947	0.936	0.807	0.753	0.809	0.942
	(22.98)	(18.73)	(15.39)	(11.87)	(8.38)	(9.12)
$b_1 b_2$	0.195	0.231	0.600	0.769	0.615	0.222
	(1.56)	(1.54)	(3.85)	(4.06)	(2.12)	(0.71)
$b_1 b_3$	0.006	0.008	0.036	0.044	0.032	-0.005
	(0.60)	(0.71)	(3.35)	(3.55)	(1.68)	(0.22)
R^2_{adj}	98.41	98.43	99.09	99.14	98.64	98.38
DW	1.45	1.60	1.51	2.49	1.78	1.35
Dh	1.15	0.93	1.08	-1.05	0.48	1.48

Table 6.7. summarises the results for the linear-demand model. It can be seen that the appropriate lag is 2 or 3. All the other specifications do not produce significant estimates of the price impact. The loglinear model produces similar results which are shown in Table 6.8. Although the results do not differ very much for the lags 2 and 3, a choice had to be made. In

further analyses, covering different time periods, a lag of 3 turned out to produce slightly better results in most of the cases and, therefore, was chosen for the empirical investigation.

The results for the final version of the model are summarised in Table 6.9. Again the equations have been estimated for different subsamples. The first one (1963-73) uses the information available at the time of the first oil crises. The second period updates this information up to 1979. Information available after the oil price collapse of 1986 is contained in the samples that reach to 1987. The second of these only uses new information.

Table 6.9.: Non-OPEC supply of petroleum for different periods of observation

	linear spec.				loglinear spec.			
	63-73	63-79	63-87	76-87	63-73	63-79	63-87	76-87
b	-.0024 (-5.40)	-.0021 (-7.38)	-.0019 (-7.03)	-	-.0013 (-3.87)	-.0009 (-2.33)	-.0004 (-3.07)	-
$(1-b_1)$	0.428 (2.51)	0.685 (4.05)	0.824 (18.21)	0.809 (27.60)	0.503 (3.48)	0.592 (3.51)	0.810 (16.67)	0.764 (30.31)
$b_1 b_2$	17.947 (2.80)	9.554 (1.97)	5.811 (4.82)	6.815 (9.97)	1.671 (2.97)	1.362 (2.58)	0.638 (4.21)	0.706 (9.26)
$b_1 b_3$	0.021 (0.02)	0.111 (2.90)	0.067 (3.24)	0.042 (3.70)	0.040 (0.35)	0.033 (2.67)	0.025 (2.70)	0.019 (2.91)
R^2_{adj}	99.63	99.15	99.70	99.77	99.66	99.30	99.67	99.73
DW	2.72	2.11	1.83	1.86	2.67	1.66	1.63	1.84
Dh	-1.45	-0.31	0.46	0.25	-1.27	0.93	0.96	0.27

Like in the case of the demand functions, *Durbin's h* indicates negative serial correlation for the first sample, the period preceding the first oil shock. For this period neither the linear nor the loglinear specification allow for detecting any significant impact of the price on non-OPEC supply. For the other periods, the following results can be summarised:

- The sixties are characterised by a strong impact of the trend variable which is indicated by a significant parameter b. This impact is getting weaker over time. In the 1976-87 sample, the trend variable was not significant any more and, therefore, was omitted. The trend impact during the sixties and early seventies can be interpreted to be a result of new findings of low-cost oil fields. This effect has disappeared during the seventies and eighties. It possibly supports the exhaustion hypothesis, but the negative trend impact in the eighties is very weak.

- In terms of the adjustment parameter, b_1, non-OPEC supply becomes less flexible over time. The estimation results show that $(1-b_1)$ increases.

- With respect to the elasticity of long-run demand, results are more ambiguous. In the log-linear model, price elasticities are constant and can easily be computed as 0.081 for 1963-79, 0.132 for 1963-87 and again 0.081 for 1976-87. In the linear model, elasticities vary with the price. For 20\$ (30\$) per barrel they turn out to be 0.187 (0.258) for 1963-79, 0.187 (0.257) for 1963-87 and 0.123 (0.156) for 1976-1987.

For the sake of simpler computation of numerical results, the linear version is chosen for the purpose of determining empirical optimal paths:

$$S_t = 0.685\, S_{t-1} + (\,9.554 + 0.111\, P_{t-3}\,)\, exp(\,-0.0021\, t^2\,) \quad \text{for 1963-79.}$$

$$S_t = 0.824\, S_{t-1} + (\,5.811 + 0.067\, P_{t-3}\,)\, exp(\,-0.0019\, t^2\,) \quad \text{for 1963-87.}$$

$$S_t = 0.809\, S_{t-1} + (\,6.815 + 0.042\, P_{t-3}\,) \quad\quad\quad\quad \text{for 1976-87.}$$

6.3.2.4. OPEC behaviour and price adjustments

OPEC as the dominant firm in the market is assumed to 'make' the price of petroleum. The estimated equation is given by

(6.3.14) $\quad P_t - P_{t-1} = \{\, c_1(\, O_{t-1} - c_2 D74_t - c_3 D79_t - c_4 D86_t + c_5(O_t - O_{t-1})\,)\,\}^n.$

The observations cover the period from the first oil shock in 1974 to the latest data available (1987). It should be noted that, with five explanatory variables, this implies that the number of degrees of freedom is only 9. The results of the estimation are listed in Table 6.10.

For the OPEC countries the following results can be reported. It turned out that the adjustment function is highly nonlinear. The best result in terms of the sum of squared residuals was obtained for $n = 18.477$.[204] The coefficients of the dummies are in the expected ranges: the desired level of demand for 1974-1978 is slightly, though not significantly, greater than for

---

[204] The adjusted R^2 is less than for $n = 17$, but this is due to the reduction in the degrees of freedom which dominates the improvement in the sum of squared residuals since the number of observations is very small.

1986-87 and the level following the second oil crisis is the highest. The differences, however, are smaller than expected. The direction of changes in production have the expected positive sign which is significant for large n. If n is endogenous, the other coefficients become less significant, probably caused by multicollinearity effects.

Table 6.10.: Price adjustments

	$n = 1$	$n = 3$	$n = 7$	$n = 17$	n end.	non-OPEC
c_1	1.045 (2.02)	0.291 (4.30)	0.204 (8.52)	0.174 (11.73)	0.173 (5.91)	-0.254 (-1.09)
c_2	28.517 (9.18)	26.155 (12.53)	25.371 (25.88)	25.055 (42.03)	25.054 (42.00)	32.672 (6.92)
c_3	19.799 (5.74)	22.670 (12.90)	23.530 28.80	23.916 (42.87)	23.949 (22.62)	39.575 (7.05)
c_4	27.466 (4.33)	25.975 (12.22)	25.380 (26.11)	24.729 (37.20)	24.729 (13.17)	34.767 (6.24)
c_5	1.230 (1.21)	0.467 (1.31)	0.386 (2.75)	0.336 (3.83)	0.329 (1.45)	0.020 (0.02)
n	1	3	7	17	18.477 (0.47)	5
R^2_{adj}	25.90	39.18	59.13	68.57	64.68	28.52
DW	2.14	2.19	1.87	1.68	1.67	2.23

These results are in agreement with the conclusions from the theoretical model. Before the second oil crisis, demand for OPEC oil was nearly 31.5 million barrels per day and by far exceeded the estimated desired level of 25.1. The new desired level of 23.9 was reached within two years (1981) and demand fell to 17.2 in 1985.[205] The new desired level is slightly higher than the 1979-85 value.

One might argue that the results mentioned above do not represent causal relationships but are merely the result of some more or less accidental correlations among variables. This

---

[205] Data are taken from *BP Annual Review of World Energy* 1987.

suspicion especially arises from the importance of the dummy variables in this model. In order to check this, the same equation was estimated for the group of the non-OPEC countries. The best results, obtained for a parameter value of $n = 5$, are shown in the last column of Table 6.10. It can be seen that the performance of this equation is poor for the non-OPEC countries. Neither the adjustment parameter nor the coefficient of production change are significant. The former even has the 'wrong' sign. The fit, measured by R^2, is substantially weaker than for OPEC data.

6.3.3. Summary of the empirical results

The regression results suggest that our theoretical model of the world petroleum market has succeeded the empirical tests in some respects. In some other respects, the results are rather ambiguous:

- The adjustment functions specified in the theoretical model had to be modified. Especially the lag in the adjustment of supply turned out to be of major importance. Introducing a three-year lag into a theoretical model might change the results. The direction of this change is, however, not clear. It will probably increase the importance of rigidity effects.

- It was not possible to detect exhaustion effects. The negative impact of the quadratic trend in the supply function hints at the fact that exogenous growth has faded out during the late seventies and the eighties. Whether this trend turns into a decline in the nineties still remains an open question.

- For data prior to the first oil crisis, the estimates of the price impact on demand and non-OPEC supply are insignificant. This finding supports the hypothesis that the magnitude of reactions to price changes could not be foreseen at that time.

- According to the theoretical model, there should have been changes in the estimated parameters after the second oil price shock. This in particular concerns the adjustment speeds of demand and non-OPEC supply and the elasticities of the long-run demand and supply functions. These changes can only partially be identified empirically. In the case of the demand function it remains unclear whether the adjustment parameter or the elasticity has changed. On the contrary, the data showed a distinct decoupling of GDP growth and oil consumption.

- The desired levels of OPEC production, estimated from the price equation, are in agreement with the ones postulated from the theoretical model. The desired levels of production in the periods 1974-79 and 1986-87 are higher than the 1980-85 level. This is in accordance with the hypothesis of an underestimation of demand flexibility by OPEC in the first half of the eighties. From the theoretical model one might, however, have expected greater differences between these levels.

These results concern the qualitative features of the model: do signs of the estimated model correspond to the properties of the theoretical model? In most respects the answer is affirmative, and this seems to support the approach. But there still remains another open question concerning the magnitude of the parameters. Even if the parameters have the 'correct' signs, they do not necessarily have the right size. For instance, given the estimated parameters, optimising behaviour can result in prices and quantities that are significantly different from historical values.

6.4. Optimal pricing policies in the empirical model

This section represents the link between the theoretical optimisation model and the regression results presented in the preceding sections. Due to the fact that many of the functions have been specified in a linear fashion, computations are relatively simple.

Two types of scenarios are imaginable. On the one hand, the model can be closed via the estimated price equation. The equilibria derived from this approach are not necessarily optima but scenarios based on past experience with OPEC behaviour. It may also be possible to derive forecasts of future price fluctuations. On the other hand, one can use the parameter estimates of the demand and non-OPEC supply functions and insert them into the optimality conditions of the theoretical model. This leads to estimates of long-run equilibrium prices and quantities. The latter approach will be chosen here and the estimated OPEC supply function will be used for the purpose of comparisons. Moreover, it will be shown how optima computed on the basis of the information available at the time of the second oil shock differ from those that include all the information. Before this can be done, a methodological remark has to be made.

6.4.1. Misspecification of adjustment processes

It has been mentioned above that the findings concerning the changes in the adjustment speeds and in the long-run demand elasticities are rather ambiguous and only partially support the hypotheses stated in the theoretical parts of the analysis. There are reasons to suspect that these empirical results to a certain extent only reflect problems of the estimation method employed here. There can be a systematic bias in the parameters if the adjustment process is not specified correctly. Therefore, before these results will be used as a test of the theory established in Chapter 5, it is useful to show which direction the bias is likely to have.

The theoretical as well as the econometric models of demand and supply have used special assumptions on the nature of the adjustment processes. In particular, these processes have been modelled in an a-historical manner. The change in demand (supply) depends on demand (supply) itself, on the price and other explanatory variables. The underlying idea is that, given the values of the exogenous variables, there exists a long-run equilibrium, and the distance of actual demand (supply) from its equilibrium level determines the intensity of adjustment. In the econometric model this simply was the Euclidian distance. Such an adjustment process is depicted in Figure 6.4. It is characterised by drastic initial adjustments that become smoother as the dependent variable approaches its equilibrium.[206]

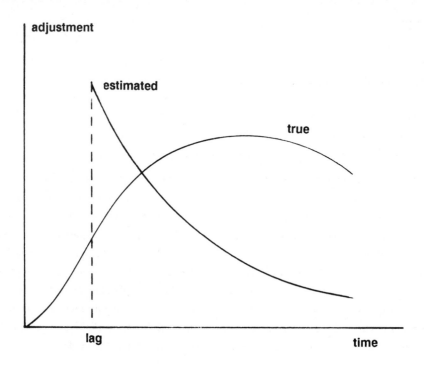

Figure 6.4.: Different adjustment processes

It is, however, unlikely that adjustment functions in the energy sector have such a shape. When lagged adjustments were introduced into the theoretical model at the beginning of Chapter 4, it was argued that oil price increases induce investments into energy-saving technologies, a restructuring of the capital stock, and additional exploration and development of new oil fields. These measures affect demand and supply of petroleum. Nonetheless, the adjustment process significantly differs from the geometrically declining function implied by the econometric specification. One can expect that, since maturing times of new technologies must be taken into account and intensified exploratory effort results in increased production only with a substantial lag, the initial adjustments are small whereas, after some years, major demand and supply

---

[206] Since we have used lagged prices in the regressions and we assume that disequilibria have been caused by price shocks, Figure 6.4 shows a lag in the adjustment function.

changes become visible. Thus, a reasonable adjustment function should look like the density function of a normal rather than an exponential distribution (see Figure 6.4).

How these specifications affect the estimates of the adjustment speeds and long-run elasticities can be illustrated if we turn to cumulative adjustment functions. This is done in Figure 6.5. The true adjustment function resembles a normal distribution. It can now be shown that the estimated adjustment functions are decisively affected by the length of the observation period. If the observation period is short (T_1), then the analysis uses informations only from the beginning of the adjustment process when changes are small. The true and the estimated adjustment functions intersect. Initial adjustments will be overestimated and the long-run response to the shock will considerably be underestimated. This effect is dampened by a longer period of observation (T_2) that allows the true adjustment process to come closer to its end. The basic argument, however, does not change.

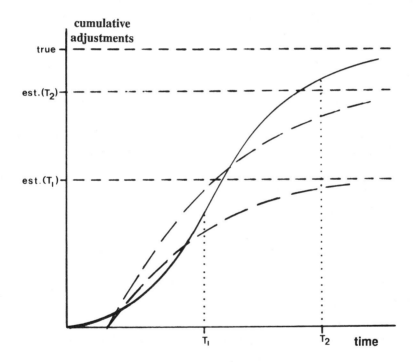

Figure 6.5.: Cumulative adjustments

These considerations have the following implications:

- Adjustment parameters tend to be overestimated.

- Long-run responses to price shocks tend to be underestimated.

- These effects are more important the shorter the period of observation.

The last proposition casts some new light on the estimation results presented in the preceding sections. The changes in the parameters over the different periods can be interpreted not only as an outcome of changed behaviour but as an artifact caused by misspecification of the econometric model. Since this misspecification effect is particularly strong for smaller samples, the results for the 1976-86 sample are - at least - questionable.

A final remark shall be devoted to the question why to use a specification which is likely to produce biased results. For the theoretical model, the answer refers to the issue of operation-ality; for the econometric model, the reason is a lack of observations. In both cases the underlying reasoning is the same. If one wanted to model an adjustment process like the one described above, one would have to consider the history of events instead of the state of the system and its change at a certain point of time. This would imply that complicated and long lag polynomials would have to be taken into account.[207] Therefore, the shrinking number of degrees of freedom could become a serious problem in the econometric model. In the theoretical model, the con-sideration of more realistic lag structures would complicate the analysis substantially.[208] So the model used here should be interpreted as an approximation of a more realistic one.

6.4.2. Adjustment processes and long-run demand and supply functions

Among the estimated functions, some have already been chosen to be used here. The criteria of this choice have been mentioned above. The estimates are valid for different periods.

The demand functions assume lagged reactions to price as well as to income changes:

(6.4.1) $\quad D_t = 0.626\, D_{t-1} + (\, 29.07 - 0.171\, P_{t-1}\,)\, Y_t^{1.061}$ $\qquad$, 1961-79.

(6.4.2) $\quad D_t = 0.771\, D_{t-1} + (\, 19.90 - 0.210\, P_{t-1}\,)\, Y_t^{1.036}$ $\qquad$, 1961-86.

(6.4.3) $\quad D_t = 0.547\, D_{t-1} + (\, 33.02 - 0.198\, P_{t-1}\,)\, Y_t^{0.218}$ $\qquad$, 1976-86.

The corresponding long-run demand functions can be determined by setting D_{t-1} equal to D_t.

---

[207] Two obvious candidates of lag distributions are the *Almon* lag and the *Pascal* lag distributions, both of which should be able to produce the desired shapes. See *Kmenta* (1971), pp. 487-495.

[208] Intertemporal models of this type are difficult to handle and may turn out to be intractable. See *Feichtinger/Hartl* (1986), 517-521, for a discussion of optimal control problems with delays or distributed lags.

$$(6.4.4) \qquad D_t = (77.67 - 0.457 P_{t-1}) Y_t^{1.061} \qquad\qquad , 1961\text{-}79.$$

$$(6.4.5) \qquad D_t = (86.74 - 0.914 P_{t-1}) Y_t^{1.036} \qquad\qquad , 1961\text{-}86.$$

$$(6.4.6) \qquad D_t = (72.99 - 0.437 P_{t-1}) Y_t^{0.218} \qquad\qquad , 1976\text{-}86.$$

The function derived from the 1961-86 sample is different from the two others with regard to the slope. The 1976-86 demand function is characterised by a low income elasticity.

Non-OPEC supply is a function of the price and the quadratic trend, except for the 1976-87 sample for which the trend did not have a significant influence.

$$(6.4.7) \qquad S_t = 0.685\, S_{t-1} + (9.554 + 0.111 P_{t-3})\, exp(-0.0021\, t^2) \quad , 1963\text{-}79.$$

$$(6.4.8) \qquad S_t = 0.824\, S_{t-1} + (5.811 + 0.067 P_{t-3})\, exp(-0.0019\, t^2) \quad , 1963\text{-}87.$$

$$(6.4.9) \qquad S_t = 0.809\, S_{t-1} + (6.815 + 0.042 P_{t-3}) \qquad\qquad , 1976\text{-}87.$$

The long-run supply functions are

$$(6.4.10) \qquad S_t = (30.36 + 0.352 P_{t-3})\, exp(-0.0021\, t^2) \qquad , 1963\text{-}79.$$

$$(6.4.11) \qquad S_t = (32.94 + 0.377 P_{t-3})\, exp(-0.0019\, t^2) \qquad , 1963\text{-}87.$$

$$(6.4.12) \qquad S_t = (35.71 + 0.220 P_{t-3}) \qquad\qquad\qquad , 1976\text{-}87.$$

The long-run supply functions are characterised by increasing constant terms. This represents an increase in the flexibility of demand for OPEC oil. On the other hand, there is a sharp decline in the slope for the period 1976-87 which indicates a decline in flexibility.[209]

The demand for OPEC oil can now be determined as the difference of global demand and non-OPEC supply. From the specification of the equations and the resulting parameter estimates it is obvious that the adjustment processes cannot be aggregated into a form

$$O_t = c_1 O_{t-1} + w(.),$$

---

[209] Similar findings have been stated above when supply elasticities were computed from the loglinear version of the model.

where w is a function of the exogenous variables. What can be done is to compute long-run demand functions for OPEC oil. For this purpose we neglect the lags of the price impact. The determination of the long-run demand schedule is particularly easy for the year 1980 which is the base year of the income time series and the trend variable. In this case, $t = 0$ and $Y_t = 1$. It follows that

(6.4.13) $O_{1980} = 40.31 - 0.825\,P_{1980}$, 1961/3-79.

(6.4.14) $O_{1980} = 53.80 - 1.292\,P_{1980}$, 1961/3-86/7.

(6.4.15) $O_{1980} = 37.28 - 0.657\,P_{1980}$, 1976-86/7.

Given these equations, it is possible to determine a crude approximation of an optimal oil price. For a linear demand function, the optimal price is the intercept divided by twice the slope of the demand function. Since this procedure neglects production costs, resource scarcity and appropriable rigidity rents, these prices are lower bounds of true optimal oil price. For the different samples the estimated cartel prices are 24.43 $/b (1961/3-79), 20.82 $/b (1961/3-86/7), 28.37 $/b (1963-86/7). The last estimate contradicts the results of the theoretical oil market model. The other two prices support the theory. The optimal price of 1980 based on the knowledge of that time is below the historical price, i.e. there remains a gap that might be filled with production costs, scarcity rent, rigidity rent, and short-run price overshooting. The new optimal price, based on all the available information, is lower than the 1979 price. This might indicate that the flexibility of demand had been underestimated in the late seventies.

6.4.3. Long-run equilibrium prices and quantities

The purpose of this section is twofold. On the one hand, one can use the estimates to test theoretical hypotheses on OPEC behaviour. Is there empirical evidence that OPEC would have underestimated the flexibility of demand during and after the second oil crisis had it used the information available at that time? On the other hand, it is possible to suggest price paths that are likely to be attained if OPEC acts as a cartel.

For the following analysis we neglect extraction costs, the scarcity rent which cannot be quantified in such a complex model, anyhow, and the effect of exogenous demand growth on the equilibrium price. So the prices to be derived here can be interpreted as lower boundaries of optimal prices that can be set by OPEC as a cartel. The prices are determined according to equation (4.5.13):

$$(4.5.13) \qquad p^* - k' - z/y = \left(\frac{g_s S_p}{g_s - r} - \frac{f_d D_p}{f_d - r} \right)^{-1} (D - S).$$

The informations necessary to compute the price can be obtained fom equations (6.4.1) to (6.4.12).

To quantify the impact of the discount or interest rate, different values for r are chosen, namely 0.00, 0.05, 0.10 and 0.20. Results are documented for the years 1980, 1986, 1995 and 2000. For the latter two years, it has been assumed that worldwide economic growth is 2% per year and that there is no exogenous decline in OPEC production.[210] Moreover, supply has been set equal to demand for all the years. This is a simplification since data on oil consumption and oil production have been used in the estimations as proxies for supply and demand. However, due to stockpiling and transportation lags, there are gaps between consumption and production that can be positive or negative. This is neglected here.

The computed prices show considerable variability over time which is due to the economic growth impact on demand. In order to obtain comparable results, the rigidity mark-ups, MU, are expressed as percentages of the price:

$$(6.4.16) \qquad MU(r) = 1 - p^*(0)/p^*(r)$$

Table 6.11.: Rigidity mark-ups (share of the price)

		$r = 0.05$	$r = 0.10$	$r = 0.20$
old data	1980	0.063	0.112	0.183
(ending 1979)	1986	0.063	0.111	0.182
	1995	0.062	0.111	0.181
	2000	0.062	0.110	0.180
new data	1980	0.068	0.118	0.188
(beginning 1976)	1986	0.068	0.117	0.187
	1995	0.067	0.116	0.186
	2000	0.067	0.116	0.185
complete	1980	0.096	0.160	0.243
sample	1986	0.095	0.160	0.242
	1995	0.094	0.158	0.240
	2000	0.094	0.158	0.240

---

[210] This implies that t^2 is 49 in the supply function since the base year is 1980.

Results are presented in Table 6.11. It can be seen that - as one must expect - the rigidity mark-up is an increasing function of the interest rate. Variability of the percentages over time is negligible. The most striking observation is the substantially higher rigidity mark-up computed on basis of the whole sample. It supports the arguments put forward in the preceding section: the longer the observation period, the smaller is the estimated adjustment speed compared to the long-run elasticity of demand and the greater is the rigidity rent compared to the pure monopoly rent.

Tables 6.12. and 6.13. report estimated optimal prices and levels of OPEC production, respectively, given a 10% discount rate. In addition to the parameter sets described above, another one has been constructed as a combination of the estimates derived from the complete sample and the sample containing only the latest data. It reflects some of the considerations made above. On the one hand, the complete sample can be expected to produce the least biased estimates of price impacts. On the other hand, the empirical results suggest that after the oil crises petroleum demand has been decoupled from economic growth. This can be taken into account by substituting the original income elasticity (1.036) by the corresponding estimate derived from 1976-86 subsample (0.218).[211] Then the demand function for the years following 1986 is:

$$(6.4.17) \qquad D_t = 0.771\, D_{t-1} + (\,19.90 - 0.210\, P_{t-1}\,)\, Y_{1986}^{1.036}\, (Y_t/Y_{1986})^{0.218} \,.$$

The following results can be reported:

- The lowest prices have are obtained for the parameters based on the complete sample. Since we have shown that for this sample the rigidity share in the price is particularly large, one can conclude that the result is due to the high long-run variability of demand.

- Price increases over time depend on the income elasticity of petroleum demand. The greater the estimated elasticities is, the higher the growth rate of the price.

- Optimal prices computed on basis of the information available at the time of the second oil crisis (truncated sample) are considerably higher than prices based on the complete information. In particular, the simulated prices for the early eighties are close to the prices prevailing on the world petroleum market at that time.

- For the complete sample and the one containing data up to 1979, OPEC production levels for the year 1980 are not too different from the equilibrium levels estimated from the price

---

[211] *Saunders* (1984b) argues that the decoupling of growth and energy demand can only be a transitory phenomenon after a price shock since, in the long run, there is no incentive to change the energy-income ratio in the presence of constant prices. This may be true but one can argue that the substitution process induced by a sudden price increase lasts for ten, fifteen or even twenty years if maturation times of new technologies are taken into account. Moreover, one can expect substantial implementation lags in less industrialised countries. Therefore, it is not misleading to assume a low income elasticity until the year 2000.

adjustment equation (see Table 6.10.). The latter were 24.7 and 23.9 whereas the corresponding optimal values are 21.8 and 20.7. Changes in the interest rate affect the optimal production levels significantly: without discounting, they turn out to be 26.9 and 23.7, respectively.

- For the future, one of the scenarios based on the complete sample appears to be the most appropriate. If the income elasticity of demand is low, the estimated optimal price at the end of the century is 30.28 $/b. This price underestimates the monopoly price insofar as extraction and user costs are neglected. Moreover, it is based on the assumption of non-declining supply by non-OPEC countries. Global demand and non-OPEC supply at the end of the century are estimated to be 72.0 and 39.6 million barrels per day, respectively. The high-elasticity scenario implies 83.6 mbd demand and 42.0 mbd non-OPEC supply. The residual demand for OPEC, however, looks unrealisticly high in this case.

Table 6.12.: Equilibrium prices for $r = 0.10$

	truncated sample	complete sample	complete sample income-inelastic
1980	32.93	24.82	24.82
1986	39.01	28.39	28.39
1995	47.50	33.30	29.85
2000	50.78	34.99	30.28

Table 6.13.: OPEC oil production for $r = 0.10$

	truncated sample	complete sample	complete sample income-inelastic
1980	20.67	21.76	21.76
1986	25.20	26.27	26.27
1995	35.23	36.36	28.46
2000	40.49	41.64	29.35

These results, obtained from inserting the empirical parameter estimates into an optimality condition, can now compared to historical figures. Table 6.14 indicates that the conclusions drawn from the theoretical model are supported by the data:

- The equilibrium price computed on the basis of the information available in 1979, 32.93 $/b, was higher than the full-information price, 24.82 $/b. The historical price after the crisis, in 1981, was even higher than the expected optimal price. This corresponds to the initial overshooting of the price in the theoretical model when the level of demand is high.

- In 1985, the year before the oil price collapse, the market price was near the equilibrium price computed from the complete-sample estimates. Demand for OPEC oil, however, was much too low: some 17 mbd instead of 26 mbd. According to the model, this requires a price reduction in order to attain the saddle path that approaches the long-run equilibrium.

Table 6.14.: Historical prices and equilibrium prices

	second oil crisis 1979/80	price collapse 1986
price before shock	12.95	27.63
price after shock	35.82	13.48
equil. price (truncated sample)	32.93	39.01
equil. price (complete sample)	24.82	28.39

The scenarios that compute end-of-the-century prices should be viewed with caution. On the one hand, we have neglected extraction and user costs. Moreover, the used income elasticity of 0.218 may well be too low and non-OPEC supply may decrease considerably during the 1990s. These are effects in favour of a price higher than 30.28 $. On the other hand, demand may be much more elastic in the very long run than estimated above. This is supported by the fact that in 1987 a price increase well below the equilibrium price made demand for OPEC oil decline again (see Figure 2.3. on p. 29). So there are also effects that tend to lower the price. Which of these will dominate, is hard to say, but a price below 30 $ per barrels seems to be a rather low estimate of a monopoly price. Finally, it should be noted that all what has been argued above is based on the assumption that OPEC behaves as a cartel. Problems of cartel stability can always lower the price considerably - as we have seen in 1986.

7. Final remarks

7.1. Summary and conclusions

In this study, the process of oil-price formation has been explored. The theoretical framework of the analysis was a dynamic dominant-firm model of the world petroleum market. We have used the assumption that OPEC acts as a monolithic block and plays the role of the residual supplier or swing producer in the market. Thus, OPEC has some monopoly power that allows the Organization to determine the price of oil. Given lagged reactions of demand and non-OPEC supply, an optimal pricing policy is sought. It has been shown that there is a long-run equilibrium price that exceeds the static *Cournot* monopoly price. There exists a rigidity rent in addition to the known monopoly rent. It depends on the adjustment speeds of demand and non-OPEC supply, the interest rate (which in this case turns out to be the appropriate discount rate), and the exogenous growth of demand.

This equilibrium is stable. It has been shown, however, that the optimal price is not necessarily monotonous over time. Scenarios in which the price decreases in an initial period, then changes its direction and approaches the equilibrium from below as well as the opposite case in which the price rises initially are possible. If demand and non-OPEC supply are aggregated into one variable, demand for OPEC oil, this non-monotonicity vanishes and the optimal path is a saddle path which is strictly increasing in the price-quantity diagram. If the initial level of demand is high, then the optimal price overshoots the long-run equilibrium price. This strategy permits the dominant firm to exploit the initial rigidity of demand. Combining this type of price adjustment with OPEC's optimal resources policy can yield various shapes of price paths one of which is the U-shaped price profile: in the beginning the adjustment of demand dominates and the price goes down; in the long run, however, the *Hotelling* rule becomes more important and the price is driven up again.

The most interesting results of the model, concerning the shapes of real rather than optimal oil price paths, are obtained when incomplete information and incorrect expectations are introduced into the model. Wrong expectations about the state of the world lead the planner, here OPEC, to choose suboptimal paths. One can argue that OPEC has overestimated the flexibility of demand in the beginning of the seventies. Thus, in setting the price at its new level in 1973/74, OPEC did not exert all its monopoly power. Demand increased again even after the quintupling of the price. The second oil crisis provided an opportunity to correct the pricing policy. The new price, however, was too high since in the beginning of the eighties it turned out that demand was unexpectedly flexible. When OPEC's production had decreased to levels less than half its capacity, another correction was necessary and this, in connection with problems of cartel stability, led to the collapse of the oil price in early 1986.

At a first glance, the oil price path derived from the theoretical model resembles the real-world price path very much. A more detailed investigation was carried out by means of econometric methods. Nonlinear-least-squares methods were used to analyse demand and supply functions. The estimated parameters were then inserted into the formula that determines the long-run equilibrium price in the theoretical model. This yielded the following results.

- In a first step it turned out that rigidity rents indeed are important. Depending on the discount rate and the observation period used to estimate the parameters, the rigidity-rent share in the price amounts to 6-25%.

- The pre-crisis years did not produce any significant coefficients. This supports the hypothesis that the mid-seventies level of the oil price is a result of trial-and-error search rather than of well-informed planning.

- Using observations up to the time of the second oil crisis produced significant parameter estimates and the optimal price computed on the basis of these estimates was close to the price prevailing on the world oil market. So the oil prices of the early eighties were in accordance with the information available at that time.

- When data of the eighties are included, important changes in some of the parameters can be observed. The elasticity of demand with respect to income is decreased considerably. On the other hand, the long-run price elasticities of demand and non-OPEC supply are increased. Although part of this increase may be attributed to misspecification, the result is striking. It supports the hypothesis that, due to an underestimation of demand flexibility, the oil price was much too high in the eighties.

- The 1986 oil price collapse lead to prices below the long-run optimal level. This corresponds to the theoretical result that, if initial demand is low, the price approaches its optimal level from below.

Finally, the estimates have been used to compute some forecasts of future oil prices. The lowest estimate was a real price of 30.82 $ per barrel (in 1980 $) for the year 2000. This estimate neglects extraction costs, user costs and the depletion of non-OPEC reserves which is expected to diminish production, especially from North Sea oil fields, from the middle of the nineties. On the other hand, it must be borne in mind that the attainability of the optimal price level requires monopolistic behaviour, i.e. the stability of OPEC as a cartel. Cheating by OPEC member countries can drive the price below this level. It has to be considered, however, that if demand for OPEC oil increases over the next years, the problem of cartel stability will be relaxed considerably. Therefore, a real oil price of 30 $ or more can be viewed as a realistic estimate for the turn of the century.

7.2. A remark on policy implications

The theoretical approach to the problem of oil price formation has placed the emphasis on the supply side or, more strictly speaking, only on a part of the supply side. OPEC's optimal and actual behaviour in the presence of sluggish demand reactions has been modelled in detail. The other groups acting on the world petroleum market have been characterised by rather mechanistic reaction functions. Since their behaviour has not been modelled explicitly, it is hard to derive economic-policy recommendations for non-OPEC countries.

It has been shown that oil exporters profit from cartelisation. This implies that OPEC should place much effort on the stability of collusion. How this can be done, exceeds the scope of this study, however. We have only used the assumption that a cartel exists but the question why it exists has not been addressed.

Another recommendation concerns oil price policies in the presence of incorrect expectations. According to the model considered here, OPEC had waited too long before the necessary correction was ultimately made, especially in the middle of the eighties. This delay was one of the reasons of the cartel stability problem that OPEC experienced in 1986. If corrections are made in time, frictional losses can be reduced.

The amount and the quality of information available increase over time. This implies that expectations tend to converge to the true parameters that describe the state of the world (provided that the state of the world itself does not change too much). If knowledge increases, deviations from optimal paths become smaller and only minor corrections of pricing policies will be necessary. Therefore, one can expect a tendency towards price stabilisation in the future. This optimistic scanario is, however, based on the assumption of cartel stability. If OPEC does not manage to keep production low during times of glut, the era of fluctuating oil prices is likely to continue.

It is difficult to derive policy implications for oil-importing states and non-OPEC petroleum exporters. It has been shown, especially in the application of estimation results, that OPEC profits a lot from the inflexibility of demand. Moreover, demand inflexibility is of major importance in times of price changes. For oil-importing countries it is therefore advisable to increase their flexibility in the utilisation of oil.

Flexibility has two dimensions. On the one hand, the term refers to long-term substitution possibilities, i.e. nuclear power or coal for fuel oil in electricity generation or capital for energy in all sectors of the economy. On the other hand, it refers to the time interval during which these substitution processes are implemented or - to use the terminology of the preceding chapters - the speed of adjustments. Perhaps it is the second dimension in which improvements are possible. After the oil crises of the seventies, there has been substantial progress in this respect. For instance, the share of dual-fire capacities in the electricity generating and industrial sectors has increased substantially over the last decade. This allows the users of oil (in particular fuel oil) to switch to other energy sources such as gas and coal without delay when relative prices change.[212] Notwithstanding the fact that such a high degree of flexibility will probably not be attainable in all applications (e.g. air-traffic), further dissemination of such technologies is desirable.

7.3. Areas of future research

Before discussing possible extensions of the model, it is useful to review its shortcomings and weaknesses. Of course, since every model to a certain extent abstracts from reality, there is always a variety of possible extensions that can make an approach more realistic. For instance, the demand for OPEC oil could be disaggregated further, or the exhaustibility of non-OPEC reserves could be taken into account explicitly. These issues can in principle be discussed within the framework of the model. But there are also conceptual weaknesses that cannot be solved by introducing additional variables but rather require a different framework.

The first conceptual shortcoming is the assumption that OPEC acts as a monolithic entity. This implies that differences among the member countries are neglected, that conflicts of interest within the cartel and the problem of cartel stability are disregarded. An economic theory of exhaustible-resources cartels would be the adequate framework within which to deal with this problem. However, such a theory does not yet exist. There are models that address the cartelisation and stability issues by means of repeated games. But this approach disregards the intertemporal relationships that characterise resource allocation problems. In order to treat the cartel stability issue appropriately in an intertemporal context, one could develop dynamic versions of static models that do not use game-theory arguments.[213] It is, however, questionable whether such an approach allows to derive interpretable results when lagged demand reactions are considered.

The other major shortcoming of the approach chosen here is its simplistic view of the demand side. Demand and non-OPEC supply are modelled by simple reaction functions that lack an exact microeconomic foundation. Certainly, it is plausible that adjustments depend on the distance between the actual and the desired state of the system. This assumption, however, neglects the occurrence of implementation lags and other delays. As we have shown, this can lead to a misspecification of the adjustment process. Therefore, the specification chosen in the theoretical model and in the empirical analysis is highly objectionable - even if an explicit formulation of the underlying microeconomic decisions is not sought.

---

[212] See *Renner* (1988), pp. 52-53.

[213] Such models have been developed by *Donsimoni* (1985) and *Donsimoni/Economides/Polemarchakis* (1986).

As a first step, one could try to implement more realistic adjustment processes by specifying equations that incorporate a memory of historical events. At least in the econometric analysis this can be done by means of *Almon* lag structures or a *Pascal* lag distribution. Especially the *Almon* lag, however, can involve a serious loss of degrees of freedom.

Both, the *Almon* lag and the *Pascal* lag distribution may improve the quality of the estimations, but they lack an exact economic foundation. Thus, the more satisfying approach is an explicit behavioural model of the demand side and the competitive fringe. Both groups of actors face an intertemporal optimisation problem in which the putty-clay nature of the capital stock and the existence of implementation lags have to be considered. This, however, is not an easy task since it complicates the analysis considerably, probably at the expense of the unambiguity of results, and as a second and perhaps even more serious problem one would obtain a *Stackelberg* situation from which, as *Newbery* (1981,1984) has shown, problems of dynamic inconstency can arise.

To conclude - simple extensions of the model are relatively easy to make; major changes as they have been discussed above, however, lead to much more complex structures, and it is questionable whether the effort pays in terms of applicable results. In this context, the present study can be viewed as a viable compromise of realism and tractability. The empirical results suggest that it has been successful and that it offers some good explanations of oil market developments. So the dominant-firm approach, extended by demand sluggishness, turns out to be a useful analytical tool in the analysis of oil price formation.

APPENDIX: Optimal control theory

In this appendix some important theorems of optimal control theory will be presented. The presentation is restricted to problems with infinite planning horizon, as they are dealt with in the theoretical chapters of the study. The formulation of the problem as well as necessary and sufficient conditions for optima are taken from the literature on optimal control theory.[214] Generalised versions of the theorems can be found there. The stability of optimal solutions is of particular interest. For a survey on stability theory see *Cesari* (1963), *Barnett/Storey* (1970) or *Takayama* (1985), ch. 3. Special attention is devoted to problems with a positive discount rate and cases in which the number of state variables exceeds the number of control variables. In order to deduce stability conditions, standard methods of linear algebra are used which the reader is supposed to be familiar with.[215]

The following notation will be used: A dot above a variable denotes its derivative with respect to time, a subscript (except numbers and the letters i, j and n) its partial derivative with respect to the variable in question. The subscript zero represents the initial value of a time-dependent variable. Subscripts i, j, n and numbers denote elements of a vector or a matrix. Superscripts T and -1 indicate the transpose and the inverse of a matrix, respectively.

A.1. The problem

Let D be the class of programs

$$z: \ (x(t), u(t)), \qquad\qquad t \ \epsilon \ [0, \infty),$$

where $x(t)$ is a real continuous n-dimensional vector-valued function and $u(t)$ is a real piecewise continuous m-dimensional vector-valued function of t. $x(t)$ and $u(t)$ are named state and control variables, respectively. In economic as well as in technical applications, t in general measures time. In the following the argument t will be omitted for convenience.

---

[214] See *Hestenes* (1966), *Long/Vousden* (1977), *Kamien/Schwarz* (1981), *Takayama* (1985), ch. 8, *Feichtinger/Hartl* (1986), *Seierstad/Sydsaeter* (1986) and *Carlson/Haurie* (1987). For an economic interpretation of optimal control theory see *Dorfman* (1969).

[215] See the first three chapters of *Barnett/Storey* (1970) or textbooks like *Hadley* (1961) and *Noble* (1969).

A finite function

$$\text{(A.1.)} \qquad I(z) = \int_0^\infty e^{-rt} F(x,u) \, dt$$

is to be maximised on the class D with respect to the restrictions

$$\text{(A.2)} \qquad \dot{x} = G(x,u,t),$$

$$\text{(A.3)} \qquad x(0) = x_o,$$

$$\text{(A.4)} \qquad \lim_{t \to \infty} x_i \geq 0 \qquad\qquad\qquad\qquad \text{for } i = 1,...,n' \leq n.$$

A.2. Necessary and sufficient conditions

THEOREM A.1. (Necessary conditions)

Let (x^o,u^o), $t \in [0, \infty)$, be a program, that maximises (A.1) and satisfies the restrictions (A.2)-(A.4). Then there are multipiers $p^\#$ ϵ R and $p(t)$ ϵ R^n not vanishing simultaneously on the interval $t \in [0, \infty)$ and a function

$$\text{(A.5)} \qquad H(x^o,u^o,p,t) = p^\# F(x^o,u^o) + p G(x^o,u^o,t),$$

such that the following conditions are satisfied:

(i) $\qquad p^\#$ is constant.

(ii) $\qquad$ The multipliers p are continuous and piecewise continuously differentiable.

(iii) $\qquad \dot{p} = rp - H_x(x^o,u^o,p,t).$

(iv) $\qquad H_u(x^o,u^o,p,t) = 0.$

(v) $\qquad H$ is continuous for $t \in [0, \infty)$.

(vi) $\qquad H(x^o,u^o,p,t) \geq H(x^o,u,p,t).$

REMARK A.1.

H is named 'current value Hamiltonian'. p is the vector of costate variables or shadow prices. $p^{\#}$ can in most cases be set equal to 1.

REMARK A.2.

If the integral in (A.1) does not converge, the determinitation of the maximimum becomes more difficult. Optima can then be derived by the application of overtaking and catching-up criteria, that have been introduced by *von Weizsäcker* (1965). For a recent systematic treatment of this topic, see *Stern* (1984).

REMARK A.3.

Transversality conditions which are well known from the finite horizon maximum principle cannot always be applied to the infinite horizon problem. It seems natural to let the terminal time go to infinity and then take limits. The transversality (or complementary slackness) conditions would then turn out to be

(A.6) $\qquad \lim_{t \to \infty} e^{-rt} p_i x^o_i = 0 \qquad\qquad$ for $i = 1,...,n'$,

(A.7) $\qquad \lim_{t \to \infty} e^{-rt} p_i = 0 \qquad\qquad$ for $i = n'+1,...,n$.

There are cases in which this equivalent to the finite-horizon transversality condition can be applied to infinite-horizon problem. See *Arrow/Kurz* (1970), ch. 1. However, *Halkin's* (1974) counterexample suggests that (A.6) and (A.7) are not always necessary conditions for an optimum. A necessary condition has been established by *Michel* (1982):

THEOREM A.2.

A necessary condition for (x^o, u^o) to be an optimal solution of the problem (A.1)-(A.4) is that the limit of the maximum of the present-value Hamiltonian is zero when t goes to infinity.

REMARK A.4.

Michel's theorem has rarely been applied to the investigation of concrete economic models. An exception is *Toussaint* (1985), who shows that *Michel's* theorem can indeed be used to derive transversality conditions of type (A.6). Her analysis, however, is restricted to a special optimal control problem which is relatively easy to tackle.

THEOREM A.3. (Sufficiency)

The necessary conditions of Theorem A.1. are sufficient for optimality provided that

(i)   (a) either $H(x,u,p,t)$ is concave in (x,u) or

(b) $M(x,p,t) = Max\ H(x,u,p,t)$ is concave in x,

(ii) $lim_{t \to \infty}\ p\ (x^o - x^1) \geq 0$ where x^1 is any other admissable program.

REMARK A.5.

See *Long/Vousden* (1977), p. 28, and *Seierstad/Sydsaeter* (1977). It can be seen that (a) implies (b):

COROLLARY A.1.

If $H(x,u,p,t)$ is (strictly) concave in (x,u), $M(x,p,t)$ is (strictly) concave in x and convex in p. If, additionally, the number of state variables exceeds the number of control variables, $M(x,p,t)$ cannot be strictly convex in p.

PROOF

Let (x^o, u^o) be a solution of the optimal control problem. Then $H_u = 0$. The implicit function theorem then implies:

$$H_{uu}\ du^o + H_{ux}\ dx^o + H_{up}\ dp = 0.$$

We can now define a function $m(\cdot)$

$$u^o = m(x^o, p,t),\quad m_x = -H_{uu}^{-1} H_{ux},\quad m_p = -H_{uu}^{-1} H_{up},$$

and M_{xx} and M_{pp} turn out to be:

$$M_{xx} = H_{xx} + H_{xu}m_x = H_{xx} - H_{xu}H_{uu}^{-1}H_{ux},$$
$$M_{pp} = H_{pu}m_p = -H_{pu}H_{uu}^{-1}H_{up} = -G_u^T H_{uu}^{-1} G_u.$$

From the first equation it can be seen that (strict) concavity of M in x implies (strict) concavity of H in (x,u).[216] The second equation implies convexitity of M in u since H_{uu} is negative definite or semidefinite. If the number of state variables exceeds the number of control variables, the $n{\times}n$-matrix $- G_u^T H_{uu}^{-1} G_u$ has rank $m < n$ and, therefore, can only be semidefinite.

REMARK A.6. (Existence)

For recent results concerning the existence of solutions of the infinite horizon optimal control problem see *Toman* (1985).

A.3. Saddle points and the stability of optimal solutions

ASSUMPTION A.1.

$$G_t(x,u,t) = 0.$$

REMARK A.6.

This assumption is needed to obtain a stationary equilibrium.

ASSUMPTION A.2.

Let (x,u) be an optimal program.

ASSUMPTION A.3.

There exists an equilibrium (x^*,u^*) such that $\dot{p} = \dot{x} = \dot{u} = 0$.

---

[216] *det* $(H_{xx} - H_{xu} H_{vu}^{-1} H_{vu})$ equals the determinant of the Hessian of H with respect to (x,v). This follows from the theorem on determinants of partitioned matrices. See *Barnett/Storey* (1970), p. 10.

DEFINITION A.1.

The system consisting of the differential equation (A.2) and condition (iii) of Theorem A.1. can be linearised in the equilibrium such that

(A.8) $\qquad \dot{x} = A\,(x\text{-}x^{*}) + B\,(p\text{-}p^{*}),$

(A.9) $\qquad \dot{p} = C(x\text{-}x^{*}) + (rI\text{-}A^{T})\,(p\text{-}p^{*}),$

where

$$A = M_{px}, \quad B = M_{pp}, \quad C = -M_{xx},$$

and M is the maximum of the Hamiltonian. It follows from Corollary A.1. that C is positive definite and B is positive semidefinite.

REMARK A.7.

(A.9) follows directly from condition (iii) of Theorem A.1.. (A.8) can be obtained by noting that the definition of the Hamiltonian (A.2) implies $\dot{x} = H_{p}$.

DEFINITION A.2.

The matrix J,

(A.10) $\qquad J = \begin{bmatrix} A & B \\ C & rI\text{-}A^{T} \end{bmatrix}$

is called the Jacobian matrix of the system (A.8)-(A.9). J is an $2n\text{x}2n$ matrix.

THEOREM A.4. (Conditional stability)

Let

$$\dot{z}(t) = Kz(t)$$

be a linear system of k differential equations having an equilibrium $z^{*} = 0$. Assume that j eigenvalues of K have negative real parts and $(k\text{-}j)$ eigenvalues of K have positive real parts. Then there exists a j-dimensional manifold containing the equilibrium such that any solution starting on the manifold approaches the equilibrium as t goes to infinity. Moreover, there exists a neighbourhood of the equilibrium that cannot be entered by any other path.

REMARK A.8.

This theorem is due to *Liapunov* (1907), p. 253. The above formulation is taken from *Coddington/Levinson* (1955), p. 330, where also a proof of the theorem is given.

Conditional stability is closely related to the saddle-point property of optimal control models. (A.8)-(A.9) is a system of $2n$ differential equations with n given initial values x_o. If the matrix J, as defined above, has at least n eigenvalues with negative real parts, then it is possible to determine the initial values of the shadow prices such that the optimal path is the stable manifold.

THEOREM A.5.

Assume $r=0$. If e is an eigenvalue of J, then $-e$ is an eigenvalue of J too. Moreover, J has no purely imaginary eigenvalues.

PROOF

Applying the theorem on determinants of partitioned matrices (See *Barnett/Storey* (1970), p. 10), the characteristic equation for the eigenvalues e of J turns out to be

$$(A.11) \qquad det \, (B + (A\text{-}eI) \, C^{-1} (A^{T}+eI)) \; = \; 0.$$

Take the transpose of argument of the determinant. Since the determinant of a matrix equals the determinant of its transpose,

$$det \, (B + (A+eI) \, C^{-1} (A^{T}\text{-}eI)) \; = \; 0,$$

and $-e$ is an eigenvalue of J too.

For a proof that purely imaginary eigenvalues cannot occur see *Levhari/Liviatan* (1972, p. 91).

REMARK A.9.

Different proofs have been given by *O'Donnell* (1966), p. 584, and *Samuelson* (1972).

DEFINITION A.3. (Controllability)

Let D and E be two $n \times n$ matrices. The ordered pair (D,E) is said to be controllable if the $n \times n^2$ matrix

$$(E \; DE \; D^2E \; .... \; D^{n-1}E)$$

has rank n.

REMARK A.10.

See *Coppel* (1974), pp. 378-379, *Lancaster/Rodman* (1980), p. 285 and *Barnett* (1971), p. 169. Controllability means that a system can be driven to its equilibrium from any initial state within finite time. The equivalence of this interpretation and the definition has been proved by *Kalman* (1960). Controllability plays an important role in the stability analysis of optimal control solutions.

THEOREM A.6. (*Liapunov's* second method)

Let

$$\dot{z}(t) = f(z(t))$$

be a system differential equations having an equilibrium $z^* = 0$. The system is uniformly globally stable, if there exists a real-valued continuously differentiable function $L(z)$ such that

(i) $L(z) > 0$ for $z \neq 0.$

(ii) $L(z) = 0$ for $z = 0.$

(iii) $\dot{L}(z) < 0$ for $z \neq 0.$

(iv) $L(z) \rightarrow \infty$ for $z \rightarrow \infty.$

$L(z)$ is called *Liapunov* function of the system.

REMARK A.11.

The theorem is due to *Liapunov* (1907), p. 259. See also *Takayama* (1985), pp. 350-351, and *Jordan/Smith* (1977), ch. 10, for instance. A *Liapunov* function can be interpreted as a distance function. If the distance from the equlibrium to the actual state of the system always shrinks, the equlibrium must be stable.

THEOREM A.7.

If $(A-(r/2)I, B)$ is controllable, then there exists a negative definite matrix W such that $(p-p^*) = W(x-x^*)$. If $r=0$, $(p-p^*) = W(x-x^*)$ is the stable manifold of the system.

PROOF

For a proof see *O'Donnell* (1966) and *Barnett* (1971), ch. 5.3. Here we will only present a sketch of the proof. Set

(A.12) $(p - p^*) = W(x - x^*)$ and $\dot{p} = Wx$

in (A.8) and (A.9) and premultiply (A.8) by W:

(A.13) $W\dot{x} = (WA + WBW)(x - x^*),$

(A.14) $W\dot{x} = (C + rW - A^T W)(x - x^*).$

This implies:

$$WBW + WA + A^T W - C - rW = 0,$$

or

(A.15) $WBW + W(A - (r/2)I) + (A - (r/2)I)^T W - C = 0.$

(A.15) is an algebraic *Riccati* equation. See *Coppel* (1974), *Lancaster/Rodman* (1980) and *Gohberg/Lancaster/Rodman* (1986) for a detailed discussion of this type of quadratic matrix equations. A negative definite matrix W solves the Riccati equation under the assumptions stated above.[217] It can than be shown that

(A.16) $L(x) = -(x - x^*)^T W(x - x^*)$

is a *Liapunov* function of (A.13) - (A.14). $L(x)$ satisfies conditions (i), (ii) and (iv) of Theorem A.6.. Its derivative with respect to time is:

$$\dot{L}(x) = -\dot{x}^T W(x - x^*) - (x - x^*)^T W\dot{x}.$$

Inserting from (A.13) and (A.14):

---

[217] *O'Donnell* (1966) and *Barnett* (1971) get a positive definite solution, since they consider a minimisation instead of a maximisation problem and assume C to be negative definite. By multiplying (A.15) by -1 it can easily be seen that both results are equivalent.

(A.17) $\dot{L}(x) = -(x - x^*)^T (WBW + C + rW) (x - x^*).$

Since $WBW + C$ is positive definite, $L(x)$ is a *Liapunov* function if $r = 0$.

COROLLARY A.2.

Using the notation that has been introduced in the proof of Corollary A.1., it follows from Theorem A.6. that the stable manifold of the linearised system in the (x,u) space is

(A.18) $(u - u^*) = (m_x + m_p W) (x - x^*).$

REMARK A.12.

It would be useful for the determination of optimal paths to have an explicit solution of the *Riccati* equation. But in general, such a solution cannot be determined, since the matrix equation consists of $n(n + 1)/2$ single quadratic equations with the same number of unkowns.

REMARK A.13.

It can be seen from equation (A.17) that the system is not necessarily stable for $r > 0$. Using the same argument as for Theorem A.5., it can be shown that if e is an eigenvalue of J, then $(r - e)$ is an eigenvalue of J too. It cannot be excluded that there exist pairs of eigenvalues with real parts in the interval $[0,r]$. Therefore, if the rate of discount is positive, the number of eigenvalues having negative real parts can be less than n. If this is the case the optimal solution is not stable in the saddle-point sense.

Stability conditions for the discounted control problem have been a primary concern of mathematical economists during the seventies. The following stability conditions have been proved:

THEOREM A.8.

Let b be the smallest eigenvalue of B and c the smallest eigenvalue of C. If

(A.19) $bc < r^2/4,$

the system is stable.

REMARK A.14.

See *Rockafellar* (1976) and *Brock/Scheinkman* (1976). The theorem has two disadvantages if applied to practical problems: The stability condition is not independent of the discount rate and, therefore, requires strong assumptions on the curvature of the functions involved, especially if r is large. Second, if the number of state variables exceeds the number of control variables, B is singular and its smallest eigenvalue is zero such that this stability condition cannot be satisfied.

THEOREM A.9.

If

(A.20) $A^T B^{-1} + B^{-1} A$

is negative semidefinite, then the system is stable.

PROOF

The theorem as well as the proof are due to *Brock/Scheinkman* (1977), p. 186-187. The distance function is chosen as

$$L(x) = (x - x^*)^T B^{-1} (x - x^*).$$

$$\dot{L}(x) = \dot{x}^T B^{-1} (x - x^*) + (x - x^*)^T B^{-1} \dot{x}.$$

Using (A.8) and $(p - p^*) = W(x - x^*)$ yields

$$\dot{L}(x) = (x - x^*)^T (A^T B^{-1} + B^{-1} A + 2W) (x - x^*).$$

Since W is negative definite, $L(x)$ is a *Liapunov* function if the matrix (A.20) is negative semidefinite.[218]

REMARK A.15.

If B is singular, its inverse does not exist and the theorem cannot be applied.

---

[218] It follows that for $A = 0$, i.e. if the adjustment function is separable, the system is stable. See *Scheinkman* (1978).

THEOREM A.10.

    If

(A.21) $(rI - A)C^{-1} + C^{-1}(rI - A)^T$

is negative semidefinite, then the system is stable.

PROOF

    See *Magill* (1977), p. 186-188. The distance function is chosen as

$$L(x) = (p - p^*)^T C^{-1} (p - p^*).$$
$$\dot{L}(x) = \dot{p}^T C^{-1} (p - p^*) + (p - p^*)^T C^{-1} \dot{p}.$$

Using (A.9) yields

$$\dot{L}(x) = 2 (p - p^*)^T (x - x^*) + (p - p^*)^T [(rI - A) C^{-1} + C^{-1} (rI - A)^T] (p - p^*)$$

Since $(p - p^*)^T (x - x^*)$ is negative, $L(x)$ is a *Liapunov* function if the matrix (A.21) is negative semidefinite.

REMARK A.16.

    Theorem A.10. is not independent of the rate of discount. The greater r is, the less the probability that the condition is violated.

REMARK A.17.

    Both, Theorem A.9. and Theorem A.10., need not be satisfied for $r=0$, although the system is unambiguously stable in the saddle-point sense. Theorem A.9. and A.10. hold for different types of stability. This hypothesis can easily be verified for the case of an optimal control problem with only one state variable. Then the submatrices of J simply are real numbers and Theorem A.9. states that A must be nonpositive, while Theorem A.10. requires A to be greater or equal r. For an analysis of the one-dimensional problem with an illustrative graphical representation see *Kamien/Schwartz* (1981), p. 159-165.

REMARK A.18.

There exists no general stability condition on the basis of *Liapunov* functions which is independent of the discount rate and can be applied, if B is singular. A necessary and sufficient condition for the stability of the two-state-variable problem has been given by *Dockner* (1985). He has shown that there is a relatively simple formula for the eigenvalues of the 4x4 matrix J. For a proof of the following theorem see *Dockner* (1985)

THEOREM A.11.

Let a_{ij}, b_{ij} and c_{ij} be the elements of the matrices A, B and C, respectively. Let K be a constant defined as

(A.22) $\qquad K = \begin{vmatrix} a_{11} & b_{11} \\ c_{11} & r\text{-}a_{11} \end{vmatrix} + \begin{vmatrix} a_{22} & b_{22} \\ c_{22} & r\text{-}a_{22} \end{vmatrix} + 2 \begin{vmatrix} a_{12} & b_{12} \\ c_{12} & \text{-}a_{21} \end{vmatrix}.$

Then, the eigenvalues of J are

(A.23) $\qquad e_{1,2,3,4} = r/2 \pm \sqrt{r^2/4 - K/2 \pm \sqrt{K^2/4 - det(J)}}.$

THEOREM A.12

If C and B are positive definite or semidefinite and A is a stability matrix, then K is always negative.

PROOF

(A.22) can be rewritten by solving the determinants.

$$K = r(a_{11} + a_{22}) - a_{11}^2 - a_{22}^2 + 2a_{12}a_{21} - b_{11}c_1 - b_{22}c_{22} - 2b_{12}c_{12}.$$

Since A is a stability matrix, its trace $(a_{11} + a_{22})$ must be negative. Adding and subtracting $2a_{11}a_{22}$, one therefore obtains

$$K < -(a_{11} - a_{22})^2 - 2(a_{11}a_{22} - a_{12}a_{21}) - b_{11}c_1 - b_{22}c_{22} - 2b_{12}c_{12}.$$

The second term in brackets is *det A*, which is positive since A is a stability matrix. This implies:

$$K < -b_{11}c_{11} - b_{22}c_{22} - 2b_{12}c_{12}.$$

Since $b_{11}b_{22} \geq b_{12}{}^2, c_{11}c_{22} \geq c_{12}{}^2, b_{11} > 0, c_{11} > 0, b_{22} > 0$ and $c_{22} > 0$,

$$K < -b_{12}{}^2 c_{12}{}^2 / (b_{22}c_{22}) - b_{22}c_{22} - 2b_{12}c_{12}.$$

Rearranging terms yields

$$K < -(b_{22}c_{22})^{-1}(b_{12}c_{12} + b_{22}c_{22})^2.$$

From $c_{22} > 0$ and $b_{22} > 0$ follows that $K < 0$.

COROLLARY A.3.

The following propositions follow from Theorem A.12.:

- If and only if $det(J) < 0$, there is one negative eigenvalue and three eigenvalues have positive real parts. The optimal solution is unstable.[219]

- If and only if $0 < det(J) < K^2/4$, all eigenvalues are real and two of them are negative. This is the conventional result of saddlepoint stability.

- If and only if $det(J) > K^2/4$, all eigenvalues are complex, two of them having negative real parts. The optimal path is stable in the saddlepoint sense but cyclical.[220]

REMARK A.18.

A bifurcation occurs for $det(J) = 0$. This is the borderline between non-cyclical stable solutions and unstable solutions. A Hopf bifurcation, leading to closed orbits, is not possible unless one of the conditions of Theorem A.12 is violated.[221]

---

[219] One could argue that, if all eigenvalues of A had negative real parts, the system would be stable. This, however, is not true. *Brock* (1977), p. 234-235, has shown that, for large discount rates, it can be optimal to destabilise such a system which, without control, would be stable.

[220] Cyclical solutions of optimal control models have been discussed by *Magill* (1979).

[221] For the occurrence of Hopf bifurcations in solutions of optimal control problems see *Benhabib/Nishimura* (1979) and *Medio* (1987).

References

Aarrestad, J., 1978. Optimal Savings and Resource Extraction in an Open Economy. *Journal of Economic Theory* 19, 163-179.

Aarrestad, J., 1979. Resource Extraction, Financial Transactions, and Consumption in an Open Economy. *Scandinavian Journal of Economics* 81, 552-565.

Adelman, M.A., 1972. *The World Petroleum Market*. Baltimore, London: Johns Hopkins University Press.

Adelman, M.A., 1980. The Clumsy Cartel. *Energy Journal* 1(1), 43-53.

Adelman, M.A., 1982. OPEC as a Cartel. In: J.M. Griffin, D. Teece (eds.), *OPEC and the Behavior of World Oil Prices*, London: Allen & Unwin, 37-63.

Adelman, M.A., 1986. The Competitive Floor to World Oil Prices. *Energy Journal* 7(4), 9-31.

Ait-Laoussine, N., F. Parra, 1985. The Development of Oil Supplies During the Energy Crises of the 1970s and Some Questions for the Future. *OPEC Review* 9, 29-62.

Al-Chalabi, F.J., 1980. *OPEC and the International Oil Industry: A Changing Structure*. Oxford: Oxford University Press.

Al-Chalabi, F.J., 1982. A Second Oil Crisis? A Producer's View of the Oil Developments of 1979. In: W.L. Kohl (ed.), *After the Second Oil Crisis*, Lexington, Toronto: Heath. 11-22.

Al-Chalabi, F.J., 1988. The Causes and Implications for OPEC of the Oil Price Decline of 1986. *OPEC Review* 12, 1-16.

Al-Chalabi, F.J., A. Al-Janabi, 1982. Optimum Production and Pricing Policies. In: R. El Malakh, *OPEC: Twenty Years and Beyond*, Boulder (Col.): Westview, 47-76.

Al-Sowayegh, A., 1984. *Arab Petropolitics*. London, Canberra: Croom Helm.

Arrow, J.K., S. Chang, 1982. Optimal Pricing, Use, and Exploration of Uncertain Natural Resource Stocks. *Journal of Environmental Economic and Management* 9, 1-10.

Arrow, J.K., M. Kurz, 1970. *Public Investment, the Rate of Return, and Optimal Fiscal Policy*. Baltimore: Johns Hopkins University Press.

Baldwin, N., R. Prosser, 1988. World Oil Market Simulation. *Energy Economics* 10, 185-198.

Banks, F.E., 1985. Some Aspects od Petroleum Futures Markets: Open Interest, Clearing Houses and Market Failure. *OPEC Review* 9, 149-161.

Banks, F.E., 1986. Economic Theory and the Price of Oil. *OPEC Review* 10, 321-334.

Barnett, S., 1971. *Matrices in Control Theory with Applications to Linear Programming*. London: Van Nostrand Reinhold.

Barnett, S., C. Storey, 1970. *Matrix Methods in Stability Theory*. New York: Barnes and Noble.

Barrett, S.A., 1986. The Economics of Oil Supply Dynamics: Theory and Practice. *Energy Economics* 8, 237-250.

Barrow, M., G. Heal, 1981. Empirical Investigation of the Long-term Movement of Resource Prices: A Preliminary Report. *Economics Letters* 7, 95-103.

Behling, D.J., R.S. Dobias, N.J. Anderson, 1985. *Capital Investments of the World Petroleum Industry 1984*. New York: Chase Manhattan Bank.

Baumol, W.J., 1968. On the Social Rate of Discount. *American Economic Review* 58, 788-802.

Benhabib, J., K. Nishimura, 1979. The Hopf Bifurcation and the Existence and Stability of Closed Orbits in Multisector Models of Optimal Economic Growth. *Journal of Economic Theory* 21, 421-444.

Berndt, E.R., C.J. Morrison, G.C. Watkins, 1981. Dynamic Models of Energy Demand: An Assessment and Comparison. In: E.R. Berndt, B.C. Field (eds.), *Modeling and Measuring Natural Resource Substitution*. Cambridge: MIT-Press, 259-289.

Berndt, E.R., D.O. Wood, 1984. *Energy Price Changes and the Induced Revaluation of Durable Capital in US Manufacturing during the OPEC Decade*. Cambridge (Mass.): MIT Energy Laboratory Report 84-003.

Berndt, E.R., D.O. Wood, 1986. Energy Price Shocks and Productivity Growth in US and UK Manufacturing. *Oxford Review of Economic Policy* 2(3), 1-31.

Bina, C., 1985, *The Economics of the Oil Crisis*, London: Merlin Press.

Bird, G., 1984. Recycling and OPEC: The Need for New Instruments. *Energy Policy* 12, 33-45.

Bird, P.J.W.N., 1987. Continuity and Reversal in Oil Spot Price Movements. *Energy Economics* 9, 73-81.

Blair, R.D., D.L. Kaserman, 1983. *Law and Economics of Vertical Integration*. New York, London: Academic Press.

Bohi, D.R., M.A. Toman, 1987. Futures Trading and Oil Market Conditions. *Journal of Futures Markets* 7, 203-221.

Boulding, K.E., 1971. The Economics of the Coming Spaceship Earth. In: H. Jarrett (ed.), *Environmental Quality in a Growing Economy*, Baltimore: Johns Hopkins University Press, 3-14.

British Petroleum Company, various issues. *BP Statistical Review of World Energy*. London: British Petroleum Company.

Brock, W.A., 1977. The Global Asymptotic Stability of Optimal Control: A Survey of Recent Results. In: M.D. Intriligator (ed.), *Frontiers of Quantitative Economics*, Vol. IIIa. Amsterdam, New York: North Holland, 207-237.

Brock, W.A., J.A. Scheinkman, 1976. Global Asymptotic Stability of Optimal Control with Applications to the Theory of Economic Growth. *Journal of Economic Theory* 12, 164-190.

Brock, W.A., J.A. Scheinkman, 1977. The Global Asymptotic Stability of Optimal Control with Applications to Dynamic Economic Theory. In: J.D. Pitchford, S.J. Turnovsky (eds.), *Applications of Control Theory to Economic Analysis*. Amsterdam: North Holland, 173-205.

Bruno, M., 1984. Raw Materials, Profits, and the Productivity Slowdown. *Quarterly Journal of Economics* 99, 1-29.

Carlson, D.A., A. Haurie, 1987. *Infinite Horizon Optimal Control: Theory and Applications*. Berlin et al.: Springer.

Casson, M., 1984. The Theory of Vertical Integration: A Survey and Synthesis. *Journal of Economic Studies* 11, 3-43.

Cesari, L., 1963. *Asymptotic Behaviour and Stability Problems in Ordinary Differential Equations*. 2nd ed., Berlin et al.: Springer.

Chen, K.C., R.S. Sears, D.-N. Tzang, 1987. Oil Prices and Energy Futures. *Journal of Futures Markets* 7, 501-518.

Choe, B.-J., 1984. *A Model of World Energy Markets and OPEC Pricing*. Washington: World Bank Staff Papers No. 633.

Choucri, N., 1981. *International Energy Futures*. Cambridge: MIT-Press.

Coddington, E.A., N. Levinson, 1955. *Theory of Ordinary Differential Equations*. New York et al.: McGraw-Hill.

Collitti, M., 1981. Size and Distribution of Known and Undiscovered Petroleum Resources in the World with an Estimate of Future Exploration. *OPEC Review* 5, 9-65.

Coppel, W.A., 1974. Matrix Quadratic Equations. *Bulletin of the Australian Mathematical Society* 10, 377-401.

Corden, W.M., 1984. Booming Sector and Dutch Disease Economics: Survey and Consolidation. *Oxford Economic Papers* 36, 359-380.

Crémer, J., M.L. Weitzman, 1976. OPEC and the Monopoly Price of World Oil. European Economic Review 8, 155-164.

Daly, G.G., T.H. Mayer, 1983. Reason and Rationality during Energy Crises. *Journal of Political Economy* 91, 168-181.

Danielsen, A.L., 1979. The Role of Speculation in the Oil Price Ratcheting Process. *Resources and Energy* 2, 243-263.

Danielsen, A.L., 1980. The Theory and Measurement of OPEC Stability. *Southern Economic Journal* 47, 51-64.

Danielsen, A.L., S. Kim, 1988. OPEC Stability: An Empirical Assessment. *Energy Economics* 10, 174-184.

Dasgupta, P.S., 1974. On Some Alternative Criteria for Justice between Generations. *Journal of Public Econcomics* 3, 405-423.

Dasgupta, P.S., 1978. Fairness between Generations and the Social Rate of Discount. *Resources Policy* 4, 172-177.

Dasgupta, P.S., R. Eastwood, G. Heal, 1978. Resource Management in a Trading Economy. *Quarterly Journal of Economics* 92, 297-306.

Dasgupta, P.S., G.M. Heal, 1974. The Optimal Depletion of Exhaustible Resources. *Review of Economic Studies (Symposium)*, 3-28.

Dasgupta, P.S., G.M. Heal, 1979. *Economic Theory and Exhaustible Resources*. Welwyn: Nisbet.

Devarajan, S., A.C. Fisher, 1981. Hotelling's "Economics of Exhaustible Resources": Fifty Years Later. *Journal of Economic Literature* 19, 65-73.

Devarajan, S., A.C. Fisher, 1982. Exploration and Scarcity. *Journal of Political Economy* 90, 1279-1290.

Diewert, W.E., T.J. Wales, 1987. Flexible Fuctional Forms and Global Curvature Conditions. *Econometrica* 55, 43-68.

Djajic, S., 1984. Exhaustible Resources and the Dynamics of Comparative Advantage. *Journal of International Economics* 17, 55-71.

Djajic, S., 1988. A Model of Trade in Exhaustible Resources. *International Economic Review* 29, 87-103.

Doan, T.A., R.B. Litterman, 1984. *RATS: Regression Analysis for Time Series*. Minneapolis: VAR Econometrics.

Dockner, E., 1985. Local Stability Analysis in Optimal Control Problems with Two State Variables. In: G. Feichtinger (ed.), *Optimal Control Theory and Economic Analysis 2*. Amsterdam: North-Holland. 89-103.

Donsimoni, M.-P., 1985. Stable Heterogeneous Cartels. *International Journal of Industrial Organization* 3, 451-467.

Donsimoni, M.-P., N.S. Economides, H.M. Polemarchakis, 1986. Stable Cartels. *International Economic Review* 27, 317-327.

Dorfman, R., 1969. An Economic Interpretation of Optimal Control Theory. *American Economic Review* 59, 817-831.

Durbin, J., 1970. Testing for Serial Correlation when Some of the Regressors Are Lagged Dependent Variables. *Econometrica* 38, 410-421.

Eckbo, P.L., 1976. *The Future of World Oil.* Cambridge: Ballinger.

Eswaran, M., Lewis, T.R., 1985. Evolution of Market Structure in a Dominant Firm Model with Exhaustible Resources. In: A. Scott (ed.), *Progress in Natural Resource Economics*, Oxford: Clarendon Press, 242-257.

Evans, G.C., 1924. A Dynamic Theory of Monopoly. *American Mathematical Monthly* 31, 76-83.

Farrow, S., 1984. Testing the Efficiency of Extraction from a Stock Resource. *Journal of Political Economy* 93, 452-485.

Farzin, Y.H., 1984. The Effect of the Discount Rate on Depletion of Natural Resources. *Journal of Political Economy* 92, 841-851.

Farzin, Y.H., 1986. *Competition in the Market for an Exhaustible Resource.* Greenwich (Conn.), London: JAI Press.

Feichtinger, G., R.F. Hartl, 1986. *Optimale Kontrolle ökonomischer Prozesse: Anwendungen des Maximumprinzips in den Wirtschaftswissenschaften.* Berlin, New York: De Gruyter.

Fertig, K., 1986. *Ölangebotsmodelle: Entscheidungshilfe für die Wirtschaftspolitik?* Hamburg: Weltarchiv.

Fesharaki, F., D.T. Isaak, 1983. *OPEC, the Gulf, and the World Petroleum Market: A Study in Government Policy and Downstream Operations.* Boulder (Col.), London: Westview.

Fesharaki, F., D.T. Isaak, 1984. *OPEC and the World Refining Crisis.* London: Economist Publications.

Fesharaki, F., M. Johnson, 1982. *Short Term and Medium Term Outlook for Oil: A Review and Analysis of Recent Studies.* Honolulu: East West Resource Systems Institute, Working Paper 82-2.

Fesharaki, F., H. Razavi, 1986. *Spot Oil, Netbacks and Petroleum Futures: The Emergence of a New Oil Market.* London: Economist Publications.

Fisher, A.C., 1981. *Resource and Environmental Economics.* Camridge: Cambridge University Press.

Fisher, A.C., F.M. Peterson, 1977. The Exploitation of Extractive Resources. *Economic Journal* 87, 681-721.

Fisher, I., 1930. *The Theory of Interest.* New York: Macmillan.

Fitzgerald, M.D., G. Pollio, 1984. The Relationship between Spot and Official Crude Oil Prices. *OPEC Review* 8, 341-349.

Forrester, J.W., 1971. *World Dynamics.* Cambridge (Mass.): Wright-Allen.

Frank, J., M. Babunovich, 1984. An Investment Model of Natural Resource Markets, *Economica* 51, 83-95.

Gallant, A.R., 1987. *Nonlinear Statistical Models.* New York et al.: Wiley.

Gandolfo, G., 1986. *International Economics.* Berlin: Springer.

Gately, D., 1983. OPEC: Retrospect and Prospects, 1973-1980. *European Economic Review* 21, 313-331.

Gately, D., 1984. A Ten-Year Retrospective: OPEC and the World Oil Market. *Journal of Economic Literature* 22, 1100-1114.

van Geldrop, J., C. Withagen, 1987. *A General Equilibrium Model of International Trade with Exhaustible Natural Resource Commodities.* Eindhoven: University Research Memorandum COSOR 87-10.

Geroski, P.A., A.M. Ulph, D.T. Ulph, 1987. A Model of the Crude Oil Market in which Market Conduct Varies. *Economic Journal (Conference Papers)* 97, 77-86.

Gjoberg, O., 1985. Is the Rotterdam Spot Market for Oil Products Efficient? Some Rotterdam Evidence. *Energy Economics* 7, 231-236.

Gohberg, I., P. Lancaster, L. Rodman, 1986. On Hermitian Solutions of the Symmetric Algebraic Riccati Equation. *SIAM Journal of Control and Optimization* 24, 1323-1334.

Goldfeld, S.M., R.E. Quandt, 1972. *Nonlinear Methods in Econometrics.* Amsterdam: North-Holland.

Granger, C.W.J., 1969. Investigating Causal Relations by Econometric and Cross-spectral Methods. *Econometrica* 37, 424-438.

Granger, C.W.J., 1980. Testing for Causality: A Personal Viewpoint. *Journal of Economic Dynamics and Control* 2, 329-352.

Gray, L.C., 1914. Rent under the Assumption of Exhaustibility. *Quarterly Journal of Economics* 28, 66-89.

Griffin, J.M., 1985. OPEC Behavior: A Test of Alternative Hypotheses. *American Economic Review* 75, 954-963.

Griffin, J.M., 1988. A Test of the Free Cash Flow Hypothesis: Results from the Petroleum Industry. *Review of Economics and Statistics* 70, 76-82.

Griffin, J.M., C.T. Jones, 1986. Falling Oil Prices: Where Is the Floor? *Energy Journal* 7(4), 37-50.

Griffin, J.M., H.B. Steele, 1980. *Energy Economics and Policy*. New York et al.: Academic Press.

Hadley, G., 1961. *Linear Algebra*. Reading (Mass.): Addison-Wesley.

Halkin, H., 1974. Necessary Conditions for Optimal Control Problems. *Econometrica* 42, 267-272.

Hanson, D.A., 1980. Increasing Extraction Costs and Resource Prices: Some Further Results. *Bell Journal of Economics* 11, 335-342.

Hart, O., B. Holmström, 1987. The Theory of Contracts. In: T.F. Bewley (ed.), *Advances in Economic Theory*, Cambridge: Cambridge University Press, 71-155.

Hartshorn, J.E., 1985. Government Sellers in a Re-structured Crude Oil Market. In: D. Hawdon (ed.), *The Changing Structure of the World Oil Industry*, London et al.: Croom Helm, 59-69.

Harvey, A., P. Collier, 1977. Testing for Functional Misspecification in Regression Analysis. *Journal of Econometrics* 6, 103-119.

Heal, G., M. Barrow, 1980. The Relationship between Interest Rates and Metal Price Movements. *Review of Economic Studies* 47, 161-181.

Helmedag, F., 1986. Long-Run and Short-Run Demand Response, Discount Rate, and Pricing. *Zeitschrift für Wirtschafts- und Sozialwissenschaften* 106, 275-286.

Hestenes, M.R., 1966. *Calculus of Variations and Optimal Control Theory*. New York et al.: Wiley.

Hickman, B.G., H.G. Huntington, J.L. Sweeney, 1987. *Macroeconomic Impacts of Energy Price Shocks*. Amsterdam: North-Holland.

Hirshleifer, J., 1970. *Investment, Interest and Capital*. Englewood Cliffs: Prentice Hall.

Hnyilicza, E., R.S. Pindyck, 1976. Pricing Policies for a Two-part Exhaustible Resource Cartel: The Case of OPEC. *European Economic Review* 8, 139-154.

Hoel, M., 1981. Resource Extraction by a Monopolist with Influence over the Rate of Return on Non-Resource Assets. *International Economic Review* 22, 147-157.

Hotelling, H., 1931. The Economics of Exhaustible Resources. *Journal of Political Economy* 39, 137-175.

Hubbard, R.G., 1986. Supply Shocks and Price Adjustment in the World Petroleum Market. *Quarterly Journal of Economics* 100, 85-102.

International Energy Agency, 1982. *World Energy Outlook*. Paris: OECD.

Jacoby, H.D., J.L. Paddock, 1983. World Oil Prices and Economic Growth in the 1980s. *Energy Journal* 4(2), 31-47.

Jacquemin, A.P., 1972. Market Structure and the Firm's Market Power. *Journal of Industrial Economics* 20, 122-134.

Jacquemin, A.P. and J. Thisse, 1973. Strategy of the Firm and Market Structure: An Application of Optimal Control Theory. In: K. Cowling (ed.), *Market Structure and Corporate Behaviour: Theoretical and Empirical Analysis of the Firm*. London: Gray-Mills, 61-84.

Jaidah, A.M., 1983. *An Appraisal of OPEC Oil Policies*. London, New York: Longman.

Jenkins, G., 1985. *Oil Economist's Handbook 1985*. Barking: Elsevier.

Jenkins, G., 1986. *Oil Economist's Handbook, 4th ed.*. Barking: Elsevier.

Jevons, W.S., 1865. *The Coal Question*. London: Macmillan.

Johany, A.D., 1979. OPEC and the Price of Oil: Cartelization or Alteration of Property Rights. *Journal of Energy and Development* 5, 72-80.

Johany, A.D., 1980. *The Myth of the OPEC Cartel*. Chichester et al.: Wiley.

Johnston, J., 1984. *Econometric Methods*. 3rd ed., New York et al.: McGraw-Hill.

Jordan, D.W., P. Smith, 1977. *Nonlinear Ordinary Differential Equations*. Oxford: Clarendon Press.

Kalman, R.E., 1960. Contributions to the Theory of Optimal Control. *Boletin de la Societad Matematica Mexicana* 5, 102-119.

Kalymon, B.A., 1975. Economic Incentives in OPEC Oil Pricing Policy. *Journal of Development Economics* 2, 337-362.

Kamien, M.I., N.L. Schwartz, 1981. *Dynamic Optimization: The Calculus of Variations and Optimal Control in Economics and Management*. Amsterdam: North-Holland.

Kaufman, G., 1983. Oil and Gas: Estimation of Undiscovered Resources. In: M.A. Adelman et al. (eds.), *Energy Resources in an Uncertain Future: Coal, Gas, Oil, and Unranium Supply Forecasting*. Cambridge (Mass.): Ballinger, 83-294.

Kemp, M.C., N.V. Long, 1984. The Role of Natural Resources in Trade Models. In: R.W. Jones, P.B. Kenen (eds.), *Handbook of International Economics, Vol 1*. Amsterdam: North-Holland, 367-417.

Kemp, M.C., K. Okuguchi, 1979. Optimal Policies for Exhaustible Resources in Open Economies. *Zeitschrift für die gesamte Staatswissenschaft* 135, 207-215.

Kennedy, M., 1974. An Economic Model of the World Oil Market. *Bell Journal of Economics and Management Science* 5, 540-577.

Kennedy, M., 1976. A World Oil Model. In: D.W. Jorgenson, *Econometric Studies of US Energy Policy*. Amsterdam: North-Holland, 95-175.

Keynes, J.M., 1936. *The General Theory of Employment, Interest and Money*. London, Basingstoke: Macmillan.

Kmenta, J., 1971. *Elements of Econometrics*. New York: Macmillan.

Kobrin, S. J., 1984. The Nationalisation of Oil Production 1918-1980. In: D.W. Pearce, H. Siebert, I. Walter (eds.), *Risk and the Political Economy of Resource Development*, New York: St. Martin's Press, 137-164.

Koopmann, G., K. Matthies, B. Reszat, 1984. *Oil and the International Economy: Lessons from Two Price Shocks*. Hamburg: Weltarchiv.

Kouris, G., 1981. Elasticities - Science or Fiction ? *Energy Economics* 3, 66-70.

Kouris, G., 1983. Energy Demand Elasticities in Industrialized Countries: A Survey. *Energy Journal* 4(3), 73-94.

Krämer, W., H. Sonnberger, 1987. *The Linear Regression Model under Test*. Heidelberg, Wien: Physica.

Lancaster, P., L. Rodman, 1980. Existence and Uniqueness Theorems for the Algebraic Riccati Equation. *International Journal of Control* 32, 285-309.

Lasserre, P., 1985. Discovery Costs as a Measure of Rent. *Canadian Journal of Economics* 18, 474-483.

Léonard, D., 1987. Co-state Variables Correctly Value Stocks at Each Instant. *Journal of Economic Dynamics and Control* 11, 117-122.

Levhari, D., N. Liviatan, 1972. On Stability in the Saddle-point Sense. *Journal of Economic Theory* 4, 88-93.

Lewis, T.R., 1977. Attitudes towards Risk and the Optimal Exploitation of an Exhaustible Resource. *Journal of Environmental Economics and Management* 4, 111-119.

Liapunov, M.A., 1907. Problème Géneral de la Stabilité du Mouvement. *Annales de la Faculté des Sciences de Toulouse* 9, 203-474.

Loderer, C., 1985. A Test of the OPEC Cartel Hypothesis: 1974-1983. *Journal of Finance* 40, 991-1008.

Long, N.V., 1974. International Borrowing for Resource Extraction. *International Economic Review* 15, 168-183.

Long, N.V., 1975. Resource Extraction under the Uncertainty about Possible Nationalization. *Journal of Economic Theory* 10, 42-53.

Long, N.V., 1977. Optimal Exploitation and Replenishment of a Natural Resource. In: J.D. Pitchford, S.J. Turnovsky (eds.), *Applications of Control Theory to Economic Analysis*. Amsterdam: North Holland, 81-106.

Long, N.V., 1984. Risk and Resource Economics: The State of the Art. In: D.W. Pearce, H. Siebert, I. Walter (eds.), *Risk and the Political Economy of Resource Development*, New York: St. Martin's Press, 59-73.

Long, N.V., N.J. Vousden, 1977. Optimal Control Theorems. In: J.D. Pitchford, S.J. Turnovsky (eds.), *Applications of Control Theory to Economic Analysis*. Amsterdam: North Holland, 11-34.

Loury, G.L., 1986. A Theory of 'Oil'igopoly: Cournot Equilibrium in Exhaustible Resource Markets with Fixed Supplies. *International Economic Review* 27, 285-301.

Luciani, G., 1984. *The Oil Companies and the Arab World*. London, Canberra: Croom Helm.

Lymbery, P., 1988. Futures Markets - What They Are and How They Work. *Petroleum Economist* 55, 55-57.

Mabro, R., R. Bacon, M. Chadwick, M. Helliwell, D. Long, 1986. *The Market for North Sea Crude Oil*. Oxford: Oxford University Press.

MacAvoy, P.W., 1982. *Crude Oil Prices: As Determined by OPEC and Market Fundamentals*. Cambridge (Mass.): Ballinger.

Maddala, G.S., 1977. *Econometrics*. Tokyo et al.: McGraw-Hill.

Magill, M.P.J., 1977. Some New Results on the Local Stabilty of the Process of Capital Accumulation. *Journal of Economic Theory* 15, 174-210.

Magill, M.P.J., 1979. The Origin of Cyclical Motion in Dynamic Economic Models. *Journal of Economic Dynamics and Control* 1, 199-218.

Malthus, T.R., 1798. *An Essay on the Principle of Population as it Affects the Future Improvement of Society, with Remarks on the Speculations of Mr. Godwin, M. Condorcet and other Writers*. London.

Marshalla, R.A., 1979. *An Analysis of Cartelized Market Structures for Nonrenewable Resources*. New York: Garland.

Massarat, M., 1980. *Weltenergieproduktion und Neuordnung der Weltwirtschaft*. Frankfurt: Campus.

Maurice, C., C.W. Smithson, 1984. *The Doomsday Myth: 10,000 Years of Economic Crises*. Stanford: Hoover Institution Press.

Mead, W.J., 1986. The OPEC Cartel Thesis Reexamined: Price Constraint from Oil Substitutes. *Journal of Energy and Development* 11, 213-242.

Meadows, D.H., D.L. Meadows, J. Randers, W.W. Behrens, 1972. *The Limits to Growth*. New York: Universe Books.

Medio, A., 1987. Oscillations in Optimal Growth Models. *Journal of Economic Behaviour and Organization* 8, 413-427.

Meyer, A., 1988. *Ökonomische Analyse von Vertrags- und Steuersystemen im Rohstoffsektor.* Konstanz: Unpublished doctoral thesis.

Michel, P., 1982. On the Transversality Condition in Infinite Horizon Optimal Problems. *Econometrica* 50, 975-982.

Mikesell, R.F., 1984. *Petroleum Company Operations and Agreements in the Developing Countries.* Washington: Resources for the Future.

Molle, W. E. Wever, 1984. *Oil Refineries and Petrochamical Industries in Western Europe: Buoyant Past, Uncertain Future.* Aldershot: Gower.

Moran, T.H., 1981. Modeling OPEC Behavior: Economic and Political Alternatives. *International Organization* 35, 241-272.

Morey, E.R., 1986. An Introduction into Checking, Testing, and Imposing Curvature Properties: the True and the Estimated Function. *Canadian Journal of Economics* 19, 207-239.

Morrison, M.B., 1987. The Price of Oil: Lower and Upper Bounds. *Energy Policy* 15, 399-407.

Mossavar-Rahmani, B., S. Mossavar-Rahmani, 1986. *The OPEC Natural Gas Dilemma.* Boulder, London: Westview.

Nasmyth, J., A. Brinks, 1986. How the Spot Market for Brent Crude Works. *World Oil* 202 (4), 118-120.

Neary, J.P., S. van Wijnbergen, 1986. Natural Resources and the Macroeconomy: A Theoretical Framework. In: J.P. Neary, S. van Wijnbergen (eds.), *Natural Resources and the Macroeconomy*, Oxford: Blackwell, 13-45.

Newbery, D.M., 1981. Oil Prices Cartels, and the Problem of Dynamic Inconsistency. *Economic Journal* 91. 617-646.

Newbery, D.M., 1984. The Economics of Oil. In: F. Van der Ploeg (ed.), *Mathematical Methods in Economics*, Chichester et al.: Wiley, 519-567.

Niblock, T., 1985. Oil, Political Change and Social Dynamics of the Arab Gulf States. *Arab Gulf Journal* 5, 37-45.

Niehans, J., 1984. *International Monetary Economics.* Baltimore: Johns Hopkins University Press.

Niering, F.E., 1984. The Spot Market: Oil Industry's Changing Structure. *Petroleum Economist* 51, 9-16.

Niering, F.E., 1988. The Merc's Recipe for Success. *Petroleum Economist* 55, 57-59.

Noble, B., 1969. *Applied Linear Algebra.* Englewood Cliffs (N.J.): Prentice-Hall.

Nordhaus, W.D., 1973. The Allocation of Energy Resources. *Brooking Papers on Economic Activity*, 529-576.

Nordhaus, W.D., 1980. Oil and Economic Performance in Industrialized Countries. *Brooking Papers on Economic Activity*, 341-388.

O'Donnell, J.J., 1966. Asymptotic Solution of the Matrix Riccati Equation of Optimal Control. In: *Proceedings of the 4th Allerton Conference on Circuit and System Theory*. Urbana: University of Illinois.

Organization of Petroleum Exporting Countries, various issues. *OPEC Annual Statistical Bulletin*. Vienna: OPEC Secretariat.

Ott, M., J.A. Tatom, 1986. Are Energy Prices Cyclical ? *Energy Economics* 8, 227-236.

Overdahl, J.A., 1987. The Use of Crude Oil Futures by the Governmaents of Oil-Producing States. *Journal of Futures Markets* 7, 603-617.

Oweiss, I.M., 1984. Petrodollar Surpluses: Trends and Economic Impact. *Journal of Energy and Development* 9, 177-202.

Pakravan, K., 1983. Estimation od User's Cost for a Depletable Resource Such as Oil. *Energy Economics* 6, 35-40.

Pindyck, R.S., 1978(a). The Optimal Exploration and Production of Nonrenewable Resources. *Journal of Political Economy* 86, 841-861.

Pindyck, R.S., 1978(b). Gains to Producers from Cartelization of Exhaustible Resources. *Review of Economics and Statistics* 60, 238-251.

Pindyck, R.S., 1981. Models of Resource Markets and the Explanation of Resource Price Behaviour. *Energy Economics* 3, 130-138.

Pindyck, R.S., 1987. On Monopoly Power in Extractive Resource Markets. *Journal of Environmental Economics and Management* 14, 128-142.

Pindyck, R.S., J.J. Rotemberg, 1984. Energy Price Shocks and Macroeconomic Adjustments. *Natural Resources Journal* 24, 277-296.

Plaut, S.E., 1981. OPEC Is Not a Cartel. *Challenge* 24, 18-24.

Plaut, S.E., 1983. *Dependence and Import Vulnerability*. Greenwich (Conn.): JAI Press.

Plourde, L.G., A Simple Model of Replenishable Natural Resource Exploitation. *American Economic Review* 60, 528-522.

Prast, W.G., H.L. Lax, 1983. *Oil-Futures Markets*. Lexington: Heath.

Raffer, K., 1987. *Unequal Exchange and the Evolution of the World System: Reconsidering the Impact of Trade on North-South Relations*. Basingstoke: Macmillan.

202

Rampa, L., 1987. On Endogenous Oil Market Fluctuations. *Rivista Internationali di Science Economiche e Commerciali* 34, 761-769.

Ramsey, F.P., 1928. A Mathematical Theory of Saving. *Economic Journal* 38, 543-559.

Rauscher, M., 1985. *The Optimal Use of Associated Gas in a Petroleum Exporting Country: An Optimal Control Model.* Fakultät für Wirtschaftswissenschaften und Statistik, Diskussionsbeiträge Serie A, Nr.200, Universität Konstanz.

Rauscher, M., 1986. *Monopoly and Lagged Demand Adjustments.* Fakultät für Wirtschaftswissenschaften und Statistik, Diskussionsbeiträge Serie A, Nr.220, Universität Konstanz.

Rauscher, M., 1987(a). Trade with an Exhaustible Resource when Demand Reactions are Lagged. *European Economic Review* 31, 1597-1604.

Rauscher, M., 1987(b). Ein einfaches Modell zur Erklärung von Ölpreisschwankungen. *Jahrbuch für Sozialwissenschaft* 38, 333-342. English transalation: A Simple Model of Oil Price Fluctuations. *Economics: A Biannual Collection of Recent German Contributions to the Field of Economic Science* 37, 124-133. .

Rauscher, M., 1988(a). OPEC Behaviour and and the Price of Petroleum. *Zeitschrift für Nationalökonomie* 48, 59-78.

Rauscher, M., 1988(b). Intertemporal Aspects of Dominant Firm Pricing in the World Petroleum Market. Forthcoming in: H.G. Radermacher et al. (eds), *Methods of Operations Research.* Frankfurt: Athenäum.

Ray, G.F., 1979. Energy Economics: A Random Walk in History. *Energy Economics* 1, 139-143.

Razavi, H., 1984. An Economic Model of OPEC Coalition. *Southern Economic Journal* 51, 419-428.

Razavi, H., F. Fesharaki, 1984. OPEC's Push into Refining: Dilemma of Interactions Between Crude and Product Markets. *Energy Policy* 12, 125-134.

Renner, M.G., 1988. Stabilizing the World Oil Market. *OPEC Review* 12, 49-72.

Reza, A.M., 1981. An Analysis of the Supply of Oil. *Energy Journal* 2, 77-94.

Ricardo, D., 1817. *On the Priciples of Political Economy and Taxation.* London: Murray.

Riva, J.P., 1981. *World Petroleum Resources and Reserves.* Boulder: Westview Press.

Roberts, B., 1980. The Effects of Supply Contracts on the Output and Price of an Exhaustible Resource. *Quarterly Journal of Economics* 95, 245-260.

Rockafellar, R.T., 1976. Saddle Points of Convex Hamiltonian Systems Having a Positive Discount Rate. *Journal of Economic Theory* 12, 71-113.

Roeber, J., 1979. Dynamics of the Rotterdam Market. *Petroleum Economist* 46. 49-52.

Roncaglia, A., 1983. The Price of Oil: Main Interpretations and Their Theoretical Background. *Journal of Post Keynesian Economics* 5, 557-578.

Roncaglia, A., 1985. *The International Oil Market*. Basingstoke and London: Macmillan.

Roumasset, J., F. Fesharaki, D. Isaak, 1983. Oil Prices without OPEC: A Walk on the Supply Side. *Energy Economics* 5, 164-170.

Ruggeri, G.C., 1983. Market Conditions and Future Oil Prices. *Energy Economics* 5, 190-194.

Salant, S.W., 1976. Exhaustible Resources and Industrial Stucture: A Nash-Cournot Approach to the World Oil Market. *Journal of Political Economy* 84, 1079-1093.

Salant, S.W., 1982. *Imperfect Competition in the World Oil Market: A Computerized Nash Cournot Model*. Lexington: Lexington Books.

Salehi-Isfahani, D., 1986. Oil Supply and Economic Development Strategy: A Dynamic Planning Approach. *Journal of Development Economics* 21, 1-23.

Sampson, A., 1975. *The Seven Sisters*. New York: Viking Press.

Samuelson, P.A., 1972. The General Saddlepoint Property of Optimal Control Motions. *Journal of Economic Theory* 5, 102-120.

Saunders, H.D., 1984. The Macrodynamics of Energy Shocks, Short and Long Run. *Energy Economics* 6, 21-34.

Saunders, H.D., 1984. On the Inevitable Return to Higher Oil Prices. *Energy Policy* 12, 310-320.

Scheinkman, J.A., 1978. Stability of Separable Hamiltonians and Investment Theory. *Review of Economic Studies* 45, 559-570.

Schneider, 1983. *The Oil Price Revolution*. Baltimore, London: Johns Hopkins University Press.

Seierstad, A., K. Sydsaeter, 1977. Sufficient Conditions in Optimal Control Theory. *International Economic Review* 18, 367-391.

Seierstad, A., K. Sydsaeter, 1983. Sufficient Conditions Applied to an Optimal Control Problem of Resource Management. *Journal of Economic Theory* 31. 375-382.

Seierstad, A., K. Sydsaeter, 1986. *Optimal Control with Economic Applications*. Amsterdam: North-Holland.

Shwadran, B., 1986. *Middle East Oil Crises since 1973*. Boulder: Westview.

Siebert, H., 1985. *Economics of the Resource Exporting Country: Intertemporal Theory of Supply and Trade*. Greenwich (Conn.): JAI Press.

Siebert, H., 1986(a). Ricardo- und Hotelling-Paradigmen für die Preisbildung natürlicher Ressourcen. In: H. Siebert (ed.), *Angebots- und Preisbildung natürlicher Ressourcen*. München: Oldenbourg. 1-17.

Siebert, H., 1986(b). Die Auswirkungen sinkender Ölpreise. *Wirtschaftsdienst*, 203-207.

Siebert, H., 1987(a). Neue Nutzungsrechte und internationale Rohstoffversorgung. *Ifo-Studien* 33, 71-99.

Siebert, H., 1987(b). Risk Allocation in Large-Scale Resource Ventures, *Kyklos* 40, 476-495.

Siebert, H., 1988(a). Langfristige Lieferverträge im internationalen Ressourcenhandel, *Zeitschrift für Wirtschafts- und Sozialwissenschaften* 108, 195-225.

Siebert, H., 1988(b). Institutional Arrangements for Natural Resources. In: H.-J. Vosgerau (ed.), *New Institutional Arrangements for the World Economy*, Berlin: Springer, forthcoming.

Siebert, H., M. Rauscher, 1985. Vertical Integration by Oil-Exporting Countries. *Intereconomics* 20, 211-216.

Slade, M.E., 1982. Trends in Natural Resource Commodity Prices: An Analysis of the Time Domain. *Journal of Environmental Economics and Management* 9, 122-137.

Smith, V.K., 1981. The Empirical Relevance of Hotelling's Model for Natural Resources. *Resources and Energy* 3, 105-117.

Smith, V.K., J.V. Krutilla, 1984. Economic Growth, Resource Availability, and Environmental Quality. *American Economic Review (Papers and Proceedings)* 74, 226-230.

Smith, V.L., 1977. Control Theory Applied to Natural and Environmental Resources: An Exposition. *Journal of Environmental Economics and Management* 4, 1-24.

Solow, R.M., 1974(a). The Economics of Resources or the Resources of Economics. *American Economic Review (Papers and Proceedings)* 64, 1-14.

Solow, R.M., 1974(b). Intergenerational Equity and Exhaustible Resources. *Review of Economic Studies (Symposium)*, 29-46.

Stern, L.E., 1984. Criteria of Optimality in the Infinite-Time Optimal Control Problem. *Journal of Optimization Theory and Applications* 44, 497-508.

Stiglitz, J.E., 1974. Growth with Exhaustible Natural Resources: Efficient and Optimal Paths. *Review of Economic Studies (Symposium)*, 123-137.

Stiglitz, J.E., 1976. Monopoly and the Rate of Extraction of Natural Resources. *American Economic Review* 66, 655-661.

Stollery, K.R., 1983. Mineral Depletion with Cost as the Extraction Limit: A Model Applied to the Behaviour of Prices in the Nickel Industry. *Journal of Environmental Economics and Management* 10, 151-163.

Stollery, K.R., 1987. Mineral Processing in an Open Economy. *Land Economics* 63, 128-136.

Stournaras, Y.A., 1985. Is the Industrialisation of the Arab Gulf a Rational Policy? *Arab Gulf Journal* 5, 21-27.

Struckmeyer, C.S., 1986. The Impact of Energy Price Shocks on Capital Formation and Economic Growth in a Putty-Clay Technology. *Southern Economic Journal* 53, 127-140.

Struckmeyer, C.S., 1987. The Putty-Clay Perspective on the Capital Energy Complementary Debate. *Review of Economics and Statistics* 71, 320-326.

Takayama, A., 1985. *Mathematical Economics*. 2nd ed. Cambridge: Cambridge University Press.

Teece, D.J., 1982. OPEC Behavior: An Alternative View. In: J.M.Griffin, D. Teece (eds.), *OPEC and the Behavior of World Oil Prices*. London: Allen & Unwin. 64-93.

Terzian, P., 1985. *OPEC: The Inside Story*. London: Zed Books.

Toman, M.A., 1985. Optimal Control with an Unbounded Horizon. *Journal of Economic Dynamics and Control* 9, 291-316.

Toussaint, S., 1985. The Transversality Condition at Infinity Applied to a Problem of Optimal Resource Depletion. In: G. Feichtinger (ed.), *Optimal Control Theory and Economic Analysis 2*. Amsterdam: North-Holland. 429-440.

Ulph, A.M., 1980. World Energy Models: A Survey and Critique. *Energy Economics 2*, 46-59.

Ulph, A.M., G.M. Folie, 1980. Exhaustible Resources and Cartels: An Intertemporal Nash-Cournot-Model. *Canadian Journal of Economics* 13, 645-658.

Verleger, P.K., 1982. *Oil Markets in Turmoil: An Economic Analysis*. Cambridge (Mass.): Ballinger.

Verleger, P.K., 1984. Petroleum Futures: Promises and Problems. *Petroleum Economist* 51, 293-296.

Verleger, P.K., 1987. The Evolution of Oil as a Commodity. In: R.L. Gordon, H.D. Jacoby, M.B. Zimmerman (eds.), *Energy: Markets and Regulation,* Cambridge (Mass.): MIT-Press, 161-186.

Virmani, A., 1985. *Tax and Contractual Arrangements for the Exploitation of Natural Resources*. Washington: World Bank Staff Working Paper No. 752.

Vousden, N.J., 1974. International Trade and Exhasutible Resources: A Theoretical Model. *International Economic Review* 15, 149-167.

Weitzman, M.L., 1981. Sequential R&D Strategy for Synfuels. *Bell Journal of Economics* 12, 574-590.

von Weizsäcker, C.C., 1965. Existence of Optimal Programs of Accumulation for an Infinite Time Horizon. *Review of Economic Studies* 32, 85-104.

Welker, A.J., 1985. *The Oil and Gas Book.* Tulsa: SciData Publishing.

Wenz, P., 1983. Ethics, Energy Policy, and Future Generations. *Environmental Ethics* 5, 195-209.

West, J., 1988. Operators Plan to Step up U.S. Exploration, Development Work. *Oil and Gas Journal* 86 (11), 33-38.

Wilson, E.J., 1987. World Politics and International Energy Markets. *International Organization* 41, 125-149.

Wirl, F., 1985(a). Stable and Volatile Prices: An Explanation by Dynamic Demand. In: G. Feichtinger (ed.), *Optimal Control Theory and Economic Analysis 2*. Amsterdam: North-Holland. 263-277.

Wirl, F., 1985(b). Are Oil Prices Going to Remain Volatile? *Zeitschrift für Operations Research* 29, B41-B62.

Wirl, F., 1988. *Dynamic Demand, Consumer Expectations and Monopolistic Resource Extraction: An Application to OPEC Pricing Policies*. Paper presented at the Third Congress of the European Economic Association in Bologna.

Withagen, C., 1981. The Optimal Exploitation of Exhaustible Resources: A Survey. *De Economist* 129, 504-531.

Withagen, C., 1985. *Economic Theory and International Trade in Natural Exhaustible Resources*. Berlin et al.: Springer.

World Oil, 1987. World Trends: The Worst May Be over. *World Oil* 205 (2), 19-25.

G. Gandolfo

International Economics

International Economics I

The Pure Theory of International Trade

1987. 83 figures. XVIII, 319 pages.
ISBN 3-540-17971-2

International Economics II

**International Monetary Theory
and Open-Economy Macroeconomics**

1987. 50 figures. XX, 507 pages.
ISBN 3-540-17978-X

These textbooks deal with a broad range of aspects in
international economics, including new topics, topics
usually omitted from textbooks and new research
results. The books are therefore also useful as reference books. They are designed for use at both undergraduate and graduate levels. This is possible
because of their two-tier structure: the text speaks
directly to the undergraduate reader in extremely
clear verbal and graphic terms, while the appendices,
which form the second tier, are addressed to the
graduate student and the researcher. They are self-
contained treatments, in mathematical terms, of the
topics examined in the text and include generaliza-
tions and/or additional topics not dealt with there.
Each chapter contains an exhaustive and up-to-date
bibliography, which lecturers will find especially
useful in preparing selected reading lists. The ample
and balanced treatment of the various approaches to
international economics, the undogmatic and eclectic
presentation, and the clarity of exposition ensure that
the reader gains a thorough grasp of theories, facts,
and policies.

Springer-Verlag
Berlin Heidelberg New York
London Paris Tokyo Hong Kong

Yoshihiko Otani, Mohamed El-Hodiri

Microeconomic Theory

1987. Approx. 320 pages. ISBN 3-540-17994-1

This text presents a rigorous and reasonably complete statement of microeconomic theory as it exists today. It starts with a unified treatment of consumers' demand, followed by an exposition of the theory of production as well as costs and profit functions of competitive firms. Market structures are then studied in detail and finally a brief introduction to general equilibrium and welfare economics is presented.

The book contains many examples, exercises and illustrations. The method of exposition unifies several approaches to the subject. The treatment of market structure is unique and more detailed than any other book on microeconomic theory. Several parts of the book reflect the original research of the authors that has not appeared in book form before. The text attempts to give rigorous foundations to the material presented in intermediate microeconomics textbooks.

B. Felderer, S. Homburg

Macroeconomics and New Macroeconomics

1987. 97 figures. XIII, 329 pages. ISBN 3-540-18004-4

This book gives a comprehensive account of traditional and more recent developments in macroeconomic theory. It is primarily written for students at the intermediate level. The book differs from the customary expositions in that the authors do not discuss topic by topic but doctrine by doctrine. Thus, the main approaches, such as classical theory, Keynesian theory, theory of portfolio selection, monetarism, rational expectations theory, and Neokeynesian disequilibrium theory, are presented in historical order. Each of these approaches is substantiated and criticized in a self-contained chapter, and the authors have taken great efforts to bring out the relations and differences between them. A mathematical appendix contains reviews of those mathematical facts which are especially important to macroeconomic models and makes the text easy to read.

Springer-Verlag
Berlin Heidelberg New York
London Paris Tokyo Hong Kong

Springer